P9-DGQ-453

AFRICA'S SEARCH FOR IDENTITY

AFRICA'S SEARCH FOR IDENTITY

VICTOR C. FERKISS

GEORGE BRAZILLER

NEW YORK

For information, address the publisher:
George Braziller, Inc.
One Park Avenue
New York 16, New York

Library of Congress Catalog Card Number: 65–25970

PRINTED IN THE UNITED STATES OF AMERICA

CONTENTS

BY WAY OF ACKNOWLEDGMENT

Any literary work derives from all of an author's past knowledge and experience, and this book is no exception, reflecting as it does ideas and insights of mentors and colleagues and of friends both African and non-African. But several individuals deserve a special word of thanks for their direct assistance. Patricia Smoot-Walker drew the map of Africa. Two of my colleagues at Georgetown University, Dean William E. Moran, Jr., of the School of Foreign Service and Dr. William H. Lewis, late of the Department of History, generously read the manuscript and gave me the benefit of their counsel. My wife, Barbara Ellen Ferkiss, not only performed routine chores of typing and editing, but through her incisive criticism and wide knowledge of Africa is responsible for much of such merit as the book possesses. Any errors of fact and judgment are of course my own.

VICTOR C. FERKISS

Washington D.C.
September 1965

AFRICA'S SEARCH FOR IDENTITY

Map drawn by Patricia Smoot-Walke

I

INTRODUCTION

In the mid-twentieth century mankind is entering what Raymond Aron, the French journalist and sociologist, has called the Age of Universal History. No longer can events in "the West," in Africa or in Asia be thought of as occurring in isolation from the rest of the world.

Today's most pressing problems and concerns are worldwide in their scope, the problems and concerns of humanity as a whole. The unlocking of the atom has opened vast new opportunities for good and evil, while the onset of a worldwide population explosion threatens to destroy the possibility of achieving a life consonant with human dignity throughout most of the world. Both man's probings into outer space and his investigations into the basic biochemical constituents of his own being are freighted with the most far-reaching consequences for all mankind.

The United Nations symbolizes the advent of this age of universal history. Paradoxically, this new universality has been made possible only by the passing of the system of worldwide domination by the European peoples, which over the last five hundred years gave the world what unity it possessed. The ending of European dominance is not just a matter of the destruction of Western colonialism, but is, in Arnold Toynbee's terms, the result of the rest of the world's repulsing and throwing off the political and cultural aggressions by means of which Western Europe made itself master of the globe.

Despite the postcolonial spread of political independence and attendant drives for the reassertion of traditional cultural attitudes, modern industrial civilization, historically the creation of the West, has become and will undoubtedly remain dominant throughout the world. This poses an enormous problem for the newly emerging nations which seek to give political independence real meaning through greater cultural and economic independence—but in an increasingly interrelated world—and which seek the modern goals of health and a decent standard of living for all—but hope to revive traditional modes of thinking and acting.

In no area of the world has the downfall of Western imperialism been more rapid and dramatic than on the continent of Africa. Last of the continents to feel the full weight of that imperialism, Africa's reassertion of political sovereignty has been a major feature of the international political landscape in the period since World War II. Nor does any area of the world more vividly illustrate the clash of triumphant Western industrial civilization with the revival of political independence and cultural self-determination. The statement that contemporary Africa is a land of contrasts—symbolized by the primitive tribal warfare in the Congo carried on almost in the shadow of Léopoldville's ultramodern hotels and public buildings—has become a cliché, but it is no less true for being a truism.

What the rest of the world and Americans in particular have failed to realize is that what underlies African politics today, both internally and on the international level, is not just a desire to destroy colonialism and create a series of new nation-states. What is really at issue is nothing less than the nature of the role Africa will play in the age of universal history. For African independence is being sought not merely as an end in itself, but as the necessary precondition for an African presence in world affairs, for the addition of a specifically African motif to the human symphony. What the character of this motif will be is not yet certain. Developments within independent Africa, the relations of Africa with the rest of the world, and, especially, the course of events in southern Africa will determine its nature. It would be a tragedy, as much for Africa as for the rest of the world, if the dominant theme was black chauvinism and the rejection of everything connected with the European or white world. It would be tragic if Africa sought to define its personality—its "Africanness"—simply as the antithesis of everything white. Yet this note is clearly rung in the speeches of some African leaders.

Yet this is not the only possible path Africa can take in the search for its own personality, for its individuality. It can seek to distinguish what is uniquely African in order to have something special, something of its own, to contribute to the whole of mankind, something to give in exchange for what it receives from others in this new age of universal history.

Once it is understood that the search for identity is the basic dynamic of African politics it becomes obvious that one cannot understand the internal developments in the new African states without understanding the relation of these developments to the role Africa seeks to play in the world, and, conversely, that one cannot understand Africa's sometimes confusing role in world politics unless one recognizes the origins and nature of the internal dynamics of the African states. Negritude, "the African Personality," Pan-Africanism, the struggles for the liberation of southern Africa, Africa's role in the United Nations, and its position in the Cold War—all of these are aspects of the same quest for a unique political and cultural identity. Just as an adolescent comes of age and must define himself in relation to a given social environment, so Africa is seeking to come of age in the new world of the twentieth century, the age of universal history.

But the simile of adolescence is a deceptive one. For Africa was not a child before the coming of colonialism, despite the myths perpetuated by colonialist rationalization and self-deception. Africa existed before its conquest by Western imperialism; indeed, it has always played a role in world history. Africa's relations with the near Eastern and Mediterranean civilizations long antedate the birth of Christianity; many of its traditional foods and some of its population come from Southeast Asia; its contacts with China go back not to the first Chinese embassies of the post-World War II period but almost a thousand years. Africa was no isolated outpost of the human race like Australia, but part of the world complex from earliest times. Africa is not a child but rather a captive released from bondage. It seeks now to play a role in the world which is self-determined rather than determined by others, and in order to do this strives first to know its own nature. Thus it looks into itself to discover its real parentage as a people and as a culture.

Africa seeks its identity in many ways—through political independence from outside rule, by recovering its own past, and by playing an independent, a specifically African role in world politics. All of these are interrelated aspects of its quest for identity, a fact that must be recognized by anyone who wants to understand Africa's role in contemporary international politics.

What can a non-African hope to contribute to this process of defining the personality of the new Africa? Why not let Africans speak for themselves and be content to listen as best one can?

One can only fully answer such questions in the course of discussing specific African and non-African interpretations of Africa's history, development and behavior. But it is well to remember that nothing can be perceived in its totality when seen solely from the perspective of the viewer or of the viewed. Both have something to contribute.

In addition, a non-African writing about Africa for a primarily non-African audience has some advantages. Not only is he especially aware of the questions which non-Africans are asking, but he is also conscious of the often false preconceptions that many non-Africans have. Many (not excluding some persons long resident there) think of Africa as not only primitive but static, raised from barbarism only by a beneficient colonialism, incautiously and ungratefully demanding premature independence, finding in it only political and economic confusion and despair, and seeking to deflect attention from internal difficulties by irresponsible action on the world stage.

At the same time, it is possible for a non-African observer to be aware of the many misconceptions Africans themselves have about their role in the world: not only their frequent romanticizing of their history and their misreadings of the record of colonialism, but, more importantly, their misconceptions about the world political environment in which the new Africa seeks to find its place—misconceptions about the motives and interests of the other actors on the world scene and about the non-African factors which necessarily condition the possible future relationships of the new Africa to other societies. To attempt to find reality among these conflicting and frequently false perceptions is a difficult but challenging task, for it involves nothing less than playing a small role in the continuous process by which, throughout history, Africa has both shaped and been shaped by the rest of the world.

What is Africa? This is the question which lies at the heart of every problem connected with the role of the new Africa in the world. For if an African presence is to be part of the new world civilization, it is first necessary for Africans to know what it means to be African. It is not an easy question to answer. One has only to look at the voluminous literature on Pan-Africanism to realize that the problem of unifying Africa is not just one of deciding how Africa shall be politically and economically united, but of defining the entity to be united.

Geographically Africa is one continent, but it is not an ethnic or cultural unity. Throughout history successive tides of culture and peoples have swept across Gibraltar and the Red Sea. Africa begins at the Pyrenees, said Victor Hugo, and in fact the relationship between the Iberian peninsula and the Maghrib (in Arabic the "west"—Morocco, Algeria and Tunisia) has been as close as that of Iberia to the rest of Europe or of the Maghrib to the rest of Africa. The Suez Canal is a ditch (and a recent one at that) and the Red Sea a mere moat; for thousands of years movement of peoples, goods and ideas has been constant and intense between Africa and Asia Minor.

Not only does Africa as a continent have close links to Europe and the Near East, it is divided within itself. Distances are vast, climates vary greatly, and no river, save perhaps the Nile, has much value as a link between different peoples. The Sahara Desert is a significant barrier to continental interrelations. Geography alone does not unite Africans any more than it makes Alaskans and Panamanians think of themselves primarily as North Americans.

Nor is race a uniting factor—at least in any positive sense. The racial composition of Africa is still debated. The notion of race is of dubious scientific meaning in any event, and confusions between linguistically and biologically related groups have further compounded the complications present in the racial picture. Africa is the home of the Negro and the only area of the world where he is indigenous, but though Negroes make up more than two-thirds of the population, substantial numbers of Africans are not Negroes. North Africans, Sudanese, Somalis, Malagasy, and Ethiopians are not Negro but primarily Caucasian or Asiatic in background; and Pygmies, Bushmen, Hottentots and the Colored of South Africa are also non-Negro. Though Pan-Africanism was originally a worldwide movement of black men, its continued existence as a continent-wide movement must depend on more than racial background alone.

What applies to race as a unifying factor applies equally to language and culture. The inhabitants of Africa speak more than eight hundred languages: how many one counts depends largely on one's criteria for distinguishing between languages and dialects. Save for a few languages which are spoken by several million (Amharic, Hausa and Yoruba are among the foremost examples) most African languages are spoken by relatively small groups. The only indigenous language used as an official language in any independent African state is Swahili, an Arabic-influenced *lingua franca* adopted by Tanzania and spoken throughout much of East Africa; Kenya has made Swahili co-official with English, and Burundi and Rwanda have made local vernaculars co-official with French. Africans speak to one another in French, English and Arabic, and members of the revolutionary movements directed against Portugal in her African colonies must normally use Portuguese as a medium of communication. Language clearly is a divisive rather than a unifying factor, and the major languages in use among African leaders bind them to European or Near Eastern cultures as much as to their fellow Africans.

Though most Africans have a good deal in common culturally, their traditional culture is to a large extent simply a variant of the folk culture found everywhere throughout the pre-industrial world, and how much relevance it has for life in the mid-twentieth century is questionable. But a deep cultural fissure divides the Islamic peoples of North Africa from the peoples of most of the continent, and, in many respects, the urbanized Africans of South Africa have more in common with American Negroes than with their fellow Africans of the rain forests or the Sudanic grasslands or even, if South African writers such as Ezekiel Mphalele can be believed, with the urban dwellers of West Africa. Ethiopia and the Malagasy Republic—despite the role of Malagasy intellectuals in the Negritude movement—are clearly separate worlds from other African societies. Common cultural characteristics no more unite or define Africa than does geography, race or language.

Yet Africa does exist. It exists in the minds of its people who, despite great internal dissimilarities, think of themselves, from Tangier to Cape Town and from Dakar to Tananarive, as being brothers. Time may widen fissures in African unity and give differences new and more significant meanings, but Africa is one. It is one, paradoxically, because outsiders have thought of it as one, and still do. The fundamental factor uniting Africans is a common experience, the experience of European colonialism. All Africa has been in living memory under the political and economic control of non-Africans. Even Ethiopia and Liberia have suffered varying degrees of political and economic domination from abroad. From the perspective of colonialism all Africans alike were fit objects of subordination. A purely Caucasian Muslim in Algeria was as much an "other," a racial and cultural inferior, as a Negro in the Ivory Coast; a primarily Asian inhabitant of Madagascar just as much an inferior as a so-called Bantu in Rhodesia. All African languages were equally childish gibberish to most Europeans—useful only for giving simple commands to servants. All African cultures were regarded as equally barbaric, and, to the extent that they obviously were not, were assumed to have been influenced by non-African forces; all of Africa was equally picturesque or savage, equally heathen, equally dark. The unity of Africa was forged by the common experience of European domination and the common venture of overthrowing that domination. Africa is a creation not of common race or geography or culture but of a common experience in world politics.

But man does not live by negation alone, nor does he wish to see himself simply as the reverse image of something else. Africans have sought and are seeking to create an Africa out of what has been freed. This involves a twofold task, the creation of a pan-African society and polity and the creation of a distinct position in world culture and world politics.

But while Africa attempts to discover what is common to its various nations and peoples and what is unique about this common identity, it is also trying to locate itself in a historical perspective. For within Africa and within almost every African there is a pressing need to reconcile past and future, tradition and modernity, which serves as a second or vertical dimension to the African search for identity. All human beings, and all cultures, have a similar need. Individual Americans and Europeans value survivals of their cultural past and even create them out of nostalgia for that past. On one level there is the folksinger in a Greenwich Village coffeehouse or the suburbanite with his rustic mailbox and wagon-wheel gate; on another, the more studied and politically inspired folk festivals of the smaller European nationalities such as the Welsh or Danes. Modern Western man, too, seeks continuity with his past. But for the Western European and his descendants in North America and Australasia the problem is not as acute as it is for the African.

For the person of European ancestry the past is his, but so is the present. The future is therefore less troubling. His folk culture has been succeeded by modern industrial civilization, but this too is of his making. The factory is just as English as the Morris dances or the Magna Charta; the time-clock and the business suit just as American as the covered wagon or the husking bee; parliamentary government or modern public administration just as French or German as the medieval manor or Saxon law. The present may be disturbing or require adaptations but it has grown out of the Western past, however painful and discontinuous the process. Modern science and technology, government and family organization, attitudes toward nature, God and man are all relatively slow and organic outgrowths of traditional Western folk culture. Western man may yearn for the past but he has no need to feel that he betrays his origins in choosing the present—or a future in a technological, rational world which is the projection of that present.

But for many other peoples of the world, including Africans, it is not this easy. They may want to be part of this new world and share in its benefits. But the modern medicine which cures their children is a European invention; the industrial system which provides them with a higher standard of living is a Western creation; the attitude toward the world underlying scientific management in business and government is the product of non-

African traditions and developments. Is it possible to refuse modernization? The answer has to be "No" if one's goal is health, prosperity, and political and military security. But does not modernization necessarily involve Westernization and de-Africanization? The African (like the Asian, and men elsewhere as well) is desperately seeking an answer to this question. He hopes that the answer is "No."

Africa, it is claimed, will modernize technologically and economically without giving up its spiritual values, family ties, communal solidarity. It will create a new culture which is an amalgam of the best of the West and of African tradition: a culture essentially European in its material aspects, African in its social and spiritual aspects. The revival of ancient rites and traditional dress, the cultivation of indigenous art and music, the proclamation of "African democracy" and "African socialism" are all elements of this quest for a new synthesis. Whether it is possible to acquire and make effective use of the material elements of one culture while retaining the modes of thought and social institutions of another is questionable at best, but it is nothing less than this that Africans seek.

It is not all that they seek, however. Such an amalgam would provide an identity of sorts, but it would still be a subservient and inferior one. Only if Africa itself has something unique which it can contribute to the synthesis of world civilization will it be possible for its people to regard themselves as full members of the world community. African music and art, the African sense of community and of the sacralness of all aspects of life are frequently cited as possible elements of this unique contribution. Africans also hope to demonstrate to the world that it is possible to have a socialism that is democratic rather than repressive, and a democracy that is communitarian rather than individualistic. In international politics, Africa in conjunction with the rest of the *tiers monde,* expects her neutrality to soften the East-West conflict and to prepare the way for the reign of world peace. As the poorest and most exploited continent and the last to gain its political freedom, the advent of the participation of Africa in world affairs marks the end of the world of colonialism and of European domination and places Africa in the vanguard of the forces seeking a new world of human brotherhood and equality. It is in this role that Africa expects ultimately to find her identity.

II

THE AFRICAN HERITAGE

To understand contemporary Africa it is necessary to understand something about African history, but it is impossible to understand that history without first having some knowledge of its physical and human setting.

The most important single fact about Africa is its size. Its land area is three times that of the United States including Alaska. The South African black chafing under the restrictions of apartheid in Johannesburg is four thousand miles from his fellow African in Dakar. Even within countries distances are great. From the Congo capital of Léopoldville to Elisabethville, center of once rebellious Katanga, is approximately one thousand miles. The difficulty in an underdeveloped country of maintaining political control over such vast distances is obvious.

Africa's size makes air travel very important, particularly since such roads and railroads as do exist were built by the colonialists not to provide better communications within a given colony (much less between colonies) but to provide a means for draining wealth from the interior to the coast where it could then enter the stream of world commerce. This heritage is slowly being overcome, but even today capitals a few hundred miles apart may have no direct paved road link and may only be able to contact each other by telephone through circuits running through Europe.

Geologically, the continent is a vast plateau. Save for the narrow coastal plains, the Atlas Mountains of Morocco, and the great ranges of the East with their chain of lakes and once-white Kenyan highlands, Africa is virtually level—like a table top floating on the sea. It lacks natural harbors and sheltered anchorages, especially on the west coast, and sand bars, coral reefs and high surf make the coastal operation of ships and small boats perilous. The construction of artificial harbors, like those of Monrovia in Liberia or of Tema in Ghana, is necessary to make possible the loading and unloading of large ships near major population centers and industrial sites. Rivers fall rapidly from the plateau to the sea, making navigation inland from the coast difficult, but giving Africa the world's greatest hydroelectric potential.

Nature has served the African poorly in many ways. Most Africans find this difficult to accept or adjust to, since they are convinced that theirs is a phenomenally rich continent whose resources have so far either been neglected by the colonialist or else exploited by him for his own benefit. They therefore assume that development under an independent African regime can quickly create a land of milk and honey. Yet the soils, like all tropical soils, are poor in essential minerals, and lack of a glacial period has inhibited soil formation. The violence of the tropical rainfall leaches the soil and causes erosion, while extreme variations in rainfall from year to year mean years of damagingly excessive rain and years of drought. The thinness of the arable layer of soil and the extremely abrasive quality of the highly metallic lateritic soils common throughout much of Africa makes them unsuitable for deep furrowing, and perhaps also for large-scale use of mechanical farm equipment. Some elaborate colonially sponsored agricultural schemes failed spectacularly as a result of not taking these factors into account. The traditional method of coping with these difficulties has been the hand hoe and the system of shifting ("slash-and-burn") cultivation, in which land is cleared by cutting and burning and, thus fertilized, is used for several years and then left fallow for many more. But with a growing population and increasing pressure on the land new methods of conserving it must be found or much of it can become worthless. The tsetse fly, a carrier of sleeping sickness, has made some of the best land unappealing to native agriculturalists and has made the raising of cattle difficult throughout much of Africa.

Most of the continent is arid or semi-arid, with deserts advancing rather than retreating as far as can be ascertained. (The Sahara was once much less dry than it is now; it is known that most of the Sahara was habitable even as late as the beginning of the Christian era and that horses were used for transport across the desert in Roman times.) The popular notion that Africans live in a dense jungle is a misconception fostered not only by Hollywood but by the early explorers, who approached Africa from the sea, often encountering impenetrable mangrove swamps, and whose principal means of exploring the continent were its rivers, which are usually fringed by large trees and thick vegetation even though open country may be only a mile or so away. Actually most of the continent is grassland similar to the American prairies, or scrub area with a covering of small trees or high bushes. Indeed, throughout much of Africa "bush" is the popular term for the countryside or the rural area. It is probable that virtually none of Africa is virgin growth, the original vegetation having been destroyed by migratory cultivators, perhaps many times over. Only in a few areas, chiefly in West Africa and the Congo basin, do people actually live in the jungle.

Nor are most Africans likely to have seen many wild animals. Almost everywhere the pressure of protein-hungry Africans has virtually extinguished the wild-animal population. African governments today are torn between trying to save the remaining animals either as a tourist attraction or as the beginning of planned wild-livestock management for food production and giving in to the pressures of native poachers in search of food. The belief that the non-African world will continue to look upon them as savages as long as wild animals roam their land has led many to regard conservation of their wild-animal resources with indifference.

Africa's agricultural resources, properly developed and managed, could feed the current population better than they do, and could provide an increased amount of specialized tropical and subtropical agricultural products for export. But even today few go hungry. Despite dietary deficiencies, Africa is not a land of famine.

But Africa's future lies less on the land than beneath it; its greatest natural resource is not its soil but what lies under it. Diamonds, cobalt, manganese, copper, bauxite and iron ore abound. Although known resources of coal are minor except in South Africa, and oil has so far been found in significant quantities only in the north and in Nigeria, power presents no problem. It has been estimated that Africa possesses 40 percent of the world's hydroelectric power potential. Though today overwhelmingly a land of farmers and herdsmen it may take its place in the world of the twenty-first century as primarily an industrial region.

African demography is a notably treacherous and uncharted field. Some countries such as Ethiopia have never taken an adequate census. Others, like Nigeria, have apparently inflated their population figures for political purposes. An educated guess would put the population at about 250,000,000, with Nigeria, Egypt and Ethiopia by far the largest countries, the first contributing about one-fifth of the total. Thus Africa's population though larger is of the same order of magnitude as that of the USSR or the United States. It is about half that of India and about a third that of China. If little is known with certainty about the size of Africa's present population, even less is known about rates of growth, which vary widely from area to area. The overall growth rate is probably less than that of Latin America or certain parts of Asia and near the world average, but this is enough to cause the population to double in a generation.

Yet to date Africa is not overpopulated, even though individual regions or nations may suffer from population pressures, in particular, eastern Nigeria, Malawi, Rwanda and Burundi and, for artificial reasons, the native reserves of the Republic of South Africa. On the whole, migration, including short-term labor migration, has so far eased these pressures. Some areas are so sparsely populated that development is inhibited by lack of laborers and consumers, while the spread of Africa's relatively small population over vast areas makes communications, education, and political and social control more difficult.

No one can say how many tribes or ethnic groups this population is divided into. Anyone choosing his criteria carefully could devise a system of classifying African tribes which would produce as many tribes as might be desired. "Tribe" is a word with little scientific meaning. It normally refers to any group of individuals possessing a common language, culture and territory. Yet culture and even language change, people move, and above all allegiances to leaders shift. It is absurd to refer to a group such as the Ibo, who number almost six million and have never been politically united, as a tribe, and then to use the same word to denominate a tightly knit kinship group of a thousand or so individuals who happen to speak a language unintelligible to their neighbors. Ultimately, tribal membership is a state of mind, a self-definition, dependent in large measure on how others view one and how one reacts to their views.

Racial identifications are also ambiguous. Nonetheless it is possible to distinguish four quite different racial types indigenous to the African continent: Bushmen, Pygmies, Negroes and Caucasians. The continent has been the scene of much movement and consequent intermixture of peoples. But, leaving aside Europeans and Asians, the few remnants of the Bushmen and Pygmies, and the half million "Colored" in South Africa, and disregarding the ambiguous racial heritage of five million Fulani of West Africa and of the partly Indonesian Malagasy, one-third of Africa's peoples are Caucasian (mostly Arabs, Berbers, etc., in North Africa) and about two-thirds are Negroes (approximately half of the Negroes, those of eastern and southern Africa, speak so-called Bantu languages, the most widespread branch of the Niger-Congo language family). Beyond this broad, common-sense racial classification, language alone provides a sure key for making ethnographic distinctions among African groups, but language it must be remembered, though usually learned at one's mother's knee, is a cultural characteristic which can and does change.

Change. This is the crucial word in understanding the dynamics of African history. For both Africa as a physical base of human habitation and the people who inhabit it have been the source as well as the setting of historical and contemporary events. Africa's peoples have been in a state of flux throughout history and even if the continent as a land mass has been relatively unchanging, its ability to support human habitation has changed with changes in technology and customs.

Even the climate of Africa has changed. As has been suggested, the Sahara was not always so dry, and, although temperature ranges have probably remained relatively stable, Africa has, in historic times, become progressively drier. Not only were populations forced out of the Sahara as desiccation increased, but, since small changes in climatic conditions can be life-or-death matters for agricultural and pastoral peoples, much of the movement in Africa, on a permanent as well as on a cyclical basis, has been prompted by climatic pressures.

The introduction of new crops has also radically affected ways of life. New crops have enabled peoples to expand their population and thus forced them eventually to seek new domains; and they have made it possible for people to live in areas where human beings could not survive before. Prehistorians have traced Eastern food crops and agricultural and herding techniques across Africa from east to west and other crops and techniques from west to east. Southeast Asian crops such as rice, yams and bananas brought by immigrants from Indonesia have spread over the whole continent. Crops from the New World brought to Africa by Portuguese slavers and traders, such as maize, manioc and cacao, are today important in many parts of the continent.

New techniques for smelting iron or new forms of political and military organization, whether developed independently or picked up from outsiders, have led to major political and social upheavals. States based on divine kingship after the Egyptian pattern were organized in the western Sudan and throughout the lake region of East Africa and became the basis of important empires. Chaka's military genius in the nineteenth century not only resulted in Zulu conquests in South Africa but upset the equilibrium and set in motion conflicting forces throughout the whole of southern and east-central Africa. Wealth derived from the slave trade made it possible for coastal groups to revolutionize power relationships in West Africa. Outside pressures or local inventions have led to a kind of musical chairs effect throughout the continent. Changes in customs and language have accompanied changes in political, economic and demographic strength, and through migration and conquest new racial types emerged. Africa was far from static or somnolent before the coming of the European.

Nor were the Europeans of the age of discovery and colonization the first outside force to add their pressures to the calculus of movement within African life. As has been noted, Africa's relations with Asia Minor had always been intimate: for Egypt, Axum and Yemen the Red Sea was a highway not a border. West African gold was crossing the Sahara in horse-drawn chariots and entering Mediterranean commerce during the fifth century B.C. Arab slaving and colonization were carried on along the East African coast before the beginning of the Christian era. Christianity penetrated deeply into Africa in the period before the Islamic conquest—Ethiopia is its monument rather than its outpost. The Arabs not only conquered North Africa for Islam, they set in motion forces which led to a largely Islamized civilization in interior West Africa with regular communication extending from the edge of the coastal forests to the Mediterranean; though cut off from medieval Europe, the ancient Sudanic kingdoms were touched by all the currents of Muslim Mediterranean civilization. Indonesian contacts and migration have had an important and lasting effect on the East African coast, and the Malagasy Republic is today primarily Indonesian both ethnically and culturally. Much trade was carried on with India and China in the period paralleling the Middle Ages in Europe. Africa's burgeoning contacts with Christian West Europe, which have determined our image of Africa as a dark and undiscovered continent, overlapped a period of diminishing contacts with Islamic and Asian civilization, resulting from overall changes in the world balance of power.

Africa has always been part of the world—affecting it as well as affected by it. But the new Africa which seeks to play a role in contemporary world affairs is not simply playing on a new stage. She herself has changed while the scenery was being reshuffled and the plots rewritten. The new personality which she seeks to express is a product of all her experiences (including the most recent) and it is to these formative experiences that we now must turn.

Africa, it is now generally accepted, was the original birthplace of the human race. It was also the place where early manlike creatures first became tool-making animals.

Man's ancestors and collateral relatives, the great apes, roamed the continent in great numbers and variety some thirty million years ago, and from Africa they spread to Europe and Asia. About two million years ago the apelike Australopithecines ("southern apes") were to be found throughout much of Africa, living in the open away from the forests and walking erect. The Kenyan anthropologist, L. S. B. Leakey, has discovered a number of fossils of about this age in the Olduvai Gorge in Tanganyika in association with chipped pebble tools.

Throughout Africa ancient chipped pebble tools are found in profusion as is the more sophisticated hand ax which was carried to Europe either through diffusion or migration during the first and second interglacial periods.

During the Pleistocene era Stone Age peoples and cultures were moving out of and into Africa: between Spain and North Africa, over the land bridge connecting Africa with Asia, and almost certainly across the Red Sea as well. The affinities between certain North African cultures and certain European ones, the similarity of the Kenyan Capsian culture (whose members may have been the first inventors of pottery) and that of the Natufians at Mount Carmel in Palestine, the resemblance of North African rock carvings and paintings to those of the Spanish caves, and the wide diffusion of the bow and arrow (invented in North Africa) are a few of the many evidences of culture contact and migration between Africa and the rest of the old world in Paleolithic times.

During this period men similar to the present-day Bushmen were spread throughout much of southern and eastern Africa; Pygmies inhabited the Congo and the rain forests of the west coast, and a Caucasian type (known as Capsian or Cushite and resembling Combe-Capelle man in France) was present in the East and North. At a somewhat later date, possibly as recently as 6000 B.C., the Negro first appeared in the Sudanic grassland belt from the west coast to the headwaters of the Nile. Although the origin of the Negro is presently the subject of considerable controversy, it seems possible that the Negroes were a differentiated group of Cushitic stock which spread westward from the region of the upper Nile, originally perhaps as fishermen, and then increased with remarkable rapidity. In any event, by about 6000 B.C. all of the major groups considered indigenous to Africa were already on the scene.

African archaeology is still in its infancy and the final resolution of current disputes must await the unearthing of additional evidence. Nonetheless, there is now enough evidence available to enable us to venture at least tentative answers to two of the most widely discussed questions concerning African prehistory.

The first has to do with whether agriculture was independently invented by the African Negro. If so, Africa ranks with Southwest Asia, East Asia and the New World as the scene of one of the major breakthroughs in the development of human culture. The practical consequences of the truth or falsity of such a claim are negligible, but for Africans long smarting under claims of Westerners that they were a Stone Age people who had contributed nothing to human civilization and had borrowed everything they had from others (a claim which was simultaneously a justification and a consequence of slavery and colonialism), the psychological and, ultimately, the political consequences are enormous.

It does in fact appear that agriculture was independently developed by Negroes on the upper Niger River in the savanna below the Sahara when they ennobled local millets and sorghums between 5000 and 4000 B.C. It then spread throughout the Sudan (the semi-arid grassland belt running across Africa between the Sahara and the forest region) during the same millennium that Neolithic agriculture and animal husbandry were being introduced into Egypt from Palestine. The next millennium was to see this Near Eastern agriculture spread westward across North Africa to the Atlantic at the same time that Sudanic agriculture spread eastward to the Red Sea, the two traditions merging as they met along the middle and upper Nile. From their meeting came the basis for Egyptian civilization and for the second great controversy about African history.

White detractors of African abilities have claimed in effect that whatever traces of civilization (as defined or acknowledged by them) have ever been found in Africa are of Egyptian origin and that the Egyptians were a Caucasian people related to and greatly influenced by the peoples of the Near East. The African response has been increasingly either to deny that advanced forms of social organization and technology in Africa were of Egyptian origin or to claim that the inhabitants of ancient Egypt were largely black. Although probably of Cushitic (caucasoid) stock and in appearance somewhat resembling the modern Somalis, the Egyptians were undeniably African and so was their culture, although their close contacts with Asia Minor (which, as anthropologist Paul Bohannan has pointed out, could equally well be called Africa Minor) have meant that it included cultural elements derived from the Near East. But the most distinctive Egyptian institution and the one which has had the most effect on the rest of Africa, that of a bureaucratic state headed by a divine priest-king, is now coming to be recognized as having been originally invented in Egypt. Dynastic kingship in Mesopotamia apparently did not come into existence until the Fifth Dynasty in Egypt so can hardly be regarded as the source of Egyptian dynastic kingship, despite the fact that it was long believed that Egyptian civilization derived from the East.

Within a thousand years of the introduction of agriculture into Egypt from Palestine the First Dynasty was founded, and in less than two thousand years the population of the Nile Valley increased from about twenty thousand people to more than three million. Predynastic as well as dynastic Egypt was in close contact with the lands to the East and traded with the Aegean islands as well. Egypt also traded with the lands to the south, obtaining gold, incense, ostrich feathers, ivory and slaves in exchange presumably for manufactured goods of various sorts. In the third millennium B.C. a servant of the Pharaoh on a trading expedition traveled into southern Ethiopia and possibly as far south as the northern edge of the Congo forest, since one of the items he brought back to Egypt was a Pygmy.

By the end of the second millennium B.C. Egypt had already colonized much of the upper Nile, but was itself beginning to crumble under pressure from the Assyrians, and in the eighth century B.C. Egypt was conquered by the rulers of its former colony Cush, and their capital Napata, located between the third and fourth cataracts, became for a short time the capital of the old world. When the Assyrians moved into Egypt, the rulers of Cush retreated south and established a new capital at

Meroë, about one hundred miles north of present-day Khartoum in 530 B.C. The torch of Egyptian civilization had now passed to a predominantly black kingdom. Unlike Egypt, Meroë had an abundance of iron ore. It had learned the art of iron smelting from its enemies the Assyrians and it now became one of the major ironworking centers of the ancient world. It grew rich on the iron spear and the iron hoe and as an exporter of such traditional African products as ivory, hardwoods, ostrich feathers and slaves. It was from Meroë that dynastic kingship, ironworking and the new forms of political and military organization entered the whole of the eastern Sudan and spread westward and southward through conquest, migration or imitation, laying the basis for the medieval "Sudanic" kingdoms in East Africa, the Western Sudan and the central forest region.

During the period of Meroë's prosperity, Egypt was conquered by Alexander the Great and was then ruled by the Ptolemies for three hundred years. Under their reign, Alexandria, with a population of 300,000, became the intellectual capital of the world. Egypt became part of the Roman Empire in 30 B.C. when Cesarion (Ptolemy XIV), the son of Cleopatra and Julius Caesar, was murdered on order of the Emperor Augustus.

About this time, Negroes had begun to replace Bushmen around the headwaters of the Nile, and Cushites had moved into Ethiopia and across to the east coast, forcing the Bushmen south. Semitic peoples (the Sabeans or Shebans) from Yemen invaded the coast of Ethiopia and penetrated into the Ethiopian mountains, founding the kingdom of Axum. Trade across the Indian Ocean led to East African relations with India and Indonesia and the exchange of agricultural crops and techniques which then spread widely throughout both Africa and Asia. Indonesians began to dominate this trade and according to some authorities settled in East Africa in large numbers.

Phoenicia had founded its first colonies in North Africa in the eighth century B.C., and by at least the fifth century B.C.

there was a well-established trans-Saharan trade connecting the western Sudan with both Carthaginian and Roman cities on the North African coast, as attested by the numerous rock carvings of horse-drawn vehicles found in the Sahara and by the descriptions of this trade given by Herodotus. As in later times, gold was probably the principal export from the Sudan and it was probably paid for largely in salt.

From the conquest of Carthage in 146 B.C. to the fall of Rome in the fifth century, North Africa was Roman territory, the fertile granary of the Roman Empire. The control of all of North Africa by the Romans enabled Christianity to spread across Africa north of the Sahara and to penetrate south almost as far as the forest belt. In the east, Axum, now Christian, burned Meroë in the fourth century, bringing its greatness to an end. But at this very time Ghana (in the present Republic of Mali) was already on its way to becoming the first great empire of the western Sudan. The introduction of new crops, possibly of Indonesian origin, and of iron implements and weapons made possible an expansion of population and the large-scale occupation of the Guinea coast (the southern coast of West Africa). These events provided the basis for the development of large states based on a modified form of the dynastic kingship of Meroë. Prior to the development of these kingdoms the western Sudan was apparently the site of a culture known (from the northern Nigerian village where its pottery and lifelike terra-cotta figurines were first discovered) as the Nok culture, which flourished from about 900 B.C. till the third century A.D., and it was on this earlier culture that the new forms of political and military organization inherited from Meroë were probably grafted.

The Negro population explosion led to the occupation of the Camerouns and the Congo basin, where the Pygmies were reduced to dependent enclaves. The Negro group known as the Bantu expanded from the Cameroun highlands into East and Central Africa, displacing the Bushmen and mingling with them, with the result that the Bantu are generally lighter in color and slighter in build than other Negro groups. In time there developed throughout western, central and eastern Africa a number of Sudanic kingdoms, although again our knowledge is only fragmentary since the archeological exploration necessary to give a true picture of Africa in the years before European penetration is only just beginning.

In the seventh century the remnants of the eastern Roman Empire fell to the Arab followers of the new religion of Islam. Within seven years of the prophet Muhammed's death the first Arabs entered Egypt; in seventy years they had conquered the whole of North Africa. In 711 Berber converts to Islam crossed from North Africa into Europe and invaded Spain and France. The Arabs took control of the East African coastal trade, settling in coastal trading ports and on northern Madagascar. Zimbabwe in what is now Rhodesia was founded in about the eleventh century and had as its major activity the export of gold to India.

In time Arabs in large numbers moved into North Africa, forcing the Berbers southward and westward, where they achieved political dominance over the local Negro agricultural groups. The nomadic Fulani came into being as a distinct group in Senegal and began to move eastward. Ghana, which had become Islamized, fell to the Berber Almoravid Empire of Morocco in the eleventh century and its place as the leading western Sudanic empire was taken by Mali. The great Muslim kingdom of Bornu came into existence in northeastern Nigeria, to endure until the coming of the British as "protectors" in the nineteenth century, and various other Hausa states also developed in northern Nigeria, all of them eventually Muslim.

The pagan kingdom of Benin was founded in the eleventh century and lasted until it was destroyed by the British in the nineteenth century. In the Congo delta the kingdom of the Bakongo was founded in the thirteenth century, only to be superficially Christianized, destroyed and largely enslaved by the Portuguese in the fifteenth century; its solidarity remains a reality in African politics, however, as does that of many a vanished realm.

And always, always there was the slow glacial movement of the Bantu—south and east—pushing all aside until they met the Boers in the seventeenth and eighteenth centuries.

The picture one gets is thus one of constant movement, conflict and change within Africa, and of continuing contacts with the world at large. Then as now these two kinds of influence interacted and Africa's internal affairs affected and were affected by its relations with the world.

Far from being isolated from the rest of the world prior to European conquest, from earliest prehistory Africa had been sending to and receiving from the rest of the old world migrants, goods and cultural inventions. The continent was in contact with all of Muslim civilization. The Moorish societies of Spain and the Maghrib were as one. Muslim Arabia and Persia were active on the horn of Africa and far down the African east coast. There was regular trade with India and Indonesia in ivory, gold, slaves and iron. For several centuries there had even been major trade with China.

China had long been in contact with the Arabian peninsula but from the twelfth century it engaged in direct and regular trade with East Africa. The Chinese ships were of great size and on one occasion as many as twenty-seven thousand Chinese are reported to have landed in East Africa. A British archaeologist has commented that "from the tenth century onward, the buried history of Tanganyika is written in Chinese porcelain." In the eleventh century an envoy from East Africa apparently visited the imperial Chinese capital. This flourishing trade died out at the beginning of the sixteenth century as a result of China's adoption of an isolationist policy which entailed the destruction of all ocean-going vessels.

In view of all this intercontinental activity how was it possible for Europeans to think of Africa as a "dark continent," languishing in isolation? The reasons must be sought in the isolation of Europe rather than of Africa. By the height of the

Middle Ages, Christian Europe had beaten back the invaders from the north and east, the Vikings and Huns, and was looking outward. But for a long time foreign commerce was carried on in deepest secrecy, lest rivals break into lucrative monopolies, and much knowledge of early European contacts with Africa and Asia was thereby lost or obscured.

In any event, the burst of energy associated with such names as Prince Henry the Navigator, Magellan and Columbus only took place when the Iberian peninsula was finally freed from Muslim control. Europe had been cut off from sub-Saharan Africa by Islam, which had relations with both but effectively separated them from each other. Despite this, the existence of the empire of Mali, which at the time dominated the trans-Saharan gold-for-salt trade, was well known to fourteenth-century Europe, and the desire to bypass the Moorish middlemen and to deal directly with Africa's gold producers was apparently a major motive behind Prince Henry's interest in navigation. The first Portuguese trade settlement in Africa was established at Elmina in present-day Ghana in 1482 and Christopher Columbus is reported to have visited here in a Portuguese vessel about 1483.

At this time the great states of the Sudan were already declining, and the diversion of the gold trade to the coast ensured their further decline. Military and technological stagnation meant that they were fast falling behind a rapidly advancing Europe. Furthermore, the Europeans first encountered these societies at the very time European self-confidence, spurred by greed for trade in gold, slaves and other valuable African goods and bolstered by an increasing technological superiority, was at its height.

From the sixteenth century on, European power was expanding not only in Africa but throughout the habitable globe. While for a brief period in the nineteenth and twentieth centuries European domination integrated all the world's continents into a pattern of European political and economic control, it also had the effect of isolating them from each other.

Combined with the Christian beliefs and the industrial power of Europe, this new isolation of the other continents made it possible for Europeans to regard the rest of the world as backward and heathen. Reservations had to be made for the ancient civilizations of China and India, but no such reservations were considered necessary for the empires of Africa. By the time European conquest of the continent was being completed, the power of most of these empires had already been broken, and their subjects had returned to a simpler way of life in a fashion not unanalogous to what happened in Western Europe after the fall of Rome. And the twin imperatives of slavery and Christian evangelization, combined with an increasingly self-conscious concept of white racial superiority, made it convenient as well as natural for Europeans to look upon Africa as a continent dark in human achievements as well as in the color of most of its peoples.

III

THE OLD AFRICA

Most human beings throughout history have lived on and from the land. Since man is gregarious and needs and wants the company of his own kind, he has almost always lived in villages of some sort. The isolated farmsteads of modern America, Canada or Australia are anomalous exceptions, as everyone familiar even with Europe is aware. Until recently most Europeans and even many Americans lived in small rural communities. Almost half of Latin America does today. The overwhelming majority of Asians and Africans still follow this traditional pattern of humankind.

Even the existence of the great empires of the past—what the Israeli sociologist S. I. Eisenstadt has called the "historic bureaucratic societies"—did not change this pattern much. There were some great cities like imperial Rome, but most of Rome's subjects remained close to the land. So also in Africa, even though the Sudanic kingdoms were based on trade and Timbuktu at its height had a population approaching thirty thousand. All the African kingdoms had royal courts with large numbers of retainers, though often they were, like some of the courts of medieval Europe, peripatetic—moving around the kingdom in order both to rule and to sustain themselves. The Yoruba of Nigeria were living in large city-states, rather like those of the Greeks, prior to the coming of the British. But by and large even the empires were built on villages and village life.

What is a village? In Africa at least it is not just a small group of farmers, living together, going out to their fields, and supporting a few artisans; it is also a family or tribal unit of some sort with closely interrelated economic, political, social and religious functions. Amid all the flux and change of life in Africa certain elements have remained constant from time immemorial to the present. Only as folk culture begins to change under the impact of modernization—of urbanization, industrialization, and technological and cultural rationalization—will these elements change. They are the constants underlying the old Africa and much of the new as well.

The most distinctive feature of African village life is the importance of kinship. The African family is not the so-called nuclear family of modern Western man: a unit composed of parents and children, with its role limited to procreation, the upbringing of minor children and close emotional ties among its members. It is the extended family traditional throughout human history. It includes parents, children, grandparents and grandchildren, aunts, uncles, in-laws and cousins of all sorts. The fact that polygamy is common throughout Africa—indeed virtually universal save among those who are Christian, highly urbanized or unable to afford it—further extends and complicates kinship patterns. Not only do Africans feel closely related to kin whom Westerners would scarcely think of as such, but these relationships serve economic, political, social and religious functions as well as the purely sexual and personal ones they fulfill in the West. Until one reaches the level where kingdoms and empires become of significance, kinship ties are the only ties with real meaning. Even within more complex and impersonal structures they remain important; in the absence of these they must be all sufficing.

Kinship groups are the building blocks upon which larger social units are constructed, and kinship ties hold these larger units together. In the new Africa many of these ties appear to some (including some Africans) as mixed blessings at best, running counter to the impersonality and emphasis on individual achievement and reward upon which much of the modern political and economic order has been built. The primacy of kinship ties also encourages factionalism, nepotism and corruption, lack of personal ambition and diffusion of energies and resources. But the disappearance of these ties is likely to leave a gap which can be filled only by an overpersonalization and overintensification of political loyalties.

Traditional Africa is largely classless for the simple reason that there is no real economic base for a class structure. Livestock is owned by the kinship group. Land is simply not owned. Which is not to say that it is communally owned. It is communally used, and the village-kinship community allocates access to it according to the varying needs of its members, but the concept of ownership of land is meaningless to rural Africa. Land does not enter the market system, as do crops, livestock and even labor on occasion; it is simply there. This becomes easier to understand when one remembers that just as nomadic herdsmen wander over the land in search of pasture (usually of course in fixed and cyclical patterns) in Africa agriculturalists also move as land becomes exhausted, so that whole villages shift their sites. Land is farmed much as it is grazed. People have rights in it, but cannot be said to own it. As a result there is no landlord problem in Africa. (White-settler communities present a separate problem of course.) There are no *rentiers,* no tenant farmers, no landless peasantry, no debts owed to exploiting moneylenders. Everyone receives a share determined by custom. Tribute in agricultural products may be paid to chiefs or kings, but usually this is largely ceremonial and symbolic, for who could transport, much less consume, extensive quantities of most African agricultural produce? Indeed, save in exceptional cases where bureaucracies and standing armies have had to be supported, even tribute usually has become the basis for communal feasting in which the donors as well as the recipients of the gifts took part.

Political structure at the village level is extremely rudimentary. In any traditional society, custom rather than a conscious process of creation of law determines the general rules according to which society lives. Law, as in medieval Europe, is "found" not "made." Executive functions do, of course, have to be performed. Decisions must be reached about going to war against neighboring tribes, moving the village to a new location when crops begin to fail, and so on. These decisions are made by chiefs in council with their tribal elders. They are not made arbitrarily but issue from seemingly interminable conferences, designed to secure unanimity. This tradition of discussion eventuating in agreement, and its corollary of the absence of organized opposition or factionalism, survive in a somewhat distorted form in the one-party regimes of contemporary African states. In traditional society throughout most of Africa judicial decisions likewise are the result of long discussion, rules are based on custom, involved arguments are presented (Africans are a notably litigious people), and there are often elaborate hierarchies of traditional courts.

All of the functions of government, legislative, executive and judicial, may be combined in one man or group, or particular functions may be split among many individuals or groups. When the colonial powers came to Africa and sought to rule through traditional institutions they were often confused by the failure of native political institutions to conform to the neat patterns with which they were familiar. They therefore delegated authority to the wrong people, or the wrong authority to the right people, or too much authority to almost anyone, with the result that misunderstanding and discontent frequently followed.

This was a source of even graver difficulties in those areas (especially in East Africa) where there was no institutionalized political authority of any kind—where there were "tribes without rulers." Here disputes about the meaning of traditional rules and quarrels between individuals were resolved primarily by negotiation on an ad hoc basis, with kinship groups upholding the rights of the contending parties, and more distant kin of both parties acting as mediators. Paul Bohannan has aptly described this situation as a grass-roots equivalent of the balance-of-power system for settling international disputes in a world without centralized authority.

Understanding the nature of tribal political rule is important for two reasons. One is that all large-scale African political systems, from the ancient empires through much of colonial administration down to most contemporary African states, have been superimposed on traditional village society and have used chiefs and traditional courts as important building blocks in constructing their own political edifices. Another is that much nonsense is written about the chief or king as the prototype of today's charismatic leaders of nationalist regimes. The chief was often revered, the king sometimes worshiped, but their power was rarely arbitrary, because tribal custom provided a kind of constitutional shield, a framework within which the ruler was obliged to operate. No traditional ruler could act with the freedom of a modern despot (though in periods of stress and transition rulers of such African states as Buganda and Benin often engaged in the killing of social inferiors).

Africans are everywhere religious. Even nationalistic leaders like the Marxist-influenced Sékou Touré claim that their socialism is different—and distinctively African—because it does not deny God or supernatural values. The traditional religions of Africa are often described as animistic, that is, as attributing spiritual personality not only to men but to animals, trees, rocks, etc., thus making them objects of worship. This is misleading. Africans do believe in the universality of spirit and that the order of causality in the universe is such that the acts of spirits affect daily life and can be influenced through religious practices (or manipulated through witchcraft). They recognize, however, a hierarchy of spiritual beings, and all traditional African religious systems conceive of the spirits as holding their power as surrogates of a Supreme Power, generally unmentioned because ineffable, and often conceived of as having no direct concern with everyday human affairs. The religious life of traditional Africa is intertwined with village life generally because, just as in ancient Greece, particular deities are the patrons, often the supposed ancestors, of particular tribes. Rules of personal conduct and social custom not only have the sanction of religion but are of its essence. The African village, like the early Greek communities, is a religious community. The undermining of traditional religious beliefs has led to the destruction of the community and, conversely, the destruction of the village community, to the extent that this has occurred, has tended to leave Africans spiritually and morally adrift.

It can be said therefore that, while village life differs greatly from one part of Africa to another (no two villages were ever exactly alike in all respects and even the same village changes over time to a greater degree than outsiders imagine), the general pattern of village life has been the same throughout sub-Saharan Africa. Above all, throughout traditional Africa all aspects of life are closely intermeshed—religion, art, politics, economics and family life constituting a single reality. The energy derived from splitting this social atom—as it was and is being split by modernization—can provide the power for the creation of a new African society or the explosion can reduce African life to a chaotic and frustrating rubble.

Ideas, it has been said, have consequences. The concept of nationalism has proved itself one of the most potent political forces in the modern world, not least so in Africa. Nationalism presupposes shared identity, and one way to achieve a common identity is to possess a common past, especially a past that can be looked back on with pride. For Africans, long taught by colonialism that they had no past, a history they could take pride in was and is a crucial need. "We cannot live with the memories of others," Joseph Ki-Zerbo of Volta has said; "we must have our own memories." African history is a weapon in Africa's current struggle to find herself and her place in the world.

There are two dangers inherent in any discussion of pre-colonial African history. The British journalist Basil Davidson put it well in one of his pioneering books on African history when he said that it was his objective to "steer between the rock of prejudice and the whirlpool of romance," that is, between thinking of Africans either as a group of Stone Age savages or as leaders of human civilization fallen prey to superior force.

The facts about African history, though still obscure in detail, are no longer what is at issue. The controversy centers around their interpretation. There is no question that African political entities were technologically and in some respects socially inferior to the European systems which conquered them. This was especially true in the nineteenth century when the great scramble for Africa actually took place. On the other hand, there is no question but that at almost any time prior to the eighteenth century the Africans had shown themselves capable of creating political societies comparable to those of their later European masters. They had certainly earned the right to be considered in most respects the peers of medieval Europe. The question, therefore, is not one of the relative ability of different racial groups (and it is almost impossible to overemphasize the racial connotations of arguments about African history) to create civilizations, but their inclination, ability or opportunity to create modern industrial civilization. The argument is over whether ability, opportunity or inclination toward a particular kind of civilization was less present in Africa than elsewhere.

Inclination is still a moot point, since, as will be seen, even those Africans most eager to share the technological successes of modern industrial civilization do not welcome all its aspects. But the African will argue that it was lack of opportunity rather than lack of ability that made him the technological inferior and therefore the political prey of the European during the colonial era. He will strive to demonstrate this by calling attention to his achievements in the past, which until the time of the industrial revolution—the unique creation of Western Europe—were comparable to those of Europe and Asia.

We have already seen that the Africanness of Pharaonic Egypt has become an issue in this argument. Whatever may be the truth about the sources of Egyptian culture, by the beginning of the Christian era the center of civilization in Africa had passed from an Egypt devasted by invasion to Meroë, an ethnically African state by any measure. Davidson refers to Meroë as a "bronze age polity, replete with slaves and royal accumulation of wealth; literate, hierarchical, given to the building of great monuments . . . rigid in its manners." It was above all a center of ironworking—the Birmingham of ancient Africa. From it spread throughout the Sudanic region not only techniques of ironworking but political and religious ideas as well. Knowledge of ironworking reached West Africa by the first century B.C. Today the Yoruba people of modern Nigeria represent their god Shango by a ram's mask, a clear derivation from Cushitic symbolism, and Shango's devotees in Brazil and the Caribbean still today carry on a cult that goes back thousands of years to the banks of the Nile.

Armed with iron and the new techniques of political organization derived from Meroë, the kingdom of Ghana arose and grew into a powerful state. Situated some two hundred and fifty miles north of the present Malian capital of Bamako, Ghana was the first of a number of states which owed their existence and power to their location. Peoples to the south needed salt. Peoples to the north wanted gold, and to a lesser extent ivory and slaves. Great trading cities grew up like seaports where the sea of the desert met the grasslands. The position of these cities was always precarious. Competitors sought to have them bypassed. Buccaneers threatened to plunder them. Just as in the steppes of Russia, the vast open spaces of the Sudanic grasslands made consolidation and defense difficult and settled empires were often at the mercy of nomadic invaders.

Yet in this area great states developed and endured for long periods of time, and when they fell others quickly took their place, so basic and vital was the function they performed. For they were the link between the Mediterranean and the forest lands of West Africa and also between the latter and the states of the southern Nile Valley.

Ghana was founded at about the same time that Meroë was going into decline, perhaps as early as A.D. 300. It is possible that its founders may have been of Caucasian origin, but we know that after the eighth century the Mandingo, a great Negro people, were its rulers. At its height the city of Ghana had a population of 30,000—half that of medieval Florence. It ruled over a vast hinterland, and in 1067 the medieval Muslim scholar al-Bakri noted that it "could put 200,000 warriors into the field, more than 40,000 being armed with bows and arrows"; the chain-mailed cavalry of Ghana would have given the contemporary Norman conquerors of England pause. Law and order were maintained throughout the empire and there was a complex system of tariffs and taxation. A kind of feudalism prevailed, with a bureaucratic structure superimposed somewhat precariously over it, as in contemporary medieval Europe. Ancient Ghana (the glories of which are of such symbolic importance that its name was chosen for the first black African colony to achieve its freedom—the nation designed by its founder Kwame Nkrumah to be the cornerstone of a united Africa) fell to the Moroccan-based religious warrior empire of the Almoravids in 1076. The Almoravids, unable to consolidate their position, turned instead to conquests on their northern flank in Spain and the scepter of power in the Sudan passed eastward.

Mali, another empire from which a modern state takes its name, was Negro from its inception. Its founder Sundiata (1230–55) renounced paganism for Islam. Throughout the area it was coming to be realized that Islamic Arabic education provided a basis for creating a literate bureaucracy, and being a

Muslim meant equality of treatment from one's Muslim customers to the north. Although rulers became Muslims not all of their subjects embraced the faith, and those that did syncretized it with their traditional beliefs, a practice still common in Africa today. The greatest ruler of Mali, Mansa Musa, is famous for having made the pilgrimage to Mecca with a retinue of five hundred gold-bearing slaves and numerous elephants, astounding even the cosmopolitan and blasé Cairo of 1324. Ibn-Batuta, who traveled in Mali in 1352–53, wrote that its people "are seldom unjust, and have a greater horror of injustice than any other people. Their sultan shows no mercy to anyone who is guilty of the least act of it. There is complete security in their country. Neither traveler nor inhabitant in it has anything to fear from robbers or men of violence."

Mali's capital of Timbuktu fell in 1468, and the scepter of power passed from Mali, once again eastward, to the Songhai empire centered in the city of Gao. Songhai under Muhammed Askia swiftly restored Timbuktu to its former greatness. The noted scholar Leo Africanus wrote of Timbuktu in Askia's reign that "there are numerous judges, doctors and clerics, all receiving good salaries from the king. He pays great respect to men of learning. There is a big demand for books in manuscript, imported from Barbary. More profit is made from the book trade than from any other line of business." Visiting scholars from Fez and Cairo taught at the university in Sankore and scholars from Timbuktu lived in hostels maintained for them by their own nation when they visited either of these cities. At the height of his power Muhammed Askia reigned from Algeria to northern Nigeria. Provincial governors ruled in the king's name and there were central ministries for finance, justice, home affairs, agriculture, forests and white peoples (i.e., Moors and Tuaregs). Taken in sum, therefore, the culture and political organization of the Sudanic states was comparable to that of Spain and more developed than that of the ruder, northern parts of Europe.

Why, then, did Spain and its northern neighbors go on to rule the world while the African states declined? The answer can be sought in several factors. One is that the Renaissance, with the spur the classical revival ultimately gave to technology, did not reach them, cut off as they were by a declining North Africa. Yet, after all, much of the classical revival and the early technology was derived from Arabic sources, so that isolation from Europe was perhaps less controlling than might be imagined. Another important factor is political, and has implications for Africa even today. Although these empires were highly centralized the extended kinship groups retained their political and economic power and, in general, continued to command the primary allegiance of the individual, so that whenever outside pressures disrupted the rule of the thin layer of literate bureaucrats the empire fell apart.

Above all, perhaps, there was geography. Spain and its successors had the open sea. They could receive wealth and stimulation from the far ends of the earth. The Sudanic empires were separated from the Guinea coast by the tropical forest, its diseases and its smaller kingdoms. They looked north, across their sea, the desert. When North Africa ceased to be a source of stimulation and the flow of wealth and ideas diminished to a mere trickle, the African kingdoms were left high and dry. New kingdoms arose, especially near the Guinea coast, where Europeans were now trading directly with Africans, and the Fulani jihads led to the creation of other new empires in the nineteenth century. But culturally the area did not so much decline as stagnate. When the British came to northern Nigeria at the end of the nineteenth century they found a series of late medieval kingdoms in all their splendor. But what would have been impressive in the fifteenth century was much less so at the dawn of the twentieth. Time and technology had passed Africa by.

While African civilization was flourishing in the west, the east was not standing still. Although Christian Ethiopia slept in her mountain stronghold, offshoots of the civilization on which she had built are traceable throughout the interior of East Africa.

Although we still know very little about this era, increasingly such common characteristics as terracing of hillsides, fortification of villages and the nature of political institutions (which as in the Western Sudan seem to have derived originally from Meroë) appear to link societies throughout East Africa during the period contemporary with the European Middle Ages. Centralization of political power, widespread trade and particular techniques of irrigation and soil conservation were distinctive features of these societies as was the prevalence of mining.

One northern center of this civilization, Engaruka, was a city of well over thirty thousand in what is now Kenya. The southern center was Zimbabwe in Rhodesia (slated to become that country's new name if African nationalists have their way). Here more has been done in the way both of excavation and speculation. The ruins of Zimbabwe have been variously dated and attributed to various non-African origins. The early white visitors—who destroyed much of the stone site in search of precious metals—were sure that no "natives" could have created these imposing ruins, so eerily reminiscent of Stonehenge. The great granite walls and battlements are now generally believed to have been begun about the eleventh century by a local Bantu people who had known the use of iron from the seventh century and who developed a large-scale mining civilization which exported ore to India during medieval times. This society is associated with the neighboring one of Mapungubwe, noted for its beaten gold, developed handicrafts and complex class system. The existence of these states, vaguely known to Europeans, gave rise to the legend of the fabulously wealthy African kingdom of Monomotapa. Actually the Monomotapa was the ruler of a Bantu group which had for a time occupied Zimbabwe before abandoning it and moving north. At the time of their first contact with the Portuguese, the Monomotapas ruled much of Rhodesia and part of Mozambique, but when they were finally reduced to Portuguese vassals in 1624 the area under their control had greatly diminished. But the explorers still were greedy for Monomotapa's fabled riches and not until the exploration of what is now Zambia by Rhodes's British South Africa Company in the late nineteenth century was it realized that the kingdom had long ago perished.

The interior states owed much of their prosperity to their contacts with the civilizations of the coast and participated in their downfall. For millennia the coastal areas of East Africa had been visited by traders from Asia Minor. They often settled there and they and their descendants mingled with or were absorbed by local peoples, including the Bantu after the latter occupied the area. From such commingling of cultures Swahili, the language of Tanzania, developed in the medieval period. Coastal cities such as Kilwa, at its height in the thirteenth and fourteenth centuries, were centers of trade and commerce. Iron from the interior was worked extensively and was exported to Asia. The cities were crowded with houses, mosques, and cemeteries; the harbors with ships. Kilwa was the site of the first mint south of the Sahara. Stoneware was imported from Siam and late Sung and early Ming porcelain from China.

As has been noted, the trade with China was cut off at the source in the late fifteenth century, and the fifteenth and early sixteenth centuries spelled the end of this East African civilization. The Portuguese encountering this flourishing commerce as they rounded the Cape were too small in numbers and weak in resources to conquer the area and turned instead to raiding and destruction. They completely disrupted trade, destroying many cities in their wars with the Arab sultanates. At the close of these wars the Portuguese controlled what is now Mozambique, and the coastal sultans controlled the coast north of it. But save for Zanzibar virtually every port was in ruins. The trans-oceanic trade to the East collapsed as the Portuguese and Dutch disrupted it at its Asian end as well. The interior cultures related to the coast also declined. The remaining coastal cities stagnated and became bases for what little trade was left—mostly cloves and slaves for the Near East.

At the same time that Zimbabwe and related cultures were

flourishing in Rhodesia and Kenya, there were apparently other important states throughout East and Central Africa about which we so far know very little. In Katanga a populous and wealthy society based on the mining and working of copper is known to have existed at least as early as the ninth century. Further exploration will almost certainly reveal the existence of medieval states of the Meroitic type in the region of Lake Victoria, the forerunners of the eighteenth- and nineteenth-century states encountered by early European explorers in Rwanda, Burundi and Uganda. But so little of the necessary archaeological work has been done that there is not much that can be said with certainty about the kind of societies these were or about the nature of their relations with the rest of Africa.

The forest states of West Africa constitute a curious chapter in African history because they were the direct result of increasing European penetration. The forest tribes of the area behind the Guinea coast (the coast itself was but lightly populated until major European penetration) had long been in contact with the Sudanic empires. With these empires they traded (it was the forest Negroes who were the suppliers of the gold and slaves eventually sent across the desert to North Africa) and from them they absorbed ideas, including that of the centralized, bureaucratic state and the divine kingship of the ancient Nile. But they had scant economic base on which to grow. The coming of the Europeans to the coast in search of gold and, later, slaves provided the needed impetus to growth. Instead of supplying gold and slaves to the middlemen of the Sudanic states, these forest kingdoms became the suppliers for another trade, the growth of which struck a final blow at the prosperity of their former partners.

To attribute the development of such advanced polities as Dahomey, Benin, the Ashanti Confederation and the Yoruba city-states to the slave trade alone would be an ironic oversimplification. Yet it was the major element in stimulating their growth from the sixteenth century on. It provided the economic surpluses necessary for the creation and maintenance of centralized power and the warfare state, offered an incentive for both, and, through access to European firearms, the means both for self-defense and for expansion. Kingdoms expanded in order to have a ready source of the slaves the European traders wanted and in order to eliminate the coastal middlemen.

When the slave trade tapered off, rapacious government had acquired a momentum of its own. Benin had been described as a great city by Dutch travelers in 1602; it was a peaceable city then. But when the British conquered "Bloody Benin" in 1897 they were horrified by what they saw. Evidence of human sacrifice was everywhere. Although relatively rare in traditional African religion and reserved ordinarily for grave public emergencies, human sacrifice had become popular as a way to deal with unsalable or excess slaves during the era of the slave trade; then, as constant warfare promoted by the need to obtain large numbers of slaves dehumanized society, it became an end in itself. From contact with Christianity the rulers of Benin had hit upon the technique of crucifixion. The rows of dying slaves the British found as they entered were hanging there to preserve the city from conquest, a last perverted gesture of supplication. But they were also a grim monument to the already advanced conquest of parts of Africa by certain European values.

IV

AFRICA CONQUERED

Colonialism in Africa is a recent phenomenon. The conquest of Africa took place in a few decades at the end of the nineteenth century and endured for half a century more. Yet Africa has long been influenced by European civilization, for good or ill. For centuries after the first contacts with Western Europe, the life of Africa, of the empires and the villages alike, continued in its accustomed paths. Only slowly did it become diverted to new paths as outside forces gradually pushed or insinuated themselves into the continent. Until the late-nineteenth-century scramble began, the relations of Africa with Europe were not unlike those it had long had with the Mediterranean and Asian worlds, relations among equals, with Africa serving, as it always had, as a matrix of ideas and impulses from throughout the old world.

To understand modern Africa and its attitudes it is essential to understand this precolonial relationship. The extended and tentative nature of European contact during this period meant that European influences have affected different Africans to different degrees—from the peoples of the coastal section of what is now Ghana, in contact with Europeans constantly for over four hundred years, to those of some parts of Central Africa who have never seen a white man. For the most part

European influence in Africa was until quite recently transmitted not directly by Europeans but by other Africans. The slave trade and the importation of firearms disrupted the existing balance of power among African states and caused bitter, destructive wars and political upheavals among Africans not involved directly with white traders. The introduction of new crops and new wants as a result of European trade changed ways of life in villages remote from areas of European trading activity. Influence without responsibility was the hallmark of European contact until the end of the nineteenth century.

The Europeans of these precolonial years are important not only for their influence on Africa but for their influence on the world's view of Africa. If they were slavers they helped shape the image of black men as slaves, even as natural slaves, an image that to some degree was internalized by Africans and their descendants overseas. If they were missionaries they shaped the world's image of Africans as "heathens," a subdivision of Kipling's "lesser breeds without the law." If they were explorers, "discovering" a mountain or river where Africans had dwelt for millennia, they shaped the image of a "darkest Africa" in which the benighted inhabitants were simply part of the landscape.

Most Europeans in the early days came in search of slaves. The history of the relationship of Europe and Africa until well into the nineteenth century is almost exclusively the history of the slave trade. The history of the relationship of Africa and the Americas, of Africa and the United States is also a history of slavery. Above all, the slave relationship—transformed into the colonial relationship—has conditioned the place of Africans and Africa in world affairs until this day. It is one of the peculiarities of language (not only of European languages but of African speech as well) that the very terms which define the race relationship suggest that black men are inferior. Black means dirty, black means evil (some African newspapers have referred to opponents as "white-hearted villains" but to little avail), and black is the night which African peasants fear as much as Western peasants always have. Providing a positive connotation for blackness, as many of the poets of Negritude have sought to do, would be a difficult task even if the relationships between Africans and Europeans had been relationships of equality rather than servitude. But black also came to mean slave.

Not all blacks were slaves, and at one time in Europe and the Mediterranean white men were slaves also. But eventually only black men were slaves, and they were slaves to white men. When slavery was replaced by colonial domination, again black men were the subjects and white men the rulers. White North Africans were subjects too, but nowhere were black men the masters. Much of contemporary African politics—domestic and international—is conditioned by the desire to prove that this relationship of black as subordinate to white is simply a fact of recent history, not something inherent in the nature of things.

Slavery was not unknown in Africa prior to the coming of the European, but it was a domestic slavery in which the slave (usually a criminal or a captive taken in battle) was regarded as a member of the household even if an inferior one. He was not a chattel to be disposed of at the whim of his master, but a person with traditionally defined rights as well as obligations. Thus to say that Africa was already sunk in slavery before the coming of the European is not accurate. Yet the fact remains that Africans willingly sold fellow Africans, especially those of other tribes, into bondage, and the Africans' condemnation of the slave trade has been muted by consciousness of their own role in it.

The first explorers and traders did not come in search of slaves. Phoenician sailors under orders from Pharaoh Necho circumnavigated Africa in 596 B.C., a journey taking three years. Hanno of the North African city of Carthage a century later planted colonies as far south as Senegal and reached the coast of modern Ghana. The Arab and oriental traders with East Africa apparently rounded the Cape and made obscure voyages into the Atlantic. But it was the Portuguese who opened up Africa to contemporary contact with the West, and by their activity as slavers, as well as by their ambivalent attitudes toward the African, set the tone of much of what was to follow.

The story of Portugal in Africa is extraordinary. The oldest imperialists on the continent, they have been the last to leave. Then as now they were overextended, a small country without the resources to build but with enough power to destroy, imbued with a sense of mission which curiously mingles some of mankind's lowest and loftiest impulses. Their role is unique, though they share, indeed to a unique degree, some general characteristics of Europeans in contact with Africa, especially prior to the twentieth century. One such characteristic was the smallness of their numbers. The Portuguese with a force of soldiers and sailors numbering probably less than one hundred thousand sought to conquer the whole world—Asia, Africa and the Americas—in the fifteenth century. Their epic struggle (mirrored in their great national epic, the *Lusiads* of Camoëns) left them impoverished and exhausted, their social corpse strewn across large areas of the world. At the outset they were little ahead technologically of those whom they traded with or attacked (their first great voyages owed their success largely to Arabic instrumentation), but they succeeded through courage, luck and sheer force of unscrupulousness. These qualities characterize the whole story of Europe in Africa. The Europeans were few in numbers and their technological superiority over Africans grew only slowly. Thus for a long time they could affect and disrupt but not take possession of Africa.

In 1444 the first African slaves reached Portugal from what is now Portuguese Guinea. In 1482 the Portuguese made contact with the kingdom of Benin, even then a great state; by 1486 they were sending it emissaries and missionaries, seeking to convert it into a Christian kingdom with which they could trade. But trade in what? Already in 1482 the Portuguese had built Elmina castle (in modern Ghana) as a port of embarkation and a bastion against rival slave traders.

In 1487 Bartholomeu Diaz rounded the Cape of Good Hope. In the years 1497 to 1499 Vasco da Gama went up the east coast of Africa, then the center of a flourishing Indian ocean trade, to India and back. The way to the East was open. This being so, there seemed little to attract the Portuguese to Africa. The real prizes were in Asia and the New World. Africa was a way station. It produced no products of interest to Europe that could not be gotten more cheaply from Asia or the Americas. It had one resource—black men, potential slaves.

The slave trade was as yet small compared to what it was destined to become, but already the Portuguese found it extremely lucrative and were determined to become its masters. They made contact with the kingdom of the Bakongo, a great state at the mouth of the Congo. At first they treated it as an equal and sought to Christianize it. Henrique, prince of the Bakongo, was consecrated a bishop in Rome in 1518 and many of his people embraced Catholicism. But missionaries were few and the lure of the slave trade great. Soon Portuguese slaving activities disrupted the kingdom. Appeals made by successive Popes to Portugal to mitigate the slave trade fell on deaf ears. Since 1510 the Portuguese had been supplying slaves to Spanish plantations in the New World (the Spaniards, curiously enough, were forbidden to engage in this trade themselves) and the temptation was too great. The struggle with the Bakongo, resentful toward the Portuguese for undermining their authority over vassal states, erupted into a great battle in 1660. Both sides went into battle under Christian banners, but the Portuguese won, and the kingdom of Bakongo was no more.

But Portugal was not strong enough to maintain its position of primacy in Africa. By 1642 the Dutch, who like the English did not even bother to send missionaries until centuries later, pushed the Portuguese off most of the important slave coasts of West Africa, though some individual Portuguese traders remained active in Nigeria. The Portuguese had reached a standoff with their Arab rivals along the east coast, and had retreated south of the Rivumo River, to present-day Mozambique. Angola, like the island of Fernando Po, continued to be of importance as a source or transshipment point of slaves for the New World, especially Brazil (which remained Portuguese until 1822 and did not abolish slavery until 1888), but Portuguese domination of the European connection with Africa was over. A few missionaries and slavers lingered on the coasts, but the Portuguese exercised no real authority outside the range of the guns of their forts. However, guns sold to black slavers enabled the latter to continue to ravage their fellow Africans, and civilization in the interior declined. Until current times, when some development has been undertaken as a result both of economic motivations and of outside criticism, the Portuguese territories have been backwaters, with the natives left to their own devices save when exploited or oppressed in casual if brutal fashion by listless Portuguese overlords.

To understand the slave trade and its significance for African history it is essential to realize that what is at issue is not only its basic inhumanity but, equally, its irresponsibility. Europeans were simply not interested in Africa, save for the Dutch settlers living out their own drama in isolation far to the South. Their interest was in Africans. The prize was the New World. Except for Fernando Po, the plantations on which slaves labored were in South America, the Caribbean, or what was to become the United States. The only contact one needed to have with Africa was to anchor off the coast, or build a small trading post there, and buy Africans. This focus on slavery alone made anything else happening on the continent of little interest or in any event largely unknown. There were no plantations, no mines, no colonies, no trade except as an auxiliary to slavery. There was no European political control save for one or two small port areas, simply treaties with chiefs along the coast designed to assure the rights of the traders. The slave trade was like a giant leech sucking the blood of Africa—

what happened to the body was of no concern. Except as disrupted by the slave trade, African life was left to follow its own course. But as a result of Europe's mastery of the seas, and, increasingly, of Africa's neighbors as well, except where the slave trade was important, the isolation of African life was now complete. All that was left of previous relations with the rest of the world were the traders in the interior who still carried on a shadow of the immemorial commerce with North Africa and Eastern coastal peoples still in truncated contact with the Near East.

Slavery had a massive impact. Figures on the slave trade change as new research makes greater precision possible. But from eight to twenty million slaves were sold in the Americas over the four centuries during which the trade flourished. Other millions died en route; in one of history's ironies, conditions apparently became progressively worse as pressures against the trade mounted and smugglers had to hide their cargoes below decks. Uncounted in these figures are those Africans taken as slaves by Arabs and Egyptians in the east, a smaller but still considerable number. Uncounted also are millions of Africans, slavers and enslaved, who died in slave raids and the other millions who died in wars caused by the political upheavals which accompanied the trade. Yet somehow Africa survived. In part this was due to the fact that slavery existed over a long period of time; the average loss per year as a percentage of the population was small. In addition, slavery brought with it contact with new techniques and crops which made support of larger populations possible. It is one of the paradoxes of the slave trade that some areas—especially Nigeria and Ghana—from which the greatest number of slaves were taken are today among the most populous and developed in Africa.

The demographic, political and economic consequences of slavery not only completely changed the internal dynamics of the continent but had other less-direct consequences as well. As centralized kingdoms grew to provide slaves for Europeans, with the help of guns purchased with slaves, so also did large-scale slavery, with the slave increasingly regarded merely as property, rather than as in tradition simply a socially inferior being. Arbitrary government and gratuitous cruelty increased, too. The downward saga of bloody Benin is an extreme example of a story repeated many times over.

If slavery stimulated political development and trade in some areas while disrupting it in others, it simultaneously inhibited economic growth. Why engage in constructive economic activity when one could conquer one's neighbors and sell them to the European for coveted luxuries? The slave trade made other trade unprofitable. When it declined, many European powers lost interest in Africa and those who remained were forced to search desperately for another economic base for their activities.

We have already referred to the most important result of slavery, the creation of a situation in which political domination of black by white became part of the proper order of things. This was significant not only in Africa but in the New World too. In Brazil and the Caribbean Negroes came as slaves; they remained to form population groups which are still striving to overcome the onus of their former status. So too in the United States. In both cases the slave status of blacks made it easier to justify white political domination in Africa and vice versa. It is no accident that today these two relationships are being altered simultaneously.

The story of the impact of the legitimate traders and the missionaries upon Africa is largely the story of the movement against slavery. Explorers such as Livingstone sought to alert Europe to the horrors of the continuing Arab slave trade in East Africa; missionaries went to Africa as part of the same impulse that issued in antislavery agitation. It is to England that most of the credit for the antislavery crusade must go. Thus it was England that made the first reluctant steps toward establishing a new relationship with Africa, one that was to eventuate in modern colonialism.

It is an article of faith with most contemporary African intellectuals that the principal motivation for the European conquest was economic. Inspired usually by Marxist teachings in some form, and especially by Lenin's updating and revision of the English writer J. A. Hobson's classic *Imperialism,* they scoff at the idea that humanitarian motives played a major role in increased European activity in Africa. Yet the fact remains that just as the slave trade was a major factor in bringing Europeans into contact with Africa in the first wave of European imperialism, it was the desire to abolish slavery that was a major, if not the sole, motivation of the second, as far as Britain was concerned.

The demise of the slave trade can be laid to many factors. Economically it was becoming less intrinsically important as the eighteenth century drew to a close. An improvement in economic circumstances was also helping to create a moral revulsion against it. The seventeenth and eighteenth centuries had been an era of poverty in Europe itself; indenture and virtual slavery were common. In an England where the poor could be forced off the land and into the slums of the new cities of the industrial revolution, shanghaied into His Majesty's Navy —a brutal and degrading existence—hanged or transported for the theft of a shilling handkerchief, people could scarcely be expected to get very excited about the plight of Africans. Contrary to the romanticism of some contemporary conservatives, life even within European civilization was not unlike that which Hobbes postulated as the state of nature. If not solitary, it was often nasty, brutish and short. But increasing prosperity helped lay the groundwork for a moral revival. Especially in England increasing attention was given to ameliorating the condition of the working classes and to such moral reforms as temperance and better treatment for women and children. Out of this general movement abolitionism sprang.

In 1772 Lord Mansfield's decision made slavery illegal in

England, and soon the slave trade was outlawed throughout the empire. With the assumption of moral superiority that was to become the hallmark of Victorianism and in order to protect her general economic position, Britain began to use her overwhelming naval and economic power to see that what she had belatedly recognized as immoral was treated as such by her competitors also. In 1808 the United States forbade the importation of slaves. Between 1800 and 1820 Denmark, Portugal, the Netherlands and Spain made international trade in slaves illegal, although they did not outlaw the institution of slavery itself.

But outlawing the trade and abolishing it were two different things. Smuggling of slaves was still profitable, and only England had the desire, under pressure from abolitionist elements at home, to do much about ending it. The need to control slaving African states, the need for bases from which to police the smuggling of slaves, and the need for homes for freed slaves slowly pushed Britain back into an African involvement from which the lack of solid economic attractions should logically have removed her. In 1792 Freetown in Sierra Leone was established as a home for freed slaves, leading to the creation of a British protectorate along the coast. This example was followed half-heartedly by the French with Libreville in the Gabon, and also by a private American group, organized by George Washington's nephew Bushrod Washington, which in 1820 settled some former American Negro slaves in what was later to become Liberia. The need to do something for areas where the end of the slave trade left semi-Europeanized Africans dependent on Britain led to an increase in the British commitment in the Gold Coast. The need to destroy the sources of smuggled slaves led to the capture of Lagos in 1851 and of Benin in 1897. Having taken over these areas and destroyed their means of livelihood, the slave trade, the British found themselves in the position of having to sustain them against their enemies and provide an alternate economic base.

In order to furnish these areas with a source of livelihood, legitimate trade had to be stimulated and traders protected against hostile Africans and rivals from other nations. Missionaries taught Africans how to grow marketable crops, and corporations such as the Royal Niger Corporation, founded in 1896, sought to serve both British imperial interests and those of their shareholders by discovering and developing exploitable resources. For it was a cardinal principle of British policy that colonies had to be self-supporting. Abolitionists and missionary interests were strong enough to insist that the Royal Navy, which existed anyway, be used to suppress slavery, but except for a brief revival of imperialism as a popular creed, under Prime Minister Disraeli, British policy throughout the nineteenth century was based on the Manchester liberal belief in free trade, low taxes and limited government. Anti-imperialism was the vogue; no one save a few strange characters such as Cecil Rhodes dreamed of empire in philosophic or racial terms. Private individuals of course sought their own fortunes, but from a public standpoint colonies were not sought to make profits; profits were sought to support colonies. Like it or not Britain was being pushed deeper and deeper into Africa. By a process which might be described as the falling-domino theory in reverse, each victory brought the need for more victories; each chief who accepted British "protection" had hostile neighbors who had to be defeated and who, when defeated, had to be protected in turn. In the Gold Coast, Nigeria and Sierra Leone Britain found herself forced into the interior.

The desire to end slavery was coupled with a humanitarian desire to convert Africans to Christianity and to improve their way of life, that is to make them more European. To do this more had to be known about the interior of Africa. Despite the fact that for centuries Europeans had been in intimate contact with the coasts, their ignorance of the interior was virtually complete. Now, under the patronage of missionary and scientific societies, explorers began to crisscross the continent, not only in search of geographical knowledge, but in an attempt to expose the continuation of the slave trade, especially the slaving carried on under Arab aegis in the east. From 1841 to 1873 the great Livingstone roamed East Africa making revelations about the slave trade which forced British intervention in that area.

From time immemorial East Africa had been a source of slaves for the East. Since usually only castrated males were shipped, they made little demographic impact on the areas (as far afield as China) to which they were taken. The smaller population of East Africa made slave raids even more destructive to civilization than they had been in the West. Well into the nineteenth century, Arabs continued to trade for ivory and slaves. Native rulers such as the Kabaka of Buganda (whose successor today is the chief of state of Uganda) received arms and cloth from the Arabs and they, not the Arabs, did the slave raiding. The Egyptians (for the most part actually Turks and Albanians who then ruled the country) were more direct in searching for slaves to fill their armies. Their method of raiding was to seize the cattle which were the Africans' mainstay and hold them for ransom until slaves were produced. The British had some nominal control over what was going on in Egypt, and they controlled the Indian Ocean. Under pressure from antislavery elements at home, the government had to act, however reluctantly. The slave trade to India was outlawed in 1822. In 1827 it was outlawed in the coastal dominions of the sultan of Zanzibar, and, in 1873, under the threat of British naval bombardment, the sultan outlawed it entirely, and a Christian cathedral was built on the site of the slave market in Zanzibar.

Slavery in East Africa was a long time dying, despite the extent to which the British were drawn into the interior in attempts to check it at its source. As long as it was an accepted social institution in Ethiopia and the Arabian peninsula, clandestine trade was almost impossible to stamp out, and lingered on until well into the twentieth century. But long before it was destroyed powerful interests in England were discovering that the Africa to which the antislavery crusade had led Britain might be a source of profit after all. Trade followed the flag. Other nations, watching the growth of British power with interest and growing envy, were drawn to Africa from the outset by motives other than humanitarian. A new age of imperialism was dawning which was to lead to the rapid conquest, partition and colonization of the whole continent.

Until the middle of the nineteenth century there was no systematic extension of settlement and sovereignty comparable to the conquests of European and Asian states, to the colonization of Latin America, or to the Russian and American movements overland across their continents. A few short decades at the end of the nineteenth century were to change all this. Spurred on largely by the activities of King Léopold of Belgium and the post-Bismarckian dreams of grandeur of German monarchs, a scramble for Africa was to take place which would soon bring virtually all of the continent under European flags, and would put an end to autonomous political and social development throughout the continent.

The conquest of Africa in the last years of the century did not begin from a dead start. As we have seen, various European lodgments already existed along the coast. The story of the conquest is in part the story of the extension of these bases inland, though its principal impetus came from new forces, and the postpartition map of Africa bears little resemblance to what might have been expected from a survey of European interests at the beginning of the nineteenth century. This is so because it was not in response to interest in Africa but to other concerns of the colonial powers that the scramble took place. As Professor Fage puts it, "deeply as it was to affect all the people of the continent, the partition was in its origins essentially a projection into Africa of the politics of Europe."

What did Africa look like at the beginning of the era of conquest? North Africa had been slowly coming under European control. The British were replacing the French as the paramount economic and political influence in the tangled affairs of Egypt. France had invaded the coastal areas of Algeria, where the disorder which had led to America's "war" with the Barbary pirates still continued. France originally sought to avoid any commitment in the interior, but a holy war by the Muslims against the French in 1832 led to increased involvement. In 1840 General Bigaud began to expel hostile elements among the indigenous population and to replace them with French *colons*. But all the recalcitrant inhabitants of Algeria could not be sent to the Sahara, so that as the French colonists moved in they displaced Arabs from the land but did not form a geographically compact settlement themselves, becoming rather what was to be a fairly large upper caste of settlers, resting on a rapidly increasing indigenous population.

It is noteworthy that although Algeria had no centralized government at the time of the French invasion, it did not surrender to alien domination without a struggle. Despite their technological inferiority, Africans in many areas of the continent long resisted conquest. Algeria, which was to be the scene of the longest and bloodiest independence struggle in Africa prior to 1965, put up a spirited resistance to its loss of freedom. It was not until 1879 that resistance ceased. By this time, which marked the beginning of civil administration throughout the area, 150,000 Frenchmen had lost their lives in subjugating Algeria. It is worth noting the time dimensions involved—almost fifty years from invasion to pacification, then a stretch of seventy-five years before armed rebellion broke out against France in 1954. Memories of independence died hard. For most African peoples the span between loss of sovereignty and the struggle for independence was shorter. What cannot be overemphasized is the briefness of the period of effective European occupation and control over most of Africa. A period of long contact and influence, yes, but a short period of actual colonial rule.

While France was establishing itself in Algeria (a conquest

which resulted ultimately in the settlement in the area of a million whites among and above nine million Africans), another group of Europeans was expanding its lodgment at the opposite tip of the continent. In 1652, contemporaneous with Dutch activity in the East Indies and in New Amsterdam, the Dutch were landing at the Cape of Good Hope. They were not interested in colonization. Their governor, Van Riebeeck, was working for the Dutch East India Company. The Cape was important only as a base on the way to the real prize, the Indies, a base where ships could put in for repairs and fresh food and water. Just as slavery had arisen in response to European interests in the New World, so the beginnings of the race problem in South Africa resulted from interest in Southeast Asia. Africa was being critically affected by events in continents thousands of miles away. The Dutch attempted to discourage settlement beyond the station's immediate needs, but settlers came anyway. They soon began to move further inland, under the pressure of their own sharp population increase and the need for more pasture for their cattle. The Dutch settlers, in time augmented by Huguenots fleeing religious strife in France and by Germans as well, soon overran the hapless Hottentots in their path, reducing them to slavery. Napoleon conquered the Netherlands in the course of his wars and Britain took possession of the Dutch overseas bases; what was originally supposed to have been a temporary arrangement became permanent and the British annexed the Cape in 1806, to the great disgust of its inhabitants. In 1820, five thousand English settlers arrived. Mutual hostility between Boer (Dutch for farmer) and Briton was aggravated by the fact that the British clergy were hostile to slavery, unlike the Dutch *dikents*, who saw the world through Old Testament eyes and looked on the black men as the sons of Ham, ordained by God to be hewers of wood and drawers of water for the Chosen People (a theological justification for racial superiority which persists in South Africa to this day). Finally, crowded by the English and threatened with the loss of their slaves as a consequence of

British legislation, most of the Boers moved north and away from British control, into the wilderness. In the 1830's occurred the Great Trek, the keystone of modern South African history.

Several facts about South Africa, important for present-day politics, stand out in this story. The first is the relative recency of British settlement in South Africa. It is about 170 years from the first Dutch settlement to the first real British settlement, only 145 years from then until today. The Afrikaner can look upon the English-speaking South African in much the same way descendants of the Mayflower pilgrims looked upon the "new immigration" to the United States after the 1880's. Since the Afrikaner has been effectively cut off from the lands of his ancestors for more than 150 years (despite a trickle of immigrants) while the Englishman until recently was in intimate contact with his, the former can look upon himself as the only real South African and on his English compatriot as a mere bird of passage. Afrikaner nationalism is a real nationalism, based on common origins, culture and history, which would exist even if there was no racial problem between black and white.

Like all nationalisms Afrikaner nationalism has its myths. The Great Trek is to the Afrikaners what the Frontier is to most Americans: a symbol of victorious struggle against great odds, a conquest of the wilderness and of hostile human forces. The South African national anthem, *Die Stem,* and all the symbolism of Afrikaner nationalism derives from this seminal experience. Bitter battles with the Xhosa, Zulus and Swazis, which the Boers won not by overwhelming technological superiority or by superiority in numbers but by doggedness and determination, marked the trek northward.

The struggles of the trekkers against hostile tribes have given birth to another legend, that the Bantus were as recent arrivals in the veldt as the Boers themselves. It is true that there was considerable population movement in the area during this time, due to the rise of the Zulus and the displacement of other peoples, and the Afrikaners contend that they moved up from the south just as the Bantus moved down from the north, that they won by right of conquest, and that they permitted the Bantus to settle among them and benefit from the side effects of their industry in areas where the various tribes were no more the original inhabitants than were the Boers. This rationale is generally accepted by most white South Africans and forms a major moral justification for their claims to political supremacy. However, the evidence of shipwrecked Portuguese sailors who made their way overland from the South African coast to Mozambique indicates that all of the cultivable area was even then occupied by Negroes so that, while individual tribes may have been on the move in the mid-nineteenth century, the Bantus had preceded the Afrikaners in the occupation of this part of South Africa by at least three hundred years.

The Boer victories were to be in vain. Dingaan the Zulu was defeated by Pretorius the Boer in 1839 and the Republic of Natal proclaimed, but Natal was annexed by the British in 1845. Many of the Boers moved north again, beyond the Orange River—beyond the Vaal—but British law and suzerainty pursued them. Yet its aim was not conquest so much as stability. Britain would have preferred to leave as much of the area in the hands of the blacks as possible, to restrict its frontiers and thereby its military commitments and the taxes needed to sustain them. Not till the discovery of diamonds in 1867 and the coming of Rhodes was Britain interested in conquest in southern Africa for its own sake.

In West Africa the British and French were fitfully extending the positions they had held for hundreds of years. Freetown officially became a colony in 1808 and Lagos in present-day Nigeria was annexed to the British crown in 1861. The primary British motive in this area was still the suppression of the slave trade and its replacement by peaceful commerce, but a new note is clearly distinguishable.

The Africans of the Gold Coast, long in contact with British ways, had drawn up a constitution for a Fanti confederacy and asked for self-rule. Britain felt them unready and unable to fight off such enemies as the Ashanti to the north so, having finally given up the attempt to get the British merchants there to rule themselves, the British government made the Gold Coast a crown colony in 1874. The institution of colonial status for this area was clearly against the will of the leaders of the local population. Domination was beginning to feed upon itself.

The France of Louis Napoleon was also increasingly active in Africa. Louis Faideherbe, governor of the old colony of Senegal, slowly began to expand it economically and territorially. Little movement into the interior was yet possible, however; economic opportunity seemed meager; and the Africans further inland—descendants of the inhabitants of the great Sudanic empires of the past—were in a state of turmoil as the result of constant religious wars for the purification and expansion of Islam.

Within a few short years this almost casual European nibbling away at Africa was to be replaced by a headlong rush to conquer the continent, a change heralded and spurred on by two European monarchs, the King of Belgium and the Kaiser of Germany. Léopold of Belgium, a vain and power-hungry man, was the head of an artificial state—itself created as a buffer in European politics as late as 1830. Belgium was too small for his ambitions. Léopold toured the world looking for likely areas to conquer. Deciding on Africa, he arranged for a conference to be called under his auspices in 1876 to further the humanitarian causes of exploration, Christianization and the suppression of slavery. Ostensibly in order to advance these worthy causes, he backed the expeditions of Stanley into the vast African interior, the basin of the great Congo River. But his real aims were revealed in 1885 when the powers, led by the United States (acting under peculiar influences ranging from subornation by Léopold's agents to illusions on the part of American Negroes), recognized the Congo Free State with Léopold as its personal ruler. Under Léopold's rule all the forces of commercial rapacity suppressed by the abolition of the slave trade ravaged Africa anew. Vast fortunes were made (in a six-year period one company made a profit of three million dollars on an initial investment of forty-five thousand dollars). But the human cost was tremendous. The atrocities perpetrated included the torture, mutilation and death of hundreds of thousands if not millions of Congolese; so impenetrable is the curtain of darkness which descended upon the Congo that it is impossible to be certain of the precise extent of its suffering. The revelations of a few courageous men, such as the British consul Roger Casement (an Irish nationalist executed during World War I by Britain as a German agent), shocked the world into putting an end to the monstrosity, and in 1908, though Léopold personally retained vast wealth within the country, the administration of the Congo was turned over to the Belgian government.

In theory the creation of the Congo Free State was to have reduced imperial and economic rivalry in the heart of Africa by neutralizing the Congo basin, to which all powers were to have equal commercial access. But as one historian has put it, Léopold's skill at intrigue (to say nothing of the general villainy of his enterprises) poisoned the whole atmosphere. Largely as a result of the Free State episode both the profits to be made in Africa and the relation of political control to the making of profits was better appreciated. The Scramble for Africa was about to begin.

Imperial Germany jumped the gun. With what has been aptly described as "stealth and swiftness" German agents between 1883 and 1885 stole into various parts of Africa, signed treaties for trade and protection with bemused local chiefs, and on this basis set up the colonies of Southwest Africa, Togo, Cameroun and what were later to become Tanganyika, Rwanda and Burundi. Germany's motives were various. One was its search for a "place in the sun," which forced Bismarck to act counter to his own instincts and embark on the extra-

European adventures he had so long counseled against. The new policy made some sense even in terms of Bismarckian doctrine; the hope was to set Britain and France against each other in Africa, which required first of all making Africa itself a general bone of contention. In this Germany almost succeeded; but through her naval buildup and her general arrogance she overreached herself and ended by bringing about the Franco-British "entente cordiale" of 1904 which doomed her hopes. Here again one sees Africa used as a pawn in extra-African politics. Perhaps the best that can be said for Léopold and his successors is that at least they have in their rapacity paid Africa the compliment of wanting her for her own sake.

Key to the scramble was the Berlin conferences. In 1884 and 1885 they proclaimed the all-important doctrine that before a European power's rule over African territory could be recognized there had to be "effective occupation" of that territory, and in the 1890 Treaty of Berlin this was defined to mean effective occupation inland as well as along the coastal strip. No longer could nations claim vast tracts of African land simply because hundreds of years ago they had been the first to explore them or enslave the native inhabitants or because now a few traders or missionaries were puttering around a decrepit coastal port. One had to plant one's flag, leave officials behind and secure some recognition of one's authority from the inhabitants. This meant that nations which had been sleeping on past laurels had to look to them, that virtually everything was up for grabs, and that, even if you had no desire to acquire additional African real estate now, you had better seize it now if you thought you might want it in the future or in order to make sure your rivals did not take it first.

All over Africa new projects for exploration, conquest and exploitation were launched. In the shuffle dormant Portugal could not keep up the pace and her claim of empire from sea to sea was effectively challenged. Newcomer Germany, methodically aggressive, made off with much of the booty. Effective occupation often meant little more than token exploration or occupation, but it did mean that no local ruler could any longer deny Europeans access to his domains, and it meant that the flags of Europe flew all over the continent except in ancient Ethiopia (which took up the hunt itself and vastly enlarged its traditional domains by conquest) and in struggling Liberia, which was constantly in danger of falling into imperial clutches.

After Germany, with its rapid moves and consolidations, France was the leading contestant in the race. René Caillié had explored much of the Sahara prior to 1830. In the seventies such French Catholic missionary orders as the White Fathers and the Congregation of the Holy Ghost began to be active in Africa, thus enlarging the influence of a France ruled by an anti-clerical republican regime. While not neglecting North Africa (Tunis became a protectorate in 1881), the French in 1879 began systematically to move into the Western Sudan from their base at Senegal, and to reconstitute their old dormant holdings on the Guinea coast. The slaving kingdom of Dahomey fell in 1893. Ancient Timbuktu, by now showing little sign of its old glory, fell in 1894, Gao in 1898. But the remnants of the storied empires did not fall without a struggle. Samory, head of the Tukulor empire of the Fulani and grandfather of Guinea's president Sékou Touré, fought on for years before his defeat in 1898. The French had to fight most of the way in taking over the Sudanic regions, and it was decades before military control was succeeded by civilian rule in the interior of French Africa. Houphouët-Boigny, today the president of the Ivory Coast, was four years old when his tribe, the Baoulé, were finally subjugated by the French in 1909, and military pacification of the country did not end until 1917. In terms of history the European conquest of Africa is but a matter of days and consequently has had limited opportunity to affect the deepest springs of human behavior. In large measure the African political renascence of today is simply the reassertion of African identity after a brief period of conquest.

In East and Central Africa Rhodes and others were laying

the foundations of the settler regimes that were to be a cause of so much grief to later British statesmen. Having traded Bismarck Heligoland for Uganda, the British sought to block further German expansion up the African coast from Tanganyika. A railroad was to be built from the coast to secure Uganda. But it needed freight traffic to pay for itself, so white settlers were imported to farm the land along its route. In this way the foundations of the Kenya problem were laid, Kenya being formally constituted in 1895.

To the south the forces of history represented by gold hunger and Cecil Rhodes had caught up with the Boer republics. The Boer War of 1898–1902 meant the end of the brief efflorescence of imperial fever in late-nineteenth-century Britain, as the war dragged on and became less gallant and more sordid. British conquest subdued but did not convert the Boers, and the death of over twenty-five thousand Boer women and children in what were in effect concentration camps set up as part of Britain's anti-guerrilla campaign did nothing to lay the groundwork for further peaceful relations, though a magnanimous restoration of full self-government to the Boer republics within the Union of South Africa in 1910 deceived British statesmen and many South Africans into believing that the wounds were healing.

Rhodes had been continuously obsessed with the idea of moving north, of conquering the dreamed-of riches of the interior and giving Britain control over all Central and East Africa. By various means (unauthorized actions, bluff, and downright corruption of British governments) he succeeded in drawing a largely reluctant nation into his wake. Though thwarted by Léopold, Rhodes's agents pushed the Portuguese aside and in 1890 founded Salisbury, the capital of present-day Rhodesia. Lobengula, king of the Matabele, was finally broken in battle in 1893 and, the chiefs of the Nyasaland area having accepted British protection against incursions of Arab slavers and Portuguese in 1891, the foundations of the later Central African Federation were laid. Empty adjacent spaces became British protectorates in order to thwart the Boers, Germans or Rhodes himself, and Bechuanaland, Basutoland and Swaziland were created.

The final outlines of European partition of Africa were hardly drawn before World War I. In 1898 a British and Egyptian force under Kitchener, later to achieve dubious fame in World War I, defeated the Khalifa, leader of Sudanese religious fanatics, at Omdurman, in an unusually bloody campaign that cost the lives of twenty thousand Sudanese. The fact that the young Winston Churchill saw action as a correspondent at Omdurman underlines the recency of colonial sway in Africa; the Sudan was an independent state for almost a decade before Churchill's death. The victory at Omdurman did more than create the Anglo-Egyptian Sudan (ruled by Britain under the façade of joint sovereignty). It ended France's dreams of continental hegemony. A French force under Captain Marchand had made a brilliant forced march across the Sahara, seeking to reach the upper Nile and establish French power at its headwaters. When they reached Fashoda they found to their chagrin that the British were already established in the Sudan. The resulting Fashoda crisis almost brought Europe to war, but its settlement marked the beginning of a Franco-British rapprochement which served as the basis of the alliance system under which World War I was fought. The major African consequence was that, to Germany's diplomatic discomfiture, the French in return for backing down in upper Egypt were given a free hand in Morocco in 1904. Despite the decisions of the Europeans (Morocco was partitioned with Spain in 1912), it took almost thirty years more before the French under the great Marshal Lyautey were able to pacify the fierce Rif nomads of the interior.

Italy entered the scramble as a scavenger. She began to move in on Ethiopia by taking possession of Eritrea and Somaliland in the period 1885–92. Defeated by her intended Ethiopian victims at the battle of Adowa in 1896, she took Libya from the decadent Turkish empire in 1912.

With this action all of Africa except for Ethiopia and Liberia was now under European flags. The map of Africa, though it did not show red from Cape to Cairo as Rhodes had dreamed, was cut into strange shapes by boundary lines whose artificiality was often overtly attested to by their unnatural straightness. The infiltration of the chartered companies had been succeeded by the direct political rule of the conqueror. Most Africans had accepted foreign domination peacefully, hardly imagining what it would mean, above all unable to conceive of a form of domination that would not only tax and exploit them, as conquerors had always traditionally done, but would seek to change their habitual ways as well. But resistance smoldered in the interior of several states, and the inhabitants of German territories revolted against a savagery that was a rehearsal for Belgium in World War I and Europe in World War II; more than 120,000 Tanganyikans were killed in the revolt of 1912 and over 60,000 tribesmen of Southwest Africa were exterminated in the surrealistic nightmare of 1904. But most of the continent was quiescent. Yet change was already in the air. Nationalism was stirring in North and West Africa at the same time that Central and East Africa were still being penetrated. But this change was taking place under European domination, and in part as a result of it. Brief though the period of effective European control of most of Africa was, it was a traumatic experience for Africans, accelerating their contact with modernity, and largely shaping the Africa of today.

Once the European powers had conquered Africa they had to find a means of ruling and exploiting it. The system they created for this purpose is usually called colonialism; but it is a misnomer. What is ordinarily called the colonial period should really be called the Era of European Occupation. This distinction is not merely a matter of semantics. Failure to understand the differences between colonialism and political and economic occupation is the cause of much misunderstanding about the African past and about Africa's present role in the world.

Colonialism has hoary and varied origins as a social institution. The term itself is rooted in ancient Greece. Colonialism in the classic sense consists of the movement of members of a particular political community to a new geographic area, usually in order to find increased living space or greater economic opportunity. In some cases in the old Near East and Asia, colonies of Greeks, Phoenicians, Indians, Chinese and others settled peacefully among other peoples, usually as merchants.

The first phase of modern Western colonial expansion consisted of the planting of European settlers in areas which were virtually uninhabited, except for small groups of technologically backward peoples. In these cases it was but a short time before the overwhelming majority of the inhabitants were immigrants or descendants of immigrants from the colonizing power. Even in most parts of Latin America the colonizing race, or those with whom they had interbred, came to outnumber the purely indigenous peoples or imported slaves. These colonies were originally under the control of the motherland, but eventually rule from a distance became distasteful to local interests and, despite ties of blood and culture, the drive for political autonomy became irresistible. Beginning with the United States, colonies composed of European settlers and their progeny sought and gained their independence by various means.

But such assertions of independence were not at all analogous to those which later took place in Western-controlled areas of Asia and Africa. The former were in effect revolts of white settlers against the control of a "Colonial Office" or its equivalent. They had little in common sociologically with the uprisings of the indigenous inhabitants of conquered countries against a racially and culturally alien occupying force. Despite the fact that many contemporary non-Western rebels have been deeply influenced by and able to make use of the rhetoric and political theory of the American revolution, it derives from a cultural and political situation radically different from their own. This is one reason why the idea that the United States was the first modern nation to free itself from colonial rule and is thus destined to be a leader of the forces of anticolonialism, though sincerely proposed by Americans and non-Westerners alike, often leads to misperceptions of reality, false expectations on both sides, and eventual disillusion and hostility. By the standard of the old colonialism the United States was a leader and precursor of anticolonial revolt. But by the standards of the new colonialism—the imperialist control of subject races—the American revolution was a revolt in many ways analogous to that threatened by present-day white Rhodesians. The United States's position vis-à-vis colonialism must realistically be measured by its role in the Philippines, Puerto Rico, Hawaii and the Western Pacific islands rather than by the Boston Tea Party. For a colonial power it is a good record, but it is the record of a colonial power.

Except for a few areas such as Algeria, South Africa, Kenya, Rhodesia and Angola, all of which at one time or another have gone through periods of white-settler resentment against metropolitan domination, the African colonies of European powers were not even remotely true colonies in the older sense. They were conquered overseas provinces, and the nonwhite inhabitants (an overwhelming majority even in areas of substantial white settlement) were not "colonials" in the true political or cultural sense, but alien subject peoples.

Colonialism in Africa was, therefore, above all else a system of political rule in which ultimate power was in the hands of members of a different racial or ethnic group from overseas. Much has been written about the differences in the administrative techniques used in Africa by Britain, France, Belgium and Portugal, but although these differences had and have important consequences in Africa, the differences were both less consistent and less basic than often imagined. Much more important were the features which "colonial" rule throughout Africa had in common. It was, first of all, a system of alien domination. Even in North Africa, where racial differences between rulers and ruled were least pronounced, even in areas—especially the British-ruled areas of Buganda and Northern Nigeria —where "indirect rule" was practiced and some façade of indigenous control and administration was preserved, the ultimate fact was that final political decisions were in the hands not only of persons who were not democratically subject to the control of those ruled, but persons who were aliens. Throughout most of Africa this meant that black men were ruled by the white men who for so long and in so many areas had made them slaves. Revolt against colonial domination therefore meant not so much revolt against government without consent of the governed as revolt against government by strangers. Freedom meant self-determination on an ethnic basis, and even today Africans are less concerned, if at all, by the fact that most of them live in one-party dictatorships with minimal civil liberties than they are about at last being ruled by men of their own flesh and blood, men with whom (always allowing for tribal and social differences) they can identify.

Colonial rule in addition to being rule by outsiders, was rule by the executive. Whether the colonial civil service ruled directly, as in most French, Belgian, Portuguese and many British territories, or with the collaboration of traditional native authorities, it ruled without the effective check of legislatures representative of local interests. In traditional society discussion of tribal policy among elites before its enunciation was the usual rule and the chiefs ruled in the name of a common good which they had superior power to perceive and in accordance with customs which were unchallengeable. Under colonialism the chiefs were replaced or supplemented by white administrators who ruled in the name of an abstract wisdom and probity which was not to be subject to the play of special interests. Today rule by the executive, now intertwined with a single political movement acting in the name of a renascent Africa, is the ready successor to this colonial authority. Colonial rule was a school for subjugation, not participation. The very same "emergency regulations" under which African political leaders were imprisoned by the imperialists are once again being used in many independent African states to silence and destroy political opposition. Where traditional rulers such as chiefs and emirs still flourish or at least play a role in government, they play it, with few exceptions, in a subjugation to the new nationalist state closely akin to the role they played under colonialism.

The idea of government domination and direction of the economy is also a carryover from colonial rule. Even if the end result of colonial economic activity was primarily the profits of foreign investors, it was activity sanctioned and managed by government. In some cases instead of government running the economy, the private corporations controlled the government. For a long time in some areas essentially governmental functions, including the preservation of law and order, were directly undertaken by what the British called "chartered companies," private organizations authorized by a colonial power to exercise jurisdiction over a particular area. In any event there was no "free market" economy in the colonies. Indigenous businessmen or farmers producing for markets could not act autonomously. Colonialism was a perverse kind of socialism in that all of what the Marxists would call the "commanding heights" of the economy were government owned or regulated: railroads, ports, airlines, public utilities were almost everywhere government built and owned. What crops were encouraged or what industries developed was a matter for government decision. All real economic initiative came from above, from the political rulers. Today African governments operating under various rubrics of "African socialism" are still largely following in the footsteps of their colonial predecessors, often with their advice, and even with the use of some of their personnel.

This is not to say that the colonial economy was socialist in the sense of being egalitarian as well as planned. The extent to which colonial economies were exploitative is a matter of much controversy and myth. There is a sense in which all economies are exploitative in that they seek to maximize the use of available resources. While much poverty and social dislocation in

Africa resulted from turning from subsistence to cash crops and from the disturbance of village life caused by migrant labor, nevertheless the poorest African countries today tend to be those where there was the least economic activity under colonialism, because economic exploitation means not only the use of the labor of miners and farmers but also the creation of mines, roads, railroads, ports and marketing facilities. The British government tended to neglect the economic development of its colonies, insisting that the colonies pay their own way even in the short run and not emphasizing public investment in them, though private investment was encouraged and in a few nations—most notably Zambia—was significant. The French were more willing to invest public funds in the hope of stimulating growth, especially in agricultural productivity. Throughout Africa some private investors of course reaped huge profits, but profits to a few foreign investors may involve economic loss to the colonizing power as a whole. Colonies were often a step in a process whereby money was ultimately transferred from the pocket of one foreign national to that of another, since the cost of colonial development and government might be levied on different individuals than those with profitable investments in the colony.

Only an omniscient accountant—a deity with a CPA credential—could draw up an accurate balance sheet of who profited and who lost in the colonial relationship and to what extent. But Africans generally, along with many non-Africans, believe otherwise. Unable to accept the reasons of humanitarianism, power politics or sheer accident that brought the colonial powers to Africa and kept them there, and strongly influenced by reformist economic literature, they are convinced that the colonies were a source of great economic gain to the colonial powers as such. This would be an argument of merely moral or historical interest were it not for the fact that it has a vital corollary. If the colonies were an important source of profit to the colonizers, the termination of those profits as a result of the end of colonial political domination necessarily means that these profits are now available for distribution to the inhabitants of the former colonies. An end to colonial rule thus logically means a greatly improved domestic living standard. It was upon this expectation that much of the dynamism of African nationalism was built. Insofar as living standards have not risen spectacularly since independence, and in some cases have even declined for a variety of reasons including falls in world raw-material prices, poor economic planning or rises in population, Africa's fledgling governments are placed in a difficult position. Unable to abandon the claims already made, unable to account satisfactorily for the failure of conditions to improve, their only alternative is to postulate that economic domination and exploitation continue despite the end of overt political colonialism, that "neo-colonialism" is the new enemy of popular hopes.

One fact is clear. Whatever the hypothetical balance sheet of colonial economics might reveal, European domination brought Africa into the world economy. There was no motive for anyone to seek in Africa anything which was not marketable elsewhere; hence, on the whole, increased production for domestic subsistence needs was neglected, save for the efforts of a few individual civil servants and missionaries. Nor was there any reason for producing anything—wheat, apples, automobiles—which could be produced more cheaply and easily elsewhere. The European merchants came in search of slaves, gold and exotic tropical products such as ivory and spices. They stayed (or their successors came) to obtain two things not found as conveniently elsewhere in the necessary quantities: tropical agricultural products such as palm oil, rubber, tea, sisal, cacao, peanuts, certain kinds of cotton or minerals such as gold, diamonds and copper. They did not seek these in order to sell them to Africans, who did not need or could not pay for them, but in order to sell them to other Europeans. As a result the resources of Africa were developed in terms of what could be sold elsewhere. This was the real "crime" of colonialism economically, and altering this pattern of development is the great hope of the African nations for raising their living standards. Ports, railroads and roads were built to drain the wealth of the interior to the coast from which goods could be shipped to overseas markets. Communications networks tied African countries to Europe not to each other. In addition, though free trade was still the dominant British doctrine when the scramble for Africa began, all the colonial countries exploited Africa on a protected basis. Consequently individual African countries developed their economies not for the general European market (the United States had domestic, Latin American or Pacific basin sources of most of the important items produced in Africa) but for the markets of their particular colonial masters. The consequences of colonialist economics persist today, much to the dismay of Africans, and are an important factor in conditioning their stance in world affairs.

Basically, African economies are competitive rather than complementary, thus reducing the potentialities for intra-African trade. Africans, though they may wish to diversify their trade, are still largely dependent upon the same markets as before, and generally find it simpler and cheaper to buy where they sell. They are thus still economically dominated by the superior bargaining power of their former masters, lending credibility to the notion of neo-colonialism. The maneuverings of the African states relative to associate membership in the European Economic Community (to whose protected markets it is vitally important that they obtain access for their products), bear witness to the frustrating effects, upon African unity as well as upon African living standards, of the continuation of past patterns. Even on the level of communications and transportation, though much money and effort have been spent on creating national airlines with intra-African schedules, it is still often quicker and easier to get from African capitals to those of Western Europe than to provincial cities in neighboring African states. Telephone and telegraph connections are still on the whole less well developed among the African states than between Africa and Europe. In time, if money can be found, this will change, but it is a present reminder of the extent to which colonialism united Africans not with each other but in the spider web of world commerce and affairs.

But, as has been said, it was not economic or political domination per se that was the essence of colonial rule, but racial subordination. It is this which has determined the essence of African self-identity—not a common genetic heritage but a common reaction to a common racial attitude on the part of colonial rulers. Though racial policies and their implementation varied from area to area, what they had in common was what was most important. Throughout Africa the white government official or settler insisted, implicitly if not explicitly, on his superiority. The meanest white in most colonies had a higher standard of living than the richest African, and he certainly had a higher social status. The white European's manner of doing things set the standards in dress, housing, economic activity, education, religion and culture generally. It was his homes, clubs and farms that occupied the choicest locations, commanded the services of Africans, and excluded them as guests or competitors. All of these elements of superior status—increasingly resented by Africans, especially educated and modernized Africans—rested on the central element of the European's superiority, his political control.

The racial animosity and conflict stemming from white overlordship varied in extent and intensity from area to area and over time as well. It was most marked where there were large white-settler communities on the land and where there were large numbers of white women. But to the African particular differences in the form of racial subordination had little significance. The sheer fact of white superiority was what he found galling; its specific modes of implementation were of much less importance.

The British, even in nonsettler territories, may have been more snobbish and exclusive than the French. Belgians and Portuguese may have preached if not practiced racial equality and paternalism. But throughout Africa regardless of the particular nuances of race relations the basic facts were the same: whites from overseas ruled over Africans in the land of the latters' origin. Racial domination was the essence of the European occupation of Africa known as colonialism.

This is not the place to draw up a balance sheet for colonialism. Even if such a task were intellectually meaningful, all the evidence is not yet in. For in the last analysis colonialism must be judged by its results, by how it shaped and conditioned the new Africa. Modern African societies and perhaps above all African behavior in international politics are in large measure and will for long continue to be the product of the commingling of traditional and colonial forces. The two most obvious results of the colonial era need to be underlined, however—on the political plane, habituation to centralized, undemocratic political rule; on the psychological plane, the making of race the principal dimension of political consciousness, so that freedom and oppression came to be defined by the color of the persons involved.

V

THE TRIUMPH OF AFRICAN NATIONALISM

The recent growth of African nationalism and its result, the almost twoscore states which have now attained self-government and the status of sovereign members of the international community, has made necessary a new definition of nationalism. Traditionally the definition in a European context has focused on the desire for independent political existence on the part of nations—nations which could be defined as groups having common characteristics which differentiated them from their neighbors: differences of race, language, religion and culture. No one can dispute the fact that the Poles and the French are separate nations according to this definition; the only question is whether at any given time they should have an independent political existence commensurate with their nationhood. Not all the nations generally recognized as existing in the Western world have either sought, gained or retained political independence. Nor has it been possible to define national boundaries to the satisfaction of all in such ethnically mixed areas as Eastern Europe. But nationalism, as the West has known it, has resulted in acceptance of the principle that in general there ought to be an identification between political statehood and national consciousness.

In Africa the basis for nationalism of this type hardly exists. The one really homogeneous national group are the Somalis (the authenticity of whose nationhood on the European pattern is borne witness to by the border problems their irredentist ambitions have created). As we have seen, Africa is a patchwork of racial and linguistic groups; a separate national existence for each distinct ethno-cultural group would make the continent a crazy quilt of obviously unviable toy principalities, reminiscent of the dukedoms of pre-Bismarckian Germany. In addition, European nations defined their national existence in resistance to domination by their neighbors, the Africans in a struggle against domination by overseas imperialists. So what could be more sensible than to make Africa as a whole the unit of national identification and hence also the unit of political independence?

The history of African nationalism is largely the story, still being told, of the attempt to create and maintain that vision in the face of the political facts of life running counter to it: the fact that while it is easy to regard a neighbor as a fellow African vis-à-vis the white colonialist, local differences are still vital enough to provoke bloody riots; the fact that since all Africa was not one colony, the revolt against imperialism had to be carried on within the political framework of many colonies, creating in the process many independent states increasingly jealous of their own identities; the fact that, despite their original artificiality, the boundaries of the former colonies now enclose entities which, as a result of the introduction by the colonial powers of a particular European language and a particular set of European political and cultural institutions, as a result of the creation by the colonial powers of internal connecting links in transportation, communications and economic life, now have a distinct life of their own; the fact that local leaders are loath to surrender the power, perquisites and international prominence that separate national existence means, not to mention their own vote in the United Nations; and, finally, the fact that Africa is of a piece ethnically and ideologically only in the false perspective of subordination to Europe and the revolt against that subordination.

Africa is today many states, and these states are the creation of many different nationalist movements. The fact that in the beginning African nationalism was the result both of local reactions against the colonial powers and of visions of intercontinental unity has emphasized the narrowly local and the continental rather than the national unit as the focus of loyalty. The local struggles were carried on on the local scene, the continental struggles on a world stage. The history of African nationalism is in large part the story of the uneasy convergence of these two struggles at the level of the individual colony. Indeed, it is possible to make a sharp distinction in the beginning between two groups—those with local and those with Pan-African aims. The first consisted largely of local elites preserved or created by the colonial system; the second of Africans abroad, including members of formerly enslaved groups in the Americas who identified with the cause of African nationalism.

It is possible to date the beginning of black African nationalism from the year 1896. Like all such choices it is highly arbitrary, but the year witnessed two significant events on two different continents. In that year W. E. B. Du Bois, the first American Negro to receive a doctorate from Harvard University, published his thesis on the suppression of the slave trade and began the public career that would lead to his founding of the National Association for the Advancement of Colored People, his calling of the first Pan African Congress, and, in his last years, to his joining the Communist party and becoming a Ghanaian citizen prior to his death in Accra in 1963. If any one man can be called the father of African nationalism it is Du Bois, and he symbolizes its international, racial and continental aspects. Also in 1896 J. E. Casely-Hayford, scion of a wealthy merchant family, became the first Gold Coast African to gain admittance to the English bar. A year later he helped found the

Aborigines Rights Protective Association, which could well be called the beginning of local, on-the-scene nationalism in Africa. Its purpose was to protect both the traditional privilege of chiefs and the position of a rising educated class increasingly discriminated against by the British, especially in government employment.

Even in these early days attempts were made to link local and wider African nationalism. Casely-Hayford in 1917 founded a National Congress of British West Africa, which sought freedom for the area as a whole. It faded away, however, and the attention of politically conscious Africans was again concentrated on local problems. The chiefs and the bourgeoisie became the mainstay of the United Gold Coast Convention, which led the struggle for self-government in the colony. At the last moment the nationalist torch was seized from their hands. Kwame Nkrumah, an African of relatively humble origins who had studied in the United States and been the collaborator of Du Bois at the Pan African Congress of 1945, was called back to Africa to serve as the UGCC's organization secretary. Breaking with what he considered their conservative ways, he founded his own mass movement, the Convention People's Party, under whose leadership the Gold Coast came to independence. It was not the older elites who were to be the standardbearers of African nationalism but egalitarian, pan-Africanist-oriented men such as Nkrumah.

Du Bois and Casely-Hayford could both be said to be the products of colonialism, in that they were reacting against the impact colonialism had had upon Africa and upon them personally. But African nationalism was the creation of colonialism not only in being a local reaction against foreign domination or a continental or racial rejection of imperialism. Paradoxically it was the creation of colonialism in a positive fashion as well. Not only were its leaders products of American or British or French education, but from this training they gained ideas as well as skills. Their striving for freedom for their peoples was conceived of and couched in the language of modern Western nationalism and democracy, and was based on ideas drawn from Locke and Rousseau, Jefferson, Thomas Paine, and Abraham Lincoln. African nationalist thinking also owed much to that arch antinationalist Karl Marx, and to his successor Nikolai Lenin, as the leaders of subject peoples sought some explanation of the reasons for and mode of their subjugation.

Home-grown empires had existed in Africa as elsewhere before the coming of the European imperialists but nationalism in the modern sense was for Africa, as for the world at large, a phenomenon unknown prior to the French Revolution. The liberalism which accompanied early European and American nationalism provided Africans with a rationale for demanding individual equality and government with the consent of the governed, while strictly nationalist slogans rejected domination by strangers. The Christian religion was also a source of inspiration for the nationalist movement. Whatever the failures in deed of Christians in Africa, the universal brotherhood explicit in Christian teaching provided another rationale for equality, including political equality. Though in some areas, especially in the Gold Coast, large-scale missionary activity, including education, antedated European political control, in general it can be said that had it not been for colonialism the African would not have received the schooling at mission or state schools that set him on the path of nationalist striving. Traditional African leaders might resent encroachment on their rights, but only an educated middle class or intelligentsia could have been the vehicle for fully developed modern nationalism.

The direct relationship between colonialism and nationalism is shown by the fact that the more advanced was the process of acculturation to the imperialist (usually and often misleadingly called Westernization) in a particular African colony, the greater, by and large, the degree of nationalism. In North Africa it was the most Gallicized intellectuals of Tunisia and Algeria who led the earliest struggles for their countries' autonomy and independence. In black Africa it was in the most developed areas of West Africa that nationalism thrived—the Gold Coast and southern Nigeria. The African still in tribal society was the last to feel resentment against the imperialist unless he was one of the few who lost his land to settlers or was forced to work for their enterprises. It was the new city dweller, living on the fringes of modern technological society but unable to enjoy the life he saw lived by white residents or portrayed in the movies, who increasingly objected to colonial rule. Having been shown what it was like to live as the conqueror did, and in some cases perhaps even being treated as an equal in Europe or America, then not being permitted to live as an equal in one's own country, was what bred resentment. So it was above all the educated African—whose aspirations were raised and then left unsatisfied—who formed the core of the nationalist movement.

The relationship between acculturation and nationalism was not as clear cut in the Americas. So great had been the wrench from their homeland that the descendants of former slaves usually failed to identify with it. Men like Du Bois were the exception. Most accepted what they, like the Africans in Africa, had been taught: that Africa was a cultural vacuum, a jungle from which they should consider themselves lucky to have escaped. But to the extent that African nationalism existed in the United States and the Caribbean it was of vital importance to the growth of Pan-Africanism since Africans from the new world were among the few able to move about freely and to act politically. In recent years African nationalism and movements for improving the status and gaining the rights of persons of African descent abroad have grown together and have moved toward convergence. Negro leaders in 1965 could with some validity claim that the struggles in Alabama and in South Africa were one and the same.

African nationalism existed in the context of a history which it helped create and from the favorable course of which it drew increased strength. At the outset it was necessarily less political than cultural, both internationally and locally, and quite restrained in its demands. The first Pan African Congress was held in Paris in 1919. Inspired by Du Bois and financed by the NAACP, it was convened not only to give Negroes throughout the world a sense of identity and solidarity but to work for a definite goal. The war had ended. Woodrow Wilson's Fourteen Points, in some sense Allied war aims, held forth the promise of self-determination. Why not self-determination for Africans? African troops had fought loyally for the Allies, especially the French. Had they not earned their freedom? Besides, something had to be done with the former German colonies. Could not the mandate system be an instrument for ultimately setting them free rather than merely a means by which they exchanged one domination for another?

Neither Britain nor France extended greater freedom to their colonies as a result of the war. The existence of mandates—though to be important in laying the foundation for the United Nations Trust Territory system—had no immediate significance in advancing the goal of African liberation. But Pan African Congresses continued to meet—in 1921, 1923 and 1927—financed largely by American Negroes and consisting primarily of delegations of persons not resident in Africa. They continued to press for racial equality and the use of Africa's resources for the benefit of Africa's own peoples. But even to Africans themselves independence seemed a matter for the far-distant future. The small minority of American Negroes concerned with conditions in Africa were content to attack the more blatant abuses of the present, to guard the independence of harried Liberia and to keep lonely vigil for the future. It took World War II to break the log jam.

In Africa itself prior to World War II independence was unthinkable in the French territories (or at least subversive), any political activity was impossible in the Congo and Portuguese Africa, and freedom was still a far-off goal in British Africa. So it is not surprising that manifestations of African nationalism at this time were not directly political. It was in the field of cultural, religious and economic activities that the African sense of identity vis-à-vis the imperial peoples first asserted itself. Later these movements and organizations were, directly or indirectly, to form the core of overtly political movements aimed at obtaining independence. But at first they offered a vent for African feelings while at the same time not falling (except in the case of some labor unions and a few religious groups) under the colonial governments' bans on political action.

The story of African nationalism is necessarily a confused one since time scales varied widely. Owing to a greater or lesser degree of economic development and to the presence or absence of settler communities within them, African nations have passed through the various common stages of political development at different times. And the more repressive the political situation, the more nationalist energies were turned toward religious and cultural expressions; the less repressive the more directly political their manifestations.

Most African nationalistic religious movements exhibited features common to many religious groups involved in the Negro protest movement in the United States. The emphasis was on the Old Testament, with the black man being identified with the Jews and the white man with the Egyptian or other oppressor; suffering and eventual triumph under the protection of an overshadowing Providence were the common themes. Many of these African churches combined Christian ideas with those of African traditional religions; others made fantastic racial and political extrapolations from orthodox themes. Although for a long time and in most areas such movements led to political quiescence, gradually the secular referents of the language of oppression and struggle came to the fore. In many areas prophets arose who fed upon the chiliastic moods engendered by the churches. Many of these prophets had as their overt purpose either the overthrow of white oppression or the leading of Africans away from it.

Frequently such movements were ruthlessly repressed by colonial authorities, but the sentiments motivating them could not be destroyed. Anyone familiar with the story of Simon Kimbangu in the Congo, his claim to be Christ, his fanatical following, their harsh repression by the Belgians, and his steadfastness in his claims under torture would have no excuse for not recognizing the depths of the tensions existing in the Congo. But if the disorders and the groups that provoked them could be put down by the authorities, it was for the most part impossible to ban African churches as such even though they were an obvious breeding ground for nationalism.

Labor unions were something else again. Strikes could be looked upon as insurrections. Organized labor in the imperialist homelands was little concerned with the problems of the colonies and it was not until quite late that their pressure was strong or effective enough to lead to the toleration of free union activity in the colonies of Britain and France. The situation in Africa was complicated by the fact that most industrial laborers (with the notable exception of miners) worked for the government, usually on the railways or in similar establishments, and could be considered civil servants. Unions existed in the Gold Coast and Nigeria, and also in South Africa, where public opinion, and later government action, split white and black labor. A 1913 labor dispute brought forth from the Communists the immortal appeal, "Workers of the World Unite for a White South Africa." Unions were illegal in the French territories until the Popular Front came in 1936 and were again illegal under Vichy. They were legalized in the Belgian Congo only in 1946. Such leaders as Habib Bourguiba of Tunisia, Sékou Touré of Guinea and Tom Mboya of Kenya either rose to prominence through or owe much of their power to the trade-union movement, and trade unions have been important components of the nationalist movements of Ghana and Tunisia.

Nationalist political parties were the almost direct creations of the colonial powers in that it took only the slightest provision for African political representation to stimulate their development. Prior to such time there had been organizations that called themselves parties and, like the student and youth groups of the Sudan and Nigeria, had most of the attributes of political parties. But without elections to focus on, the stimulus of competition and reward needed for sustained and permanent growth was lacking.

The Nigerian National Democratic Party was founded in 1923 by Herbert Macaulay to contest the municipal elections in Lagos; the Senegalese section of the French Socialist party was begun by Lamine Guèye in the 1930's to fight for the seat in the French Chamber of Deputies traditionally allotted to Senegal. But while these groups helped Africans to get used to the idea of purposive political activity, trained a few leaders, and stimulated the imaginations of all, they were not the basis of the ultimate liberation movements. The colonial powers were not anxious to encourage African political life. The degree of political participation was so small under colonialism (the opportunities limited to a few of the more conservative educated class or to the traditional authorities) and the extent of the powers exercised by elective bodies so minute, that this political life could not become the direct basis of strong political parties. The gap between such political activity and self-rule was almost unbridgeable. Real African political life prior to independence existed only in the independence movements themselves.

The results have been far-reaching and unfortunate. While some Africans were trained for and allowed to gain experience in administration in the British and French colonies, it was not possible for them to get any real experience in the give and take of politics. A few French colonial Africans, especially those from Senegal, did have a chance to see real parliamentary politics at first hand when they served as deputies in Paris, but the experience was hardly an inspiring one, and part of the admiration many of them have for General De Gaulle stems from their feeling that a strong man is needed in France just as they contend that strong men are needed in Africa.

Nowhere in British Africa was there any opportunity to learn the need for getting along with opponents or for accepting defeat gracefully. Coalitions were formed; second-wave nationalists succeeded their more moderate middle-class predecessors in public favor in such countries as Ghana and Mali; but a real multiparty system could not exist under colonialism. Basically there was only the mass party of African nationalism and the party of forces representing the traditional leadership, usually in tacit alliance with the colonial power. By the same token, though both the Gold Coast and the southern regions of Nigeria had experience with several years of local self-government prior to complete independence, the restrictions upon final decision making were sufficient to deny the political leaders the opportunity to make their own mistakes and learn to live with them and with the popular opposition they engender. In any event the questions of the nature, timing and means for attaining independence overshadowed all other issues.

As a result of this background, for which blame must surely rest upon the colonial powers, many African politicians, even some who have borne the responsibilities of power since independence, are afflicted by what one American sociologist has called the "oppositional" mentality. They are best at making demands and laying blame on others. Those who have been on the outside looking in almost all their lives often find the discipline of hard facts and limited possibilities hard to bear. Even the most statesmanlike of African leaders, long habituated to claiming that all will be well after "Freedom" and beset by a population that still believes freedom to be a magic cornucopia, may be forgiven the tendency to place the promised land over just one more hill—the end of white domination in the South, the demise of neo-colonialism, the coming of Pan-African unity, or whatever. In every country there are those who would like to turn the revolutionary tactics that ousted the colonialists against the new rulers and who hope to come to the fullness of power on the cry that the anticolonial revolution has only begun. Those leaders who understand that the oppositional mentality has been inherited by a younger generation find themselves forced to resort to various means (from semi-bribery to repression) to keep power securely enough in their hands to try to make good on their own promises.

Though the lack of existence of meaningful political opposition is much to be regretted, any widespread nationalist movement has proved better than none at all. Compare for example Algeria and the Congo. In her long and bloody fight for independence, Algeria forged her unity. Whatever judgment one passes on individual Algerian politicians, the Boumedienne leadership is that of men who have learned how to put together and use power, how to separate the men from the boys among their lieutenants, how to rally and manipulate real support among the population. The future of Algeria may be troubled but complete disintegration is not in the cards. The Belgians, on the other hand, gave the Congo its independence virtually for the asking. No history of nationalist struggles separated the talkers from the doers, forced compromises and convergences, and settled the question of who was boss. It was as if an American political party had to nominate its candidate after, rather than before, winning a national election, with all the responsibilities of office already upon it. The Congo had to try to create a national consciousness and a political mechanism expressive of that consciousness at the very same time that it was being forced to deal with problems of economic distress and foreign machinations. The same maneuverings which in other African nations took place unnoticed in the villages and shanty towns, the work of minor politicians probably despised by their colonial overlords, have in the Congo taken place in presidential palaces, under the eyes of a watching and involved world—like a courtship carried on in public. The results have been disastrous. Having avoided the price of political strife before independence, the Congo has paid it doubly afterward in blood.

When World War II ended, Africa, save in the north, still lacked any deep-rooted, broadly based nationalist movements. There was a long nationalist tradition in Nigeria, but only limited nationalist activity, and the same thing was true in the

Gold Coast. The French West African territories were also stirring. But that was about it. The forces of nationalism consisted of a few traditional rulers jealous of their prerogatives, civil servants or would-be civil servants resentful of discrimination, some discontented farmers and professionals, and students abroad who had been inspired by pan-Africanism. But all this was to change overnight.

The focus of nationalism south of the Sahara was in West Africa, especially in the Gold Coast and Nigeria. The end of the war meant the return of two groups. The soldiers had seen that not all white men were gods—they had been trained to kill them, and they had seen many whites living in degradation and poverty in European countries. They wanted to be rewarded for their services and they were ready to demand rather than beg. But the real catalysts of nationalism were the returning students—men who had studied abroad and been accepted as equals in some countries for some purposes, confirming their self-confidence; men who had studied abroad and who had been denied equality in other countries, firing their resentments. Nkrumah of Ghana and Azikiwe of Nigeria, both former students in the race-conscious United States, became the fathers of modern nationalism in their countries. In French territories men such as Senghor and Houphouët-Boigny, who had found a real place in the life of Paris, sought new formulas for relating their African homelands to France.

Wartime inflation was causing economic difficulties and wartime exhortations to help in the common cause had made all Africans dimly aware that they were of some political consequence. This new restlessness was not too congenial to many of the older nationalist leadership, though they did step up their demands for Africanization of the public services and for increased home rule. But the new drives were to be ridden to power by new men—the leaders of new movements and parties in the process of formation. Few dramatic events marked the new outlook that was spreading over the continent, but pressures were mounting. They had been on the rise in many areas, despite seemingly placid surfaces, for over a generation. Now the dam of colonialism was about to burst.

How ironic it is today to read the arguments about Africa's political future that were being advanced only a scant decade ago. It was not only the mossbacked Colonel Blimps who scoffed at the possibility of African states' being ready, much less permitted to become independent within a foreseeable period of time. Even spokesmen for African nationalism tended to think of themselves as somewhat utopian when they asked for self-government within a measurable period of years. The arguments were mainly about whether and when the colonial governments should accept African self-government as their ultimate goal and about what preparations should be made to train Africans for and to grant them the gradual exercise of political power.

Not only did the growth of the movement toward independence on the African continent surprise everyone, including most Africans, but so did the rapidity with which the process of gaining freedom, once begun, was accomplished. In 1955 there were, exclusive of South Africa, four independent states on the continent. By the beginning of 1960 there were just seven; at the end of 1960, the "year of African independence," there were twenty-six. By midsummer of 1965 there were thirty-six.

Just as startling as the speed with which independence was won was the lack of serious violence—except in war-torn Algeria and disturbed Kenya—with which it came about. These two circumstances are not unrelated. Both the swiftness and peacefulness of the onset of independence have a common cause: the fact that the colonial powers—France, Britain and Belgium—were not pushed out of Africa. They retreated—indeed, in the case of Belgium, simply abdicated—rather than fight.

It is interesting to speculate about the motivations behind

this retreat, especially in the light of the broader perspectives of history. Special factors—such as the advent of a Labour government in Britain in 1945 and the policies of Mendès-France and De Gaulle in France, played a part. So too did the existence of the United Nations with its trusteeship over several former African colonies and its anticolonial Asian and Latin American blocs. The pressures of anticolonialism, at the rhetorical level, in the United States, and the Cold War between the West and the Soviet Union, a power which could have exploited conflict in Africa to its own ends, also doubtless played a part. But, above all, the colonial impulse itself was spent. The same forces that caused world opinion—as expressed by the United States, the Soviet Union, Latin America, Asia and the Near East—to be opposed to the domination of peoples by overseas colonialists were also operative within Europe itself. The rise of social democracy in Britain and France over a period of decades, the general revulsion against war and militarism, the questioning of the basic assumptions of traditional capitalism, all made it difficult even for those committed to colonialism to consider fighting to maintain it against determined opposition. Popular opposition within France to the Algerian war showed what could have happened on a broad scale had colonial wars been duplicated elsewhere.

Besides, colonialism had never presented itself simply as an instrument of domination for domination's sake. There was always an idealistic streak—represented not only by Lord Lugard's doctrine of the "dual mandate," which held that the increasing welfare of the Africans was a major objective of the colonizing power, but also by the Belgian *"Dominer pour servir."* This idealism saw in colonialism a means by which the stronger and more developed could aid the weaker and less developed, a paternalistic responsibility to bring the colonized to the point of some sort of self-rule, albeit at some hypothetical date in the unpredictable future. Education, economic development, provision of law and order, even missionary activity, were all thought of as means to this end.

One might argue about whether, given the fact of their responsibilities, the colonial powers did not withdraw in unseemly haste. The United States, though rhetorically anticolonial, was not pressing hard when it came to actual timetables for independence, although the Soviet bloc and most of the nations of Asia and the Near East were. But it must be remembered that World War II left both Britain and France exhausted. The handwriting on the wall was clear that not they but the United States and the Soviet Union were to be the dominant powers. Die-hard romantics of imperialism might object, but reasonable men increasingly saw colonies as a burden that could well be laid down. Even proponents of colonial domination came to believe that the economic and cultural hegemony of the colonial power could perhaps be more easily and cheaply maintained under the cover of independence. Thus self-interest combined with idealism and with outside pressures and the rising force of African demands to cause almost a scramble in reverse, a scramble to leave Africa, with consequences that are still debatable. Belgium's abrupt withdrawal from the Congo, which plunged that hapless country into a chaos whose depths are still unplumbed, is a special case, inexplicable save on the assumption of Machiavellianism or total political incompetence.

Nonetheless, one notion must be laid to rest once and for all—the notion that rising nationalism interfered with a planned, rational process of decolonization, whereby Africans were being prepared by the colonial powers to take over the reins of government, and that "premature" independence therefore hurt the interests of the Africans themselves in the long run. Virtually every step toward training Africans in the responsibilities of power was made only as the result of anticolonial pressures, internal or external. Had nationalism not existed, decolonization would never have taken place. In individual cases the process may have been arbitrarily speeded up, and disjunction between preparation for and the actual event of freedom may have resulted, but this was inevitable. Those who waited for freedom as a gift would be waiting still. Had not the probability of African mastery existed, an African apprenticeship in self-rule would never have taken place, or once begun would have been of infinite duration.

The speed with which decolonization occurred also sheds some light on the question of economic exploitation under colonialism. Unless one accepts the proposition that the colonies had been sucked dry prior to European withdrawal and were simply thrown away like a used orange, or that neocolonialism has meant that exploitation continues to the same degree as before, or, alternatively, that despite little change in the domestic balance of power within the colonial nations the major capitalist interests had suddenly lost all power to influence government policies, it seems likely that colonies were not the economic cornucopias to their possessors that is sometimes postulated. This is not to say that the colonial economy particularly benefited the Africans either. Like so many other arrangements in human affairs, it may have been a bad deal all around.

For several reasons North Africa (with the exception of Algeria) took the lead in the African march toward independence. Libya had been an Italian colony; therefore, it became a United Nations Trust Territory. The Soviet Union as a European belligerent was making claims to share in its administration and in that of similarly situated Somalia as well. The solution adopted was to move Libya, a dubious prospect for independence by any rational criteria, toward independence as quickly as possible. It became sovereign in 1952. Somalia was made an Italian Trust Territory with a definite date set for its independence. Morocco and Tunisia were never simply colonies in theory but were French protectorates with some minute vestiges of sovereignty. They had long-established nationalist movements, as well as French interests determined to hang on. Some disorder and much political maneuvering, both within France and within the Arab-pressured United Nations, were necessary before they finally broke free of French control,

Morocco in 1956 and Tunisia by stages which culminated in independence in 1960. In Algeria, in theory part of metropolitan France, the nationalist movement was younger, and there were a million "French" *colons* (actually largely of Spanish and Italian descent) residing there, with influence in metropolitan politics. In addition, the French army, long a haven of ultranationalism, was, after defeat in World War II and Indochina, making a last stand for its version of the "real" France. It required a long and bloody war, beginning with nationalist-inspired riots in 1954, to free Algeria. It was only the skill and determination of De Gaulle, whose advent to virtual dictatorial power in 1958 was made possible, indeed essential, by events in Algeria, which finally brought about a resolution of the situation in favor of Algerian independence in 1962.

In sub-Saharan Africa things moved somewhat more slowly though no less inexorably. The Gold Coast was the linchpin whose removal precipitated wholesale independence. The leadership in accession to freedom of Nkrumah's Ghana was paradoxical in many respects. African nationalism in the Gold Coast had, as has already been noted, a long and honorable history. But when self-government was achieved in 1951 it was not under the old leaders. The old elite, represented by the United Gold Coast Convention, was swept aside by the mass-based Convention People's Party, led by the UGCC's erstwhile organizing secretary, Kwame Nkrumah, and Nkrumah's first cabinet contained virtually none of the Africans who had received such experience in government as previous constitutional arrangements had permitted. Britain's much-touted training for independence had come to nought.

There was the further anomaly that Nkrumah had aspired to leadership of a united Africa, and had expected Ghana's independence—granted in 1957—to be the new cornerstone of Pan-Africanism. Yet the onrush of independence which the Ghanaian precedent helped set in motion had the effect—in part because of its very rapidity—of largely sweeping Ghana's and Nkrumah's pretensions aside; despite repeated and continuing efforts on Nkrumah's part, his paramountcy has never been accepted. Ghana was not only the leader and first exemplar of the nonviolent revolution in Africa but, sadly, must be credited with being the leader in the movement toward adoption of the quasi-totalitarian one-party state throughout Africa.

But Ghana did point the way to attainment of political independence. Its experience showed that Britain was ready to yield political control rather than face the possibility of continual disorder and potential large-scale violence. The lesson was not ignored, and others, not only emulating Ghana but jealous of its precedence, soon sought to follow in its footsteps. In nearby Nigeria, regional self-government had been granted to the South in 1956 under the pressure of the nationalist leaders Azikiwe in the East and Awolowo in the West. Internal suspicions among Nigeria's three regions and the lag of nationalism in the semifeudal North postponed the advent of national sovereignty, however, and it was not until 1960 that, a federal constitution having been agreed upon, Nigeria with its vast population could become independent and challenge Ghana for leadership in Africa. Conservative Sierra Leone, Britain's oldest major possession in Africa, was far from restive under the British tie, but by now to seek independence was *de rigueur;* internal dissensions were resolved and independence granted in 1961. Tiny Gambia, Britain's oldest African colony, was a backwater with less than a third of a million people. Its independence was long delayed because of its dubious economic viability, but by 1965 it too had asked for and received sovereign status.

Events in French Africa were both more dramatic and in the end more anticlimactic and diffuse than in British Africa. De Gaulle recognized that a colony held against its will was a liability. He also owed Africa a special debt of gratitude because during the dark days of World War II it had been French Equatorial Africa, under its governor Félix Eboué, a Negro born in French Guiana, which had first raised the Cross of Lorraine over a significant segment of French territory. Not only did it send a military detachment on an epic march across the Sahara to fight against Rommel's Afrika Korps in North Africa, but by giving the harassed De Gaulle a territorial base, it had made him more of a force to be reckoned with by a dubious Roosevelt and Churchill. In return De Gaulle, in a speech at Brazzaville in 1944, had promised French Africans a greater share in freedom after the war.

When the threat of an ultra-right coup mounted from Algeria ended the Fourth Republic and brought De Gaulle to power in 1958, he at once set out to put France's African house in order. He announced a plebiscite to be held later that year, in which France's overseas territories (members of the confusing and largely meaningless French Union) would have a choice of independence, becoming legal parts of metropolitan France (on the model of Martinique or Réunion), or accepting continued "association" with France in a future, loosely defined French community. Knowing the weakness both in material resources and trained manpower of overseas French territories and confident of his own personal popularity and the hold of French culture upon native elites, De Gaulle expected that all would choose the second or, more likely, the third alternative, and he embarked on a personal tour of Africa to explain his proposals.

All went well, despite occasional dissident notes, until he arrived in Guinea. There Sékou Touré declared publicly in De Gaulle's presence that his people preferred freedom in poverty to subjugation in prosperity. De Gaulle departed in a huff. The gauntlet had been dropped.

Whether Touré was simply pressing for greater freedom within association or whether he hoped to be a magnet for other states, making himself the Nkrumah of French Africa, is still a matter for speculation. In virtually every colony the vote was easily delivered by a local leadership which decided to stay with De Gaulle, in association with France. Left-wing elements friendly to Touré mustered a substantial negative vote in Niger, but Guinea alone, and with virtual unanimity, chose independence. French reaction was swift. Private French citizens stayed on in Guinea (there was, amazingly enough in view of the political passions aroused by the referendum and by its aftermath, no antiwhite violence, a tribute both to French colonial rule and to Guinean leadership), but the French administration, save for a few Communist civil servants, left at once, taking with them everything that could conceivably be construed as belonging to France—the government tax records, the uniforms of the military, even telephones ripped from the walls. Guinea had to be made an example of the perils of ingratitude.

It was at this point that Nkrumah, seeing in Touré a junior partner in his projected pan-African state, stepped in. A union of Ghana and Guinea was proclaimed, and a ten-million-pound loan made to Guinea. In deference to their NATO ally, Britain and the United States kept hands off. Touré accordingly sought support where he could find it, behind the iron curtain. It was to be years before a balance was struck in Guinea between Western- and Communist-bloc influence (a balance achieved largely as a result of Communist ineptitude and over-aggressiveness) and relations between Guinea and France somewhat healed.

But in a real sense Touré had won. Despite its difficulties Guinea was now a free agent in world affairs, with its own vote in the United Nations. Other French African leaders were envious, as well as fearful of pressures from ardent nationalists within their own countries. They began to raise the ante for continued fealty to France. Finally it was the Ivory Coast's Houphouët-Boigny, the leader who had heretofore been the most outspoken about the advantages of continued ties with France, who asked for independence for the member states of his Conseil de l'Entente (Ivory Coast, Niger, Volta and Dahomey). De Gaulle yielded, preferring to maintain intact France's economic and cultural pre-eminence. Before the year was over all of the fourteen former French African colonies save French Somaliland were independent states, as were the trust territories of Togo and the Cameroun. For a time some retained their membership in the French community, but the distinction between members and nonmembers was virtually meaningless.

Yet De Gaulle had won a victory too. French influence in economic and cultural affairs continued to be predominant in French-speaking Africa. The French continued to maintain military bases in many African nations. Most of France's former colonies followed French leadership in the United Nations most of the time, even on such controversial issues as French atomic testing in the Sahara and questions connected with the war in Algeria. English-speaking Africans and others might regard these new nations (save for Guinea and Mali) as French satellites, and talk of neo-colonialism: did not French civil servants still largely staff their governments and French citizens sit even in their cabinets? But De Gaulle had won a propaganda victory the significance of which extended beyond Africa. He had established himself in the eyes of many as a rare European statesman who understood and was sympathetic to the *tiers monde,* the underdeveloped countries. With his growing independence of American domination in NATO and of American policy in the Far East, he was laying the foundation for his bid to make France the leader of a "third force" in world politics, a force which could enable nations to be neutral in the Cold War without at the same time depriving themselves of Western economic and technical assistance.

The Belgian withdrawal from the Congo in 1960 and from the associated trust territories of Rwanda and Burundi in 1962 was the next step in decolonization, but the Congo chaos in which its small neighbors are also involved is a separate story. So too are recent developments in Malawi and Zambia, which became independent in 1964, upon the breakup of the settler-dominated Central African Federation. Malawi and Zambia are on the frontier of the "white redoubt" and are necessarily deeply involved with the struggle for black African mastery in southern Africa.

The Triumph of African Nationalism

In former British East Africa the march toward independence appears in retrospect to have been a simple one, despite incidental complications. After 1948 there never really was any doubt about the region's ultimate future as far as the issue of rule by the indigenous majority was concerned. The year 1948 marked the high point of white-settler supremacy in Kenya, the keystone of settler power in East Africa. The outbreak of Mau Mau terrorism in late 1952 served to alert the world to the racial problems of the country and to the fact that settler rule was untenable without British military support. The failure of Kenya's white community to acquire dominion status on their own terms prior to 1948, when nonwhites were given equality with whites among nonofficial members of the legislative council, was the then not fully appreciated beginning of the end for the curious society which was white Kenya. Uganda, on the other hand, had never been allowed to become an area of white settlement. African paramountcy had always been recognized. But its accession to independence, like that of Nigeria, depended on finding a solution to problems of the internal division of power—in Uganda's case the division between the more highly organized and modernized Buganda kingdom and the rest of the country.

Tanganyika not only had fewer white settlers than Kenya, but such settlers as there were were largely non-British and without substantial influence in conservative circles at home, and they did not control as much of the arable land. Though conflicts between Asian and African, Christian and Muslim (which are still mounting in intensity) did exist, there were and are no large tribal units fighting for supremacy. Most important of all, Tanganyika was a United Nations trust territory, whose future independence was assured in advance. Under the skillful leadership of Julius Nyerere who preached multiracialism and moderation, Tanganyika became independent in 1961. Uganda composed its difficulties, at least temporarily, and followed suit in 1962. In Kenya the process of whittling down white-settler power through pressure upon and from the Colonial Office in

London overlapped the growth of fear on the part of the less-advanced tribes that independence would leave them at the mercy of the Kikuyu and Luo. But by 1963 Britain was weary of the whole business and Kenya became independent under the centralizing constitution favored by Jomo Kenyatta's Kenya African National Union. Zanzibar followed Kenya to independent nationhood under an Arab rule that was to be bloodily overthrown by Africans in 1964, leading to a tenuous union with Tanganyika as the United Republic of Tanzania.

By the end of 1964, therefore, all of Africa save for a few small odds and ends was under postcolonial African nationalist rule—all, that is, north of the white redoubt of Rhodesia, the Portuguese territories and South Africa. From the point of view of militant African nationalism, these areas are an intolerable anomaly, a part of the continental African nation still under enemy occupation, which must become the object of concerted and unremitting African pressures for liberation. But between most of independent nationalist Africa and the white-dominated areas, athwart the continent, lies the giant Congo, bordering eight African states and Portuguese Angola, occupying the heartland of Africa, and rent with chaos which threatens Africa's emerging sense of identity and all the purposes, claims and aspirations of nationalism by drawing extra-African powers back into the center of the continent and making it not an island of neutrality, peace and nonalignment but a major arena of battle between Western and Communist powers.

VI

THE NEW NATIONS

Most of Africa is now free, free at least according to the African nationalist definition—free of foreign control. But this does not of itself tell us very much about what political and social life is like in these new states, and acquaintance with the quality of life within these states is essential if we wish to understand their actions on the international scene. For insofar as foreign policy is not simply a reflex of geopolitical conditions, it is deeply affected by national character. Victorian self-confidence as well as Britain's national economic needs helps explain the British role in the nineteenth century. French and German assumptions about their cultural or racial superiority provide important keys to understanding their world posture throughout modern history. America's peculiar combination of hedonistic self-satisfaction and crusading moral zeal go at least as far as its geographic and demographic position in the world to explain its vacillation between isolationism and the assumption of global responsibilities.

The foreign relations of African states reflect their internal patterns even more directly than the foreign policy of most states. The search for identity, the need for self-affirmation, the desire to confirm an independent existence the reality of which is perhaps subconsciously questioned, the personal interests of local or Pan-African ruling elites, all directly underlie the moves and countermoves, the aspirations and pretensions of African leaders in continental and global politics.

Any separation of the political, economic and social factors in the life of a nation is necessarily artificial, and this is especially true in Africa where, under colonialism, the foreign rulers openly and directly influenced all areas of life—and where today nationalist elites who seek to undo much of the colonial heritage also use political rule as a lever to create change. But for the sake of clarity it is useful to look first at the economic and social base of the new African nations before examining their political structures. For, while politics is the lifeblood of these new societies, particular political and constitutional forms are ephemeral, the projections of economic and social forces rather than causal factors in their own right.

Africa's nonsubsistence economy is the heir of its colonial parentage. It is highly dependent on world markets and is involved in patterns of trade which are the product of the colonial past, one source of the oft-repeated complaints about neocolonialism. All the African states are seeking to build up their economies and to maximize domestic production of such basic items as textiles, cement, canned goods, beverages and other consumer soft goods, both to save foreign exchange and to provide employment for domestic labor. But it will be a long time before any African economy, save that of South Africa, approaches the flexibility and relative self-sufficiency of the developed nations. The cocoa and coffee and peanuts produced by African farmers are still sold not to Africans but primarily to Europe; the copper and iron and bauxite mined in Africa still supply the raw materials not for African industries but for those of the developed nations.

The organization of the economy continues to be patterned on the colonial model in the sense that virtually the whole operation is in the hands either of the government or of foreign concerns. A legacy of colonialism perpetuated by the policies of the new governments is the absence of any important independent business class. There is no local pool of entrepreneurial skills. Even those Africans with administrative or technical training are not businessmen but the employees of large organizations. Although African planters in such nations as Ghana, Nigeria and the Ivory Coast are sometimes wealthy, they too are dependent on the government—for the price and marketing of their crops.

Not only does the state or large foreign corporations control manufacturing, mining and public utilities, but the middlemen in the distribution and service industries, who might serve as the basis of a future business class, are usually not Africans. The "market mammies" of Ghana (women traders who have been an important element in Nkrumah's following) and their counterparts in Nigeria and the Hausa traders are rare exceptions to the rule according to which Lebanese, Greeks, Indians and Arabs are the commercial class throughout the continent.

Those Africans with money they might invest in productive activities tend either to consume it in ostentatious living and the fulfillment of kinship obligations (these two are sometimes difficult to distinguish) or else turn to real-estate speculation or moneylending, activities which are fantastically profitable and easily comprehensible to the peasant mind, although not particularly conducive to economic development.

Most African governments are not anxious to see a business class arise. Save in countries such as Nigeria, Liberia, Ethiopia and Sierra Leone, which are regarded as backward in this respect by most other African nationalists, socialism is the order of the day. Official doctrine holds the emergence of a native capitalist class to be socially undesirable. A less-often-mentioned reason for denigrating independent businessmen is that they could become potential rivals to the new political elite. Foreign businessmen can be more easily controlled and they cannot become rival claimants for political power. Even where local businessmen are accepted or encouraged, as in Nigeria, business success is so highly dependent upon political favors that corruption is rife and, as a rule, politicians use their positions to make money in business rather than businessmen using their position in society to influence politics. Throughout Africa, as in the developing world generally, the businessman has little social status and probably little future. Traditional African values, which antedate colonialism, are aristocratic and downgrade the trader (a notable factor in past European history as well), while the values of African nationalism equate capitalism with colonialism and exploitation.

The ideology of "African socialism," the colonial heritage, and above all the practical exigencies of economic development combine to give the state a leading role in economic life. Economic development demands large infusions of capital into the economy, and throughout the continent the state has been the principal instrument for generating and acquiring this capital. Basically, capital can only come from two sources: external gifts, loans and investments, or savings derived from the postponement of internal consumption. Domestic savings available for investment purposes can come either from private profits or can be obtained through governmental compulsion in the form of taxes, tariffs or forced savings plans.

For African states the major source of external funds has been foreign governments or international institutions such as the World Bank. Only a government can negotiate a loan from such sources (outright grants are rare, though some long-term low-interest loans serve much the same purpose), and it is government which has the increasingly burdensome task of paying the interest on the money borrowed. Again, only a government is in a position to make the concessions and guarantees necessary to attract large-scale private foreign investment—and even the most ardently socialist states such as Guinea and Ghana want and actively seek such investment.

If capital is to be generated domestically the burden also falls upon the government, largely through necessity. No African country has a large enough or wealthy enough entrepreneurial class to begin to provide investment capital sufficient for development, and what well-to-do indigenous farmers and merchants do exist have shown little inclination to risk their funds in productive investment. Ghana, the African nation with the most substantial middle class, claims to have tried unsuccessfully to give potential domestic capitalists a role in economic development before turning completely to state socialism as a means of capital formation. But even if would-be capitalists existed, it can well be argued that the conditions under which capitalist development took place in the West could not be duplicated in modern Africa because under popular government the people would not allow their living standards to be depressed for the benefit of private accumulators of capital. Only government—and perhaps only authoritarian government—can elicit or compel the austerity necessary to generate the savings needed for investment.

Some African governments have not only tried to raise capital domestically by curtailing living standards through their economic and fiscal policies but have even attempted to follow the Chinese model in substituting labor for capital in programs such as Guinea's "human investment," using semivoluntary unskilled labor to build roads, schools and bridges. These programs have largely been abandoned since they have generally proved inefficient as well as increasingly unpopular. However, some states still use labor brigades composed of the otherwise unemployed, and in some areas locally organized community development programs have contributed to the economy in a small way.

All African governments assume that economic development requires state planning and that the execution of these plans must be subject to continuing state supervision. The major difference among states is in how projected economic activity is divided between that to be carried on by the private sector of the economy, that to be undertaken by the state directly, and that to be turned over to bodies such as cooperatives. Generally the more "socialist" states not only place greater reliance on the public sector but tend to plan for higher growth rates. Ghana's current economic plan calls for an annual rise of 3 percent in per-capita income while Nigeria's is much more modest. The plans of both countries are in difficulty, however, due in both cases to such factors as failure of planned-for foreign assistance to materialize and the fall in world market prices for the primary products upon which all African economies so largely depend. The increasingly heavy cost of servicing the foreign debt and the high recurrent expenses entailed in staffing and maintaining the many newly completed projects such as schools are also a serious drag on African economies. Rates of development, however, do not seem to depend primarily on whether a state is more or less "socialistically" inclined; despite setbacks, Ghana has had a high growth rate under the Nkrumah regime, but so too have such capitalist-minded countries as Liberia and the Ivory Coast. Whether the benefits of economic development are more equitably distributed in the doctrinairely socialist states than in states with mixed economies is open to question. In the last analysis this can perhaps best be measured by the extent to which the different governments manage to retain popular support.

Unions, where they exist, are of little independent social or political importance. Ordinarily they are merely another arm of the state (or of the ruling party in the one-party states), whose role it is to increase production along the model of unionism in the Soviet Union. Such a role is a natural concomitant of socialism, for, where the economy is the people's, to strike for higher wages or better working conditions is to wage war against the whole community. Even in countries such as Nigeria, which so far have been unable to see in socialism the answer to every ill and continue to permit strikes, the unions tend to be in the vanguard of those advocating a more nationalistic and socialistic regime, so that the paradoxical effect of their independent role may be to help bring about a new political order in which their own independence will be proscribed.

Just as most Africans still live in a subsistence rural economy, so too most Africans (usually the same ones) still live within traditional or precolonial society. But in neither case are the boundaries hard and fast. Few Africans are completely untouched by the products of modern industry. White shirts, radios, bicycles and canned goods are found in all but a few remote villages. Similarly there are few villages in which no one has a degree of literacy or at least where no one has learned that his traditional rulers and customs are not the only or the ultimate authority.

While there is no significant indigenous business class, there is a local ruling class and a local middle class. In some areas such as Northern Nigeria and Buganda the local traditional rulers retain political and social pre-eminence. In others such as Ghana they are barely tolerated and have been reduced to a minor appendage of the state, chiefs who once held the power of life or death becoming the African equivalent of justices of the peace or YMCA officials. In most places where the traditional ruling elite retains authority it is because it has become absorbed into the new currents, owing its continued power largely to wealth or literacy, less an independent aristocracy than a pool of usually low-level talent for the new rulers.

For the most part the African middle class and contemporary ruling class are identical. They have two marks: political power and education. But the relationship between power and education is not a direct one. The politicians are more powerful than the better-educated civil servants, increasingly so as the colonially transmitted tradition of neutral expertise dies out or is suppressed. And in some countries there are increasing numbers of literate or semiliterate unemployed or underemployed (a phenomenon also found in other developing nations such as India). Nonetheless, education is the key to power, even to full membership in the new society.

The new ruling class composed of politicians and civil servants—the new intelligentsia—is much closer to the traditional elite in its ethos than is often realized. One of the marks of traditional rule throughout the world (in the pre-modern West as well as in developing areas such as Africa) is an addiction to rules and order for their own sake and a distaste for innovation, experimentation and flexibility. In the Western world the combination of the technological revolution made possible by modern science and the economic revolution associated with the rise to power of an innovating business class has led to a pragmatic and individualistic approach to life and a distaste for convention and tradition. Some critics of modern American society, where this tendency has reached its apogee, hold that these trends have gone too far; in any event, in the developed countries the growth of large-scale organization has led to increasing bureaucratization and centralization of control.

But Africa has never gone through this period of pragmatism and individualism. The rule of chiefs acting according to the communal wisdom of the ages or of emirs acting according to the dictates of the Koran and the *shari'a* was succeeded by that of colonial administrators acting according to the wisdom of colonial office bureaucrats in London or Paris or the unquestionable decrees of colonial governors. In both systems veneration was given to authority, to office, to traditions or regulations purporting to incarnate the public interest, and there was no room for individualism or dissent. The new intelligentsia has taken up where the traditional authorities and colonial administrators left off. The public official is invested with an almost religious aura of legitimacy, and the most minor laws and administrative decrees are held sacred and unquestionable. Modernization has not meant the introduction of a spirit of experiment, individualism or innovation, but often simply the substitution of modern literary or technical education for initiation into the traditional ruling class of chiefs, seers or mallams. The man with the diploma is like an anointed priest, and paper qualifications outweigh any pragmatic judgments about individual abilities or potentialities. All this is done in the name of progress or socialism, but in large degree it is simply traditional autocratic or communal society in a new guise. As the American sociologist Edward Shils has pointed out, this is an almost universal phenomenon in the developing nations, and has the effect of inhibiting the growth of any counterpart of that innovating class, especially in the economic realm, responsible for the modernization of the West. That the African nations can afford this sacrifice seems unlikely.

Not only is the new ruling intelligentsia largely hidebound and authoritarian despite the surface appearance of modernity, it also enjoys an extremely high standard of living, especially by African norms. In part this reflects the example of colonial civil servants who seemed to live like kings compared to the Africans they ruled; in part it reflects sheer human greed. Not only do civil servants live well but politicians (and in parliamentary systems the distinction is often blurred at the top levels) live especially well. The latter tend to be paid higher salaries than their European counterparts although obviously they do much less work in one-party states. Congolese parliamentarians voted themselves higher salaries than their Belgian counterparts on the rationale that the Congo was much larger than Belgium; and everywhere there is little heed paid to a nation's ability to sustain such a burden. In many cases a substantial portion of the national budget is consumed by the salaries and perquisites of those on the public payroll; for instance, it has been calculated that the cost of the Gabon government constitutes a higher proportion of that nation's national product than did the cost of the French court immediately prior to the French Revolution. To high legitimate incomes are added opportunities for graft; corruption of various kinds is widespread throughout most African governments. The power of the political elite further inhibits the growth of a legitimate business class by making it harder for them to compete for talent.

These high standards of living have two consequences, aside from the strain they place on the national treasury. They lead to pressures to maintain nondemocratic government through the one-party state, electoral corruption and the like, since virtually none of those in office have the qualifications for doing nearly so well outside (indeed there are few comparable opportunities for enrichment anyway) and will do almost anything to hang on to office. Additionally, particularly since there is no local capitalist class to contest their position at the top of the economic and prestige hierarchies, any popular resentment over general economic conditions—and such is growing—inevitably focuses on them. A real gap is opening up between the rich in authority—rich because they are in authority rather than the other way round—and the poor for whom the revolution of rising expectations has not been fulfilled.

Some observers regard this situation as a hangover from colonialism and trust in its demise in the militantly socialist states. It is true that such nations as Ghana, Mali, Guinea and Tanzania have tried to eliminate high living and corruption among their ruling elites. But the possibility of such attempts meeting with permanent success rests upon two doubtful assumptions. One is that abuse of power by a ruling elite is bound up with a colonial-bourgeois mentality and is not inherent in the nature of things. The parallel difficulties experienced by the Soviet Union and other socialist states suggest that this is not so, that, as the Yugoslav leader Milovan Djilas put it in his classic description, socialist society too necessarily creates a "new class," little different from the aristocrats of old. The second assumption is that the rise of such a class can be prevented without at the same time inhibiting the growth of the nation. Perhaps economic progress necessarily implies specialization, social distance between individuals, and therefore inequality and, ultimately, privilege. Within the Communist world China, which is poor, has done better in maintaining austerity than better-off Russia, and within the African states committed to extreme forms of socialism poor Guinea and poorer Mali have done better than relatively well-off Ghana. In any event, keeping this new class in its place requires a discipline which tends to contribute to that stifling of personal liberty which is already a major problem in one-party states. Above all, as a score of fighting faiths of the past attest, it is hard to maintain devotion at the fever pitch necessary to keep human beings on the straight and narrow in situations where ordinary social checks and the rule of law are not strong enough to do so.

The problem is if anything becoming more serious with the passing of time, partly because of the continuing departure of non-African civil servants and technicians. Whatever their faults, they did usually have a sense of professional morality, based in part undoubtedly on their impersonality and lack of roots in the African community. An "expatriate" civil servant concerned with his career and the respect of his peers simply had fewer temptations than an African caught up in a web of family, tribal and often party obligations in conflict with the unbiased performance of his duties. Not only gift giving to the powerful but even outright bribery was part of the accepted traditional political morality in African society; mitigated though hardly abolished under colonialism, it is again coming to the fore. The lack of effective open political opposition and the weakness—economic, political and psychological—of the average individual African vis-à-vis the government official make checking corruption—though widespread, and generally acknowledged—difficult.

Whether and when the gap between the ruling elite and the masses will cause or contribute to outright rebellion, as to some extent it has in the Congo, is difficult to estimate. Africans are long-suffering; they have had a long habituation to authority, and sometimes to the misuse of authority, in both precolonial society and under colonial rule. But certainly there is growing disillusionment among many rank-and-file Africans who feel they have exchanged one set of oppressors for another, sufficient disillusion to be a check on that outpouring of popular energies which many African governments count on as a major asset in their drive for their countries' progress.

As one African put it, "Independence is not for us; it is for the people in the cities." This remark calls attention to another significant fact about the new African political and social elite, its almost complete urbanization and identification with city life. It is the cities above all that are the new Africa, and in them its character and identity—on a continental as well as a national basis—are being shaped. The city is the epitome of modernity, which is a synonym for development and freedom. It was the city which ruled and set the standards under colonialism and it continues to do so today. To the city Africans from the "bush" come for jobs and often for education. The city represents success or simply an opportunity for more adventure and variety than is offered by the routine of village or tribal life.

Though some Africans—notably the Yoruba of western Nigeria—lived in relatively large cities prior to the European conquest, the modern African city is the creation of colonialism. Under colonialism (and the pattern persists) there was only one real city per colony; it was the center of government (itself highly centralized) and of economic life as well. Such provincial capitals as Enugu or Kumasi, or industrial cities like Elisabethville, are obvious exceptions, and a few traditional African urban centers continue to flourish, most notably Ibadan and Kano in Nigeria. But the colonial capital was and is everywhere dominant. Such cities grew enormously in a short time, especially during and after World War II, and their tone was set by the white man. He lived in his own exclusive areas—and in some cases still does, not only in white-ruled Johannesburg and Salisbury but in independent Dakar, Léopoldville and Nairobi as well. The African lived and lives, often in squalor and unemployment, in his own part of town.

The role of the city as an agent of social and psychological modernization cannot be overestimated. It is here, more than in school or through exhortation, that the African learns of the ways of modern life and it is here that he sheds, often with unfortunate consequences, his old personality for a new one, or, more likely finds himself torn between cherished but unworkable old patterns and unassimilated and often misunderstood new ones.

When Africans move to the city they tend to settle among others from their own tribe or village in what amount to tribal quarters, often even with their own resident chiefs. The new arrivals turn to relatives, friends and fellow tribesmen for housing and for help in obtaining employment, much as European immigrants to America did in the nineteenth century. Indeed the process of African urban migration more closely resembles the peopling of urban America by rural Europeans than it does the growth of English or European towns. As in the European migration to the United States a majority of African migrants from the countryside to the town are men—men who hope eventually to return to their village and their families or who hope in time to have their families join them in the city. Like the European immigrants to this country the African migrants have created ethnic social and cultural organizations.

But if tribal identifications and loyalties are transferred from the village to the city, the reality of traditional life cannot be transferred quite so easily, any more than the life of a Polish or Sicilian village could be transferred to an ethnic ghetto in an American city. Above all there has been a breakdown in family life. In the cities not only is there a gross imbalance in the sex ratio, but the family when it exists has lost the economic role which helped hold it together in traditional society. Drunkenness and gambling feed on loneliness and boredom. Juvenile delinquency of various sorts is a serious and growing problem. Desertion, divorce and prostitution are commonplace. Wives are less dependent on their husbands and children less amenable to the authority of their elders. Although tribalism remains strong, tribal social controls have lost much of their force.

Yet the life of the African city is no more an unending round of misery than is that of depressed areas in American cities. Indeed, there are many of the same compensations, and the fierce resistance of many American slum families to being moved to make way for highways or housing projects has its counterpart in the Africans in the "locations" of urban South Africa who bitterly resisted being uprooted and moved to distant, more hygienic barracks cities. In their cities Africans live close together and largely out of doors—abetted by the climate and impelled both by crowded conditions and village tradition. Privacy and solitude are not high on the African's list of priorities and many consider the desire for these scarce commodities to be antisocial if not immoral. Noise—the human voice reinforced by the phonograph and transistor radio—abounds, as does human and vehicular traffic, above all the ubiquitous bicycle. Small stores, bars, restaurants, meeting houses and places of worship are omnipresent as are vendors of virtually every product known to traditional or modern society. Life is always bustling, sometimes gay but never lonely. The urban African is confused rather than anomic or rootless.

One must be wary of idealizing the African city and thinking of it as a large-scale, urban version of an idyllic, spontaneous peasant life. There is much insecurity—both economic and psychological. Less and less are women, children, the aged and infirm and the unemployed able to turn to the extended family or the village from which they came for assistance in the confident expectation that their needs will be met to the limit of the group's ability to do so. Traditionally the kinship group or the village community provided "cradle to grave" social security. This enormous burden is now about to fall upon the new African governments. It is a cost of modernization and urbanization which they will be hard put to meet but it is a cost which must be met if dire political consequences are not to follow.

Despite the hardships and dislocations, people usually come to urban areas voluntarily—in search of jobs, medical care, education, excitement and "progress." Above all cities are the core of political activity in the new states. Here all the elite live; indeed a major problem is how to get trained people back to the villages where they are so badly needed. Here also are the potential urban mobs which, as in eighteenth- and nineteenth-century Europe, can topple governments while the life of the countryside goes placidly on.

The new cities are not only important as centers of national life, they are also the centers of the life of a whole continent, for through them and their activities African elites and nations are linked to one another. Even as national exclusiveness is on the rise and national boundaries are hardening, the top level of society is becoming fused. At airports there is a ceaseless flow of intra-African travelers. In the hotels and offices of the cities a constant stream of visitors and a multiplicity of conferences mean increasing contact of Africans with one another. In the capital cities a new Pan-African society is being born.

This new society is above all political. There is essentially one social bond and one status system; it is based on political office and political power. Politics is primary. The central political authority in African states does not merely provide internal order, external security, and justice, and build roads and schools. It builds new villages and whole cities, runs most of the economy, and dominates all of cultural life. The political elite has no competitors in independent business, professional or intellectual elites; African society is politicized from the seats of government to the most remote villages. "Seek ye first the political kingdom," said Kwame Nkrumah. All else is derivative. Nation building means building not only a political structure but a new society and a new economy. It is through politics that the African, having won his freedom, seeks to win his unity and to find his identity.

In Africa political activity is carried on both on the national and on the continental level, but the politics of the continent are of more importance than national politics in shaping African identity. However, their primacy cannot be understood without an understanding of why it is that the internal politics of the independent states have so little direct significance.

Most African nations are one-party states. Except for Nigeria and Somalia, there is no stable pattern of electoral competition, though in some countries a truncated opposition is still tolerated. Ethiopia, still a feudal monarchy despite constitutional trappings, is a nonparty state. The Congo has not yet pulled itself together sufficiently to create any lasting political order.

The causes of one-party government in Africa (as elsewhere in the underdeveloped world) are simultaneously and interrelatedly historical, ideological and practical. Under the colonial regimes all Africans who were politically active were nationalists, the only issue was how nationalistic to be. By a process akin to the "no enemies on the left" psychology which long dominated most of French political life, the less violently and unconditionally anticolonial groups were squeezed out. "Independence now" as a slogan could always beat out a demand for independence in two or five or ten years, and the more moderate nationalists could always be represented as colonialist stooges and politically destroyed. The nationalist movement had to remain united in order to convince the colonial government that it meant business and in order to provide a setting in which colonial-administration policies of divide and rule could not succeed. As a result the moderate opposition to the dominant political movements was usually thoroughly discredited prior to independence.

Nor was there any basis for the revival or creation of a political opposition after independence. National liberation usually took place under the leadership of a charismatic revolutionary leader—an Nkrumah, Nyerere, Banda, Touré or Kenyatta. Who could challenge such a leader? After all, it was only after George Washington's death that political party conflict could arise in the United States; and long after Indian independence Gandhi's heirs still enjoy a virtual monopoly of power, while the ideological and political primacy of Mexico's Party of Revolutionary Institutions has continued for half a century after the Mexican revolution. Why should Africa be different? Julius Nyerere of Tanzania has said:

> The struggle for freedom from foreign domination is a patriotic one which necessarily leaves no room for difference.

> . . . The same nationalist movement, having united the people and led them to independence, must inevitably form the first government of the new state; it could hardly be expected that a united country should halt in midstream and voluntarily divide itself into opposing political groups just for the sake of what I have called the Anglo-Saxon form of democracy at the moment of independence. Indeed, why should it?

Where multiparty systems survive they are usually the legacy of special historical causes: the federal structure of Nigeria, the conservatism of the Creole elite of Sierra Leone, the nationalist role of the Moroccan monarchy before independence. In the case of some former French colonies, independence was granted in such an offhand fashion by De Gaulle that nationalist movements did not have time to coalesce under one leadership, but here the exigencies of government have led to coalition parties rather than opposition ones. Instead of the "*parti unique*"—the mass-based, ideologically oriented single party—one often finds the "*parti unifié*"—a coalition of feuding groups into a loosely structured party of electoral alliances, which also brooks no meaningful opposition to itself.

The historical factors promoting one-party rule have been compounded by ideological ones. Though there exist several pragmatic, ad hoc dictatorships of conservative bent (those in Liberia and Niger, for instance), the major impetus to one-party rule comes from the doctrine of African socialism, which virtually all political leaders support in some form. This inchoate creed is more a mood than a precise political philosophy, but it has several distinguishable tenets: it stands for a state-planned, state-managed economy, with a negligible private sector, for economic egalitarianism and, in general, against involvement in the Cold War. It differs from classic Marxism in several crucial respects, aside from its refusal to openly align itself with the "socialist camp." It rejects proletarian ideology—since most of Africa is pre-industrial the enemy is not the employer as such but the white colonialist, old style or new. It also rejects atheism on the grounds that all Africans are naturally religious; even Touré and Nkrumah speak of and call upon God in a manner reminiscent of American political rhetoric. Above all, African socialism holds that it is authentically African because traditional Africa was a classless, communitarian society, and therefore for Africans the class war is an unnecessary concept.

Given acceptance of the ideology of African socialism there is no reason for the existence of conflicting political parties. The African socialist generally accepts the Marxist notion that democratic politics, as practiced in the West, is a sublimated version of the class struggle, so designed as to frustrate proletarian aims and maintain the power of the oppressor. But since in Africa there is only one class—the worker-peasant class—there is no need for more than the one party which serves his interest. Those nations that still have multiparty systems are by definition nations in which the democratic aim of African socialism—the giving of political power to the masses—has been frustrated to date. Rather than regarding parties as necessary to democracy, most African political leaders regard parties and democracy as incompatible.

Social groupings, other than those based on class interest, upon which party differentiation might be based, such as loyalty to traditional authorities, ethnic identifications, or regional interests, appear to African leaders as antisocial and even subversive. To recognize the political relevance of such groupings would be to make concessions to outmoded "tribalism." Such subversive tendencies must be suppressed, by law if necessary, or made politically impotent by means of electoral systems such as those favored in many French-speaking African states which award all legislative seats to the party receiving a plurality of the votes. It is argued by African socialists that, in a popular democratic socialist state, the only legitimate political disputes are over means not ends, that discussions within the single party itself provide sufficient political freedom, and that regular ratification of the leader's position in mass elections—

albeit elections in which opposition is either illegal or impractical—guarantees that grounding of government in the popular will which is considered to be the true essence of democracy. The two- or multiparty system is regarded, if not as evidence of backwardness or class rule, as a "European" cultural phenomenon, not suitable for an Africa whose traditions and needs call for a democracy based on discussion, leading always to consensus. Finally, it is maintained as a practical matter that many African states, short of trained political and technical cadres, cannot afford the luxury of an opposition "shadow cabinet" waiting in the wings—that everyone must contribute his talents to helping govern.

Few issues have done more to confuse outside opinion about the nature of contemporary developments in Africa than this matter of one-party democracy. To most English-speaking democrats one-party democracy seems a contradiction in terms, a sham to cloak the reality of an oppression equal to that of colonialism. If African leaders are virtually unanimous in their support of the one-party state, this is attributed to political naïveté, chauvinism or political self-interest. On the other hand, most non-African specialists on African politics, especially Britons and Americans, tend to accept the rationale of the African leaders. England's Thomas Hodgkin (now teaching in Ghana) tells us that we must recall the tradition of French Jacobinism or English Radicalism if we are to understand the democratic origins of the concept of one-party democracy, while the American Gwendolyn Carter holds that such regimes are new governmental forms which it would be misleading to call undemocratic.

Where does the truth lie? Much can be said in favor of one-party democracy on pragmatic grounds. It is obviously true that some kinds of political disputes are so fundamental that they cannot be accommodated within the competition of the electoral process, nor can every disagreement be compromised. Weimar Germany fell when the ideological clash became insupportable: regional differences led to a bloody Civil War within the United States. The unity of the new states is extremely fragile; in addition, ideology aside (and African socialism, though not universally embraced in so many words has no real rival as an ideology), Africans are united on most major political issues. There is no substantial popular support for closer ties to former colonial powers or for acceptance of the regimes in Portuguese Africa or the Republic of South Africa. Most states are small, largely dependent for income on a few crops or mineral products, and without any highly differentiated and articulated social classes or special-interest groups. To be against cocoa in Ghana is like being against cotton in the old South; to be against rule by the intelligentsia almost anywhere is like being against segregation in Mississippi. Also, it must be admitted that in the past opposition groups with a regional or traditional power base were sometimes sponsored or encouraged by the colonial powers, as in the case of the *partis de l'Administration* in French-speaking Africa, as a counterweight to the nationalists.

Nonetheless, unanimity of interests and aims can be transitory, and, despite assertions that it exists or will exist, there is no substantial evidence to indicate that there is any real discussion of policy questions among the rank and file in one-party regimes as a substitute for popular participation in decision making through a competitive electoral process. Although personal feuds, factional enmities, and bitter disagreements over policy are to be found, as in any state, even the most totalitarian, these are resolved in secrecy and frequently through purges or violence. Where there is no freedom of speech and opposition it is meaningless to talk about majority rule. Majority rule actually depends upon the existence of political rights for the minority. Unless dissent and dissenters are legally protected, the majority is deprived of the information necessary for making a free and rational choice and thus lacks any real power of decision making.

Maintaining one-party rule of a supposedly democratic nature will become more rather than less difficult as the African nations develop economically. Economic growth will almost certainly be accompanied by increasing social differentiation—in incomes, occupations, ideas and styles of life. The continued monopoly of power by one party logically requires either that such differentiation be stopped at its source and that all members of society be made as alike as possible (the approach adopted by the Chinese Communists), or that any differences in circumstances, interests or ideas be denied political expression, forcibly if necessary—the position to which the Russians seem to have been driven by the growth of Soviet society. Either course is fatal to personal liberty.

In the last analysis, the argument in favor of one-party democracy involves a paradox. It contends that, although Africans are just as human as anyone else and just as capable of managing their own affairs (to claim otherwise would be to accept the premises of colonialism and even of slavery), they are nonetheless basically different in that possible ignorance or self-interest on the part of African leadership cadres does not require that the general public have a means, through constitutional safeguards and the possibility of organized opposition, of "throwing the rascals out." It may yet turn out that the multiparty system is not a peculiarity of Western culture but a fundamental requisite for democracy anywhere in the world.

Despite the abuses to which one-party monopoly of power can lead, there is a fundamental check on one-party rule often overlooked by its supporters and detractors alike. It stems from the fact that Africa is in many respects one political community rather than many. Every leader—even if he spurns world opinion and does not directly aspire to the leadership of a united Pan Africa, is extraordinarily sensitive to intra-African public opinion. Africans increasingly travel around their continent. They listen to one another's radio programs and read one another's press. Influential political figures see one another at international conferences, at the United Nations and in one another's homelands. Technological factors, administrative weakness, and concern for intra-African public opinion make it impossible to isolate Africans within a hermetically sealed iron-curtain type of totalitarianism. Banning of foreign periodicals, including African newspapers, as in the case of Ghana's intermittent conflicts with the Nigerian press, does occur, but word of their contents leaks out, especially to the elite upon whose confidence the security of the leader ultimately rests. Frontiers are still porous to anyone willing to walk a few miles through the bush, at least anyone not obviously white. African political activists have networks of friends and political associates throughout the continent, and, despite pious disclaimers at inter-African conferences, it is not difficult for men opposed to the status quo in their homelands to find sanctuary and support in exile in other African states. The leaders, despite bombastic rhetoric, usually find compromise with colleagues whose abilities they respect relatively easy as well as necessary, so that the purged frequently return, and alliances can shift with surprising rapidity. Therefore, despite the one-party states and the controlled press and radio of most African nations, a certain amount of actual dissent, ferment and freedom of action exists. Real struggles for power occur, sometimes almost in the open, as in the maneuverings over Soviet arms in Kenya in 1965. In general this sensitivity to a continentwide opinion has favored the more leftist and anticolonial movements and leaders, since in a context of continuing economic and political discontent, where the rhetoric of nationalism reigns supreme, potential opposition from the left is endemic. But no regime, regardless of its political orientation, can completely control domestic opinion, try as it may.

Nevertheless the one-party state seeks constantly to control as much of it as it can. Labor unions, educational institutions, women's and youth groups, even sports activities are generally coordinated and supervised by the single party, with only the religious groups retaining a certain freedom, provided their intervention in political and social matters is of a sort approved by government. Such elements of traditional aristocracy as have any continuing political role exercise authority at the behest of the government. Independent business and professional classes do not exist to challenge the monopoly of power. The principal check on the new ruling class and its authority, power, pretensions and living standards is intra-African public opinion.

Yet to conclude from this that the position of the new elite is unassailable and that it will retain unquestioned control indefinitely would be rash. Not only is there the possibility of peasant uprisings as in the Congo or of such widespread disaffection as led to the overthrow of the junta of General Abboud in the Sudan in 1964; beyond this the institution of the one-party state ruled by a nationalist intelligentsia has basic structural weaknesses which threaten its stability if not its continued existence. First of all, there is the problem which all regimes not periodically subject to renewal of their popular mandate have to face when their leaders pass from the scene as all eventually must—the problem of succession. It is not yet possible to tell whether any African leaders of mass party states have created political and governmental structures strong enough to hold together after their death. The assassination of Nkrumah, first and in some ways foremost of such leaders, has allegedly been attempted several times already. His death could bring chaos to Ghana, despite the façade of rule by a monolithic Convention People's Party.

The discord in Kenya, over Cold War policies especially, even while the revered Jomo Kenyatta is still alive, gives warning of what might befall that country when this elderly leader dies. The possibility of having to face a sudden change of this sort is heightened by the dependence of the one-party states on a single leader and the lack of accommodation of dissent. The only means to change is violence directed against the ruler or the state, and assassination attempts (however unsuccessful) are frequent, as are charges of plots and counterplots against the government. One-party states are thus basically unstable in two related ways: they often breed subversion by driving legitimate opposition underground, and through lack of an orderly succession procedure they make every change of ruler a major political crisis.

But the system of rule by the intelligentsia acting through a single-party state is not only unstable because of these overt and obvious problems of accommodating dissent and providing for new leadership. It is unstable because the new African political elite is not as monolithic as it sometimes seems. There are many cleavages within the elite. Politicians and civil servants in some nations eye each other uneasily. So far the civil service, often tainted with colonial associations, has had to take second place, and attempts are being made to politicize it and thus prevent it from developing a separate esprit de corps which might prove dangerous to the party's interests. Insofar as civil servants can retain their identity and resist the blandishments held out by the politicians, they may in time be tempted to seek popular support for more efficient government.

More likely, however, is a division based on age, with both the civil service and the party divided along generational lines. Throughout Africa, in both "conservative" and "radical" states, a younger generation, usually though not always more "leftist" in its leanings than the established leadership, often with superior formal education and technical competence but with limited experience of responsible political activity, is coming to the fore. The possibility that such cleavage will lead to open conflict increases insofar as age and ideological differences coincide. This generational conflict is exacerbated by the fact that in many African countries the older generation is not very old by world standards. Because those in power are only a few years the seniors of their potential successors the inevitable frustrations of subordination are magnified, since the passage of time alone is unlikely to make room at the top.

But the greatest threat to the unity of the ruling elite is presented not by cleavages between political and technical elites, nor between old and young, but increasingly by that between the military and the political leadership. The increasing importance of the military in Africa means that they are or soon will be in a position to determine which side would win out if there was an open struggle for political power among other competing groups. Until recently leaders have operated on the premise that political power was the reward for political skill and popular support, and the relative willingness of the colonial regimes to yield power confirmed them in their beliefs. Now they are faced with the necessity of testing the extent of the validity of Mao Tse-tung's dictum that political power grows out of the barrel of a gun.

For a long time Africa was unique within the underdeveloped world in that the military did not play any substantial role in its politics. As independent states Ethiopia, Liberia and Egypt had their own officer corps. But in areas under colonial rule (with the exception of the Sudan) military forces were small and Africans were not commissioned officers. Colonies gained independence, therefore, possessing few or no military forces. Nowhere save in Algeria were the processes of nationalist revolution sufficiently violent to create an indigenous people's army. The military were not rivals for power with the civilian intelligentsia.

This is now changing. Not only are African nations building up their armies, but in some areas—notably the Horn of Africa—they are on the verge of a major and economically debilitating arms race. At the same time that they are increasing their forces they are Africanizing their military leadership as rapidly as possible, replacing British or French officers with local ones. The security provided African political leaders by white professional officers, who had no motive for failing to support established authority, has diminished. The military took power in the Sudan from faltering civilian hands in 1958 and ruled for six years. By taking sides the military determined the outcome of political crises in Dahomey and Congo-Brazzaville, and military elements played a part in the crisis of power within the former Belgian Congo. In Algeria military support was the major factor in making possible Colonel Boumedienne's ouster of Ben Bella. Ethiopia was the scene of an unsuccessful military coup in 1960. While apparently not seeking to take over power generally but merely wishing to gain special benefits, the army overthrew the government in Togo and almost did so in Kenya, Uganda and Tanganyika.

African political leaders are of course seeking to minimize the threat of a military takeover. That this is possible is demonstrated by the Communist Chinese, who have done much better in this regard than the Russians. Whether African leaders will be uniformly successful in controlling the military is doubtful. We may yet see military regimes in Africa if African armies develop sufficient cohesion and national esprit to take over in a future politically deadlocked Nigeria or a chaotic post-Nkrumah Ghana. Even if they do not seize power themselves Africa's armies will increasingly become another voice that must be listened to. Whether, when it comes to world affairs, they will speak in different accents than the existing nationalist intelligentsia is as yet an open question.

The very existence of the new nations of Africa constitutes a paradox. Their political structures and economies and societies are still highly fragile. Through revolutionary élan and monopolistic mass parties their leaders strive to hold them together long enough to forge real bonds of nationhood—mutual identifications based on intercommunication and common action. Yet many of these nations are, in their present boundaries, admittedly the artificial constructs of colonialism, and all African nationalists are to some extent committed to the Pan-African ideal. This leads to serious practical and political difficulties. Why strive to make nations of such possibly economically unviable entities as Niger, Gambia, Chad or Rwanda? Why strive to bind the ethnic groups within Nigeria or Uganda together when they might be more at ease in a larger political unit where there was less danger of their being dominated by their immediate neighbors and long-time rivals?

The New Nations

Pan-Africanism seems a practical measure for political and economic growth as well as an ideological imperative. But while rival schools of thought and rival leaders debate the means to and nature of Pan-Africanism, life must go on and existing nations are strengthened. Yet the very act of nation building makes eventual African unity more difficult. National economies are planned and knit together, political structures take root, loyalties and interests become bound up with a particular nation-state. Every minute lost makes the task of creating continental unity more difficult as almost two-score nations acquire lives of their own.

VII

CREATING A NEW CONTINENT

"Africans, all over the continent, without a word being spoken either from one individual to another or from one African country to another, looked at the European, looked at one another, and knew that in relation to the European they were one."

In these words Julius Nyerere describes the effect of colonialism on Africa. Had there been no colonial regime in Africa, Pan-Africanism would probably never have come into being. Like most movements for political or social unity, it derived its consciousness and coherence from outside pressures. Africans defined themselves as such in contrast to those who oppressed or despised them.

The first impetus to Pan-Africanism was racial and came from outside—from Negroes in the United States and the West Indies who found themselves unaccepted where they lived because of something about them which could only be defined as their Africanness. In time this movement for overall African freedom, which was at first waged only on the intellectual and polemical plane, became a practical political movement carried on within particular colonial situations. The first four Pan African Congresses were the creation of non-African Negroes; the fifth, held at Manchester, England, in 1945, was the first to be dominated by Africans. World War II with its implicit promise of the Four Freedoms to all mankind was ending victoriously. Independence was in the air. George Padmore, a West Indian educated mostly in the United States, a man who had passed through Communism on his spiritual pilgrimage to Pan-Africanism, was the conference's mentor. But most of the delegates were African students or trade unionists, and two men who were later to become the heads of independent African states, Jomo Kenyatta and Kwame Nkrumah, were among the conference's leading figures. One of the Congress's resolutions was that the Sixth Pan African Congress would be held in the first African state to win its freedom. When Ghana, a state whose symbolism and ideology were permeated by Pan-Africanism, became independent in 1957 one of Nkrumah's first acts was to invite Padmore to Ghana to become his adviser on African affairs. The All-African Peoples Conference, held in Accra in December, 1958, was considered by many to be the Sixth Pan African Congress.

But no one argues over which was the seventh, for by 1958 it was becoming obvious that the onward march of independence was going to be on a local basis and that the various parts of Africa once separately freed would become increasingly difficult to unify. The political structures and social and economic patterns created by colonialism were obstacles enough to continental integration; the disparate pace of independence compounded the problem.

In the French colonies, a weakening colonialism left one last legacy of disunion—the Loi Cadre of 1958, which broke French West Africa into eight separate political units, French Equatorial Africa into four. This was in large part a deliberate attempt by France to balkanize these areas in the expectation that the bargaining power of the resulting units vis-à-vis the metropole would be less than that of the former federations and the need for continued ties to France greater. In the course of the confused process by which these states either seized independence, as in the case of Guinea, or drifted into it, ideological, personal and economic differences completed the process of disunification. Touré of Guinea, Senghor of Senegal, and Houphouët-Boigny of the Ivory Coast saw the world through different eyes as well as being personal rivals, and the rich states were reluctant to carry the burden of the poorer ones. Differing degrees of dependence upon French assistance increased the difficulties of reintegration.

In British West Africa the process of fragmentation was even simpler, since the British colonies were not contiguous. Despite its Pan-African ideology Ghana was forced by the logic of its independent status to break such unifying links as had existed. Though remaining within the sterling bloc, it established its own currency, abandoning the British West African pound, and it withdrew from British West African Airways, setting up its own national airline. The net result was to make intercommunication, travel and trade among the British West African countries more difficult than before. As Nigeria and Sierra Leone became independent they followed the Ghanaian precedent. Throughout independent West Africa, both former British and former French territories were less integrated with nations of the same colonial background than they had been, while at the same time British and French Africa had not grown any closer to each other.

In East and Central Africa the British had made some attempt to integrate their territories. East Africa had a common currency, a common university college and many jointly operated services. But Africans in Uganda and Tanganyika feared that closer unification might mean domination of the new unit by the white settlers of Kenya and fought it. Julius Nyerere, leader of Tanganyika's nationalist movement, who realized what effect unsynchronized independence was likely to have, expressed a willingness to delay Tanganyikan independence until the problem of white-settler domination in Kenya and of Buganda separatism in Uganda could be solved so that all three states might become independent at the same time. But the march of events could not be halted and Tanganyika alone was granted its independence in 1961. Though only a few years separated effective freedom for the three territories and for neighboring Zanzibar, the process of rebuilding even the degree of functional economic unity which had existed under British rule has proved difficult. National planners are wary of each other since the different nations have different economic problems, different growth rates and different basic resources. Tanganyikans especially fear that in an East African Common Market Kenya's head start in industrialization will be intensified at their expense. Hostility between Uganda and Kenya, as a result of Kenyan seizure of Communist arms transported to Uganda across Kenyan territory without authorization, has dealt a further blow to hopes for closer economic cooperation among the three countries.

The Central African Federation was created by the British over African objections, in an attempt to further the interests of the white settlers of the region. However, the Federation did make some sense economically since it united the mineral resources of Northern Rhodesia, the agricultural productivity of Southern Rhodesia, and the labor surplus of Nyasaland. But the Federation dissolved under nationalist pressures for independence, first in Nyasaland and then in Northern Rhodesia, while in the south the white settlers became increasingly intransigent. Though certain parts of the Central African economic omelet are almost impossible to unscramble—especially the hydroelectric projects and the rail links—the black-run nations of Zambia and Malawi (the independent successors to Northern Rhodesia and Nysasaland) are in a state of increasingly uneasy coexistence with Rhodesia. Zambia and Tanzania have been planning a new rail link which will make it possible for Zambia, one of Africa's richest nations, to bypass Rhodesia and Mozambique in marketing her copper. But railroads are not built overnight. By even the most pessimistic African nationalist timetables Rhodesia and Mozambique should be liberated before the railroad can be completed, much less amortized, so that it seems likely that what these nations seek is an end to economic domination by Salisbury and Nairobi, whether their rivals are white settlers or fellow Africans.

Is regional integration a step toward continental unity? Or does it merely mean new and more rigid boundaries—the creation of superstates sufficiently viable to make their integration in an overall unit even more difficult? Should political unity come first, as Nkrumah advocates, or should steps toward economic integration precede it, as others, such as Nigeria, Liberia and most French-speaking states, insist? What form should Pan-African unification take—should Africa be a single unitary national state, a federation or simply a loose confederation?

While political leaders and intellectuals debate these questions, events continue to provide answers, or at least the beginnings of answers—since the signs can be read in differing ways. So far regional integration has made little headway. In most cases where combinations were effected immediately after independence, problems have been minimal. But elsewhere the story is different. Ghana and Guinea became one nation on paper in November, 1958; Mali joined them in a Union of African States in April, 1961. But save for a loan offered by Nkrumah to newly independent Guinea nothing came of the union and the separate parts are again going their own ways as fully sovereign states though often in agreement about broad issues of African and world politics.

The Conseil de l'Entente—a loose federation of the Ivory Coast, Voltaic Republic, Dahomey and Niger—gained independence jointly in 1960, but for long remained only a shadow, with Houphouët-Boigny declining to back up his desire for political leadership of his poorer neighbors with promised economic assistance. Lately the Conseil has revived somewhat, and Togo is now talking of joining. Gabon, the richest state in former French Equatorial Africa, has resisted overtures for the restoration of unity in this region; she thrives on timber and mineral revenues, while Brazzaville, the region's former capital, overbuilt for the needs of the Congo Republic, is prey to unemployment and Chinese Communist influence.

The most spectacular failure of unification was the Mali Federation. Two states which originally planned to join this Federation, the Voltaic Republic and Dahomey, withdrew as a result of pressure from Houphouët-Boigny. Senghor's Senegal and Keita's Soudan found themselves alone together. Running the two one-party states in tandem—the hyper-socialist and nationalist regime of Keita and the more moderate, Paris-oriented one of Senghor and Mamadou Dia—created unresolvable tensions. A quick coup and counter coup led to the Federation's dissolution within two years. Salt was thrown into the wounds when Keita, calling his remnant Mali, diverted its peanut trade from the railway to Dakar to, of all places, Houphouët-Boigny's Abidjan, to the economic detriment of both Senegal and Mali. Amity has since been in part restored, but once-bustling Dakar remains in the economic doldrums, suffering, like post-Hapsburg Vienna, the fate of a great capital deprived of its hinterland.

The latest effort at unity, the union of Tanganyika and post-revolution Zanzibar in the United Republic of Tanzania, was apparently motivated largely by a desire on Nyerere's part to contain Communist bloc influence in East Africa. But so far little real political unification has taken place between the two units.

In several cases such unity as already exists is fading or in peril. The serious crises in Nigeria resulting from the 1963 census and the 1964 elections point up the need of many African states to concentrate on internal unity before worrying about larger unions.

But while regional union seems as far off as ever, regional cooperation on specific economic matters has been making slow and unsteady but nevertheless real progress. Regional transportation and communications networks are growing, and regional common markets, as well as other forms of economic cooperation, are under serious discussion. Though of limited economic importance because of the generally competitive nature of the economies of neighboring African states, such developments bespeak a real hunger for African unity.

Attempts to bring about continental unity face the same problems of reconciling clashing local interests as do programs for regional unity. But, in addition, they are involved not only in the cross currents of African politics but in those of world politics as well. Here at the level of Pan-African conferences African internal and international politics intersect. It is no wonder that the results are often confusing to non-Africans.

A brief historical sketch of the nature, leadership and results of conferences designed to promote unified action among the independent states of Africa illustrates the extreme fluidity of African politics. This fluidity stems not only from Africa's lack of a clear self-image but also from the tendency, common in other areas of the world also, to mistake rhetoric for action. Yet despite these factors the history of such meetings clearly evidences the belief in underlying unity and in the eventual triumph of the ideals of African nationalism and nonalignment.

From the very beginning Pan-African meetings were primarily political and consisted largely of delegates' making polemical statements, attacking common enemies, predicting future victories, and, having come to agreement on such matters, setting up committees, whose venue, powers and resources were left vague, to deal with these problems. Current conferences still reflect this heritage from a movement which could do little more than state its aims and appeal to the conscience of the world or to the emotions of largely powerless Africans. Now, when most leaders are heads of states with the military, administrative and economic means to implement their aims, they still continue to operate within the framework of the agitational politics of the past.

In the early postwar period most of the independent states participating in Pan African conferences were North African and Arab. Despite this, the Conference of Independent African States held at Accra in April, 1958, endorsed Nkrumah's doctrine of the "African Personality," a vague, somewhat less intellectualized and more politicized English version of Negritude. According to the proponents of the African Personality the differences between Africans and others are basic, and must be the foundation of all action, especially in the political sphere. The All-African Peoples Conference held at Accra the following December was dominated by Nkrumah and Tom Mboya. Though Ghana and Guinea were the only sub-Saharan African colonies to have won their independence the conference mustered three hundred delegates from twenty-eight countries and sixty-two organizations, despite the fact that few French-speaking Africans attended. It set the tone for subsequent conferences of the sort in its endorsement of the appeal (drafted by Padmore and Nkrumah) to all Africans to work to "formulate and proclaim our African personality based on the philosophy of Pan African Socialism and the ideology of the African, Non-Violent Revolution."

The next year saw a bid for a role in Pan-African affairs by Liberia. In August, 1959, Liberia called a conference of African foreign ministers to discuss ways of speeding Algerian freedom without resort to extreme measures. This conference followed a particularly clever bit of political maneuvering by Liberian President William Shadrach Tubman. Though long mocked by many other Africans for its "neo-colonialist" relationship to the United States, its rejection of African socialism, and the top hats and frock coats affected by its rulers, Liberia had managed to survive the predatory forays of the colonial period as an independent state and had gained considerable experience in the ways of diplomacy. In July, 1959, Tubman, an advocate of functional cooperation rather than political union among independent African states, helped deflate the Ghana-Guinea union by persuading Nkrumah and Touré to meet with him at Sanniquellie, a Liberian town near the Guinea border. Not only did the conference's final communiqué reflect

Tubman's views rather than those of his guests, the local Mandingo (in close touch with their kin across the frontier) greeted Touré with great enthusiasm while ignoring Nkrumah (of whom they had heard only vaguely if at all), helping bolster Touré's ego and undoubtedly making him a little less amenable to taking second place to Nkrumah.

The year 1960 was the great watershed of African political development; nineteen African states gained their independence, shifting the balance of power in African affairs to the non-Arab states and that in the so-called Afro-Asian bloc from Asia to Africa. But it also marked the beginning of a serious rift in African unity, one which was to have implications for the Cold War and the Congo debacle and which persists to this day.

The year began with the Second All-African Peoples Conference held in Tunis in January. Though Tunisian president Habib Bourguiba, a moderate and an enemy of Egypt's General Nasser, was host and keynoter, the conference chose as its secretary-general the representative of more radical Guinea, Abdoulaye Diallo. June saw a new bid for African leadership, that of Haile Selassie of Ethiopia, another moderate who was host to the second Conference of Independent African States at Addis Ababa. Old rivals Nkrumah and Nasser and their allies were being put under increasing pressure to unite on ideological and policy grounds.

Such pressures came to the surface later in 1960. In October one of the continent's most conservative leaders, Houphouët-Boigny of the Ivory Coast, made his move. A conference of former French colonies was held at Abidjan. It was followed by another in Brazzaville in December, which led to the creation of a loose organization of Francophone African states sometimes called the Brazzaville powers. Their aim was to build mutual ties on the basis of their common cultural and economic backgrounds. They rejected Nkrumah's claims to Pan-African leadership and took a somewhat more moderate position in foreign affairs, being notably loath to condemn outright French policy in Algeria, where they sought to act as mediators, or French atomic testing in the Sahara, which had aroused violent anti-French sentiments in much of the rest of independent Africa. A conference in Yaoundé in March, 1961, set up an organization for economic cooperation underlining their commitment to a loose, functional relationship based on pragmatic considerations rather than to a political union based on an extreme nationalist ideology. A follow-up meeting in Tananarive in September led to the formal creation of the Union of African and Malagasy States—the UAM.

Houphouët's challenge was quickly taken up. In January, 1961, the Brazzaville conference was followed by one in Casablanca under the anomalous patronage of a king, Morocco's Mahomet V. Here Nkrumah and Nasser joined forces with Guinea, Mali, Morocco and the Algerian provisional government. The "Casablanca powers" had come into being. They dominated the Third All-African Peoples Conference at Cairo in March, 1961, and in July they had their own economic conference at Conakry. Although it would be possible to claim that the Casablanca powers, Morocco aside, could be distinguished from other African states in being somewhat more aggressively "socialistic" in their domestic economic arrangements and more "radical" in basing their political structures directly upon the mobilized rank and file, their major distinguishing feature was in the area of international politics—in their greater willingness to criticize the Western powers and to lean toward the Soviet position in their nonalignment.

The creation of the Casablanca group led to an adherence of the more moderate non-Francophone states, such as Nigeria and Ethiopia, to a new grouping in which they were joined by the Brazzaville powers (who, however, also retained their membership in the UAM). Tubman sponsored a new conference at Monrovia in May, 1961, and the "Monrovia powers" were born. They too held an economic conference—at Dakar later that year, and another general conference at Lagos in January, 1962.

It must be emphasized that save for the UAM, which involved continuous intimate working relationships, even spawning the airline Air Afrique, no important functional organizations were established by these groups, though various agreements were signed. Although the Casablanca powers usually acted as a group in the United Nations and the Congo—supporting Lumumba and then, as long as possible, his deputy Antoine Gizenga—all of these conferences were primarily manifestations of political positions and tendencies. Nations came and went, inconsistent in their politics and unstable and overlapping in their allegiances. What resulted from these meetings was definitions of centers of gravity rather than solid alignments.

This division of Africa into the Casablanca powers and their opponents posed a grave danger to African well-being and the cause of continental unity. If the Casablanca powers could be regarded as pro-Eastern bloc, the UAM as pro-French, and the Monrovia powers as pro-Western, then the Cold War would have come to Africa with a vengeance. A larger unity had to be created to mitigate the possible consequence of such groupings. Africa could not allow itself to be divided anew by the outside world, this time not by old-style colonial rivals but by rivals for world political and ideological hegemony.

But unity required at least a tentative resolution of the conflict between the proponents of varying degrees of political unification. A conference was held at Addis Ababa in May, 1963. Thirty states attended and thirty-two (including Morocco and Togo, who did not attend) signed a charter creating the Organization of African Unity, designed to be the juridical embodiment of Pan-African unity. The creation of the OAU was a blow to Nkrumah and his followers, for this new unity was not to be the unity of a continentwide African national state (a cause Nkrumah continued to advocate in his speeches and writings) but that of a loose confederation. The OAU charter was patterned on that of the Organization of American States, and was registered as a regional organization with the United

Nations. Pan-Africanism had taken the form of Pan-Americanism, with the major difference that there was no power to play the United States's role of "Colossus of the North."

As in the case of the OAS, the OAU was to seek to solve local problems locally, and to keep foreign powers from meddling in African affairs—a kind of Monroe Doctrine for Africa. It also sought to promote economic and technical cooperation among its members. It differed from the Pan-American model in one major respect, however—its concern for the liberation of all the territory in its region. Article IV of the OAU charter proposes "to eradicate all forms of colonialism from Africa," and at the Addis Ababa conference resolutions called for the granting of independence to all remaining colonies, asked Britain not to transfer sovereignty to the white-settler government of Southern Rhodesia, opposed South African annexation of South-West Africa, and demanded the breaking off of diplomatic and economic relations with Portugal and South Africa. Such resolutions were to be expected, and have been commonplaces of African nationalist activities in world organizations as well. More significant was the fact that the OAU envisioned taking more direct action for the liberation of white-controlled territories. A committee was set up at Dar es Salaam in Tanganyika to coordinate African assistance to liberation movements, and a special fund was established to supply "necessary practical and financial aid," this aid to include military training and supplies, although the word "military" was carefully not mentioned. It is noteworthy that the coordinating committee includes African states of both the so-called "radical" and "moderate" blocs: Ethiopia, Algeria, Uganda, UAR, Tanzania, Congo-Léopoldville, Guinea, Senegal and Nigeria.

The OAU is the broadest African organization created to date and constitutes the most impressive bid for continental self-determination and nonalignment. Upon its future the hopes of Africa for these aims largely depends. Can and will it succeed?

It has already had some success in a few relatively minor matters. Intra-African mediation has solved the border dispute between Morocco and Algeria. The Moroccan claims to Mauritania have been put aside for the present. The claims of Somali irridentism against Ethiopia and Kenya have been kept from erupting into large-scale warfare. But the larger problems and issues threatening African unity and stability remain.

One problem is that of maintaining internal order. In 1964 French troops intervened in Gabon to restore President M'Ba to power after a revolution had forced him to resign. In that year also the leaders of Kenya, Uganda and Tanganyika were humiliatingly forced to call upon British military assistance to put down revolts by their own military forces; African states such as Nigeria have since helped keep order while internal security forces are reorganized. But Africa still lacks an internationally constituted force capable of assisting in similar emergencies in the future and help must still be on an ad hoc basis.

Creation of such a force is beset by many difficulties. Africa is a vast continent, and the logistic problems of a general security force, which would inevitably have to be moved and supplied primarily by air, would be considerable. More important, however, is the fact that despite an incipient arms race, few African states have sufficient internal security forces for their own needs in time of crisis. The sending of Tanganyikan police to help restore order after the revolution in Zanzibar helped pave the way for the military uprising in Tanganyika. Few leaders would care to part with their scant resources of reliable and effective forces for possibly long service in distant lands even for the sake of their weaker colleagues. In any event, given current divisions in African politics, leaders have every right to be less than confident of the political neutrality of the forces upon which they might call for help.

In the Congo rebellion Africans called upon the Belgians and Americans to stay out of the civil war, but from the outset were unwilling to provide their own troops to help put down the rebels. Aside from the general obstacles to such a force already cited, the fact was that the majority of African leaders were hostile to Tshombe and favored the rebel cause, at least to the point of wishing to grant the rebels political legitimacy and a part in any future Congolese government. Algeria, the UAR, Sudan and Uganda actively aided the rebels. Tshombe therefore realistically assumed that any Pan-African military intervention would in the long run work against his interests. By the time the issue was joined in the Congo the great powers were already involved, the attempts of the OAU to mediate were spurned with American encouragement, and the OAU's claim to be the sole arbiter of intra-African disputes rejected by events.

But the Congo is not all of Africa or even representative of it, however long its shadow. The OAU and the forces it symbolizes continue to work toward practical African unity in economic and technical fields. An African Development Bank has been established with headquarters in Abidjan, and an institute for training economic planners has been set up at Dakar with the help of the UN Economic Commission for Africa, which is the agency responsible for advising the OAU on economic development. Commissions for social and economic affairs, for scientific, technical and research matters, for educational and cultural affairs, and a defense commission meet regularly. Plans are being made for improving road and telecommunication links among African states and for establishment of an African agricultural institute. Yet the basic facts of economic life remain. The existence of the European Common Market and its attendant tariff structures continues to divide Africa, inevitably forging economic ties between member African states and member European states closer than those between African states and some of their neighbors. An African Common Market, even if it could be legislated into existence—difficult enough even leaving aside the question of existing European ties—would continue for long to be of greater symbolic than economic importance, given the character of African economies. The heritage of the colonial past and the influence of physical nature continue to militate against unity even at the most mundane levels.

However, the gravest threat to unity, especially as manifest in the OAU, is political. The OAU's inability to deal effectively with the Congo (and especially its toleration of the support given by many of its members to the rebels), its failure to get its members to cease intervening in each other's internal affairs through the encouragement and support of activities of dissident exiles, and the growth of Chinese Communist influence have led to the resurrection of the more conservative UAM under a new name. (In fact the UAM can be said to have never really died since its economic arm, the UAMCE, continued to function even after the founding of the OAU and the formal dissolution of the UAM.) A conference of representatives of thirteen French-speaking states meeting at Nouakchott, Mauritania, in February, 1965, set up a new organization called OCAM (Organization Commune Africaine et Malgache). A compromise between those who, like Houphouët-Boigny, wished to return to a strongly political UAM and those who, like Senegal and Cameroun, wished to stress the economic ties forged through UAMCE, the new organization was launched with strident denunciations of the alleged subversive activities of Ghana in neighboring countries and of Chinese Communist infiltration into Africa. The rising sympathy of most of the members of OCAM for the hitherto ostracized Tshombe on the grounds that he is after all the legitimate ruler of the Congo was apparent.

It is obvious that at present the old ideological split between different groups of African states is as real as ever, menacing both the political and spiritual unity of the continent, as rival leaders put forth what in essence are their conflicting ideas about how Africa should define its identity. The hard core of OCAM members have carried their general orientation into the councils of the OAU in opposition to the more radical powers which they in effect charge with having taken over control. Senegalese Foreign Minister Doudou Thiam at an OAU Council of Ministers meeting denounced the OAU as a forum full of "hollow verbalism and outdated phrases" and accused his fellow delegates of using words such as "neo-colonialism" and "imperialism" of whose meaning they were ignorant.

In May the Congo was admitted as a member of OCAM despite Tshombe's presence at its head. The gauntlet had been thrown down to the leaders of the more "progressive" African states. Despite the withdrawal of Mauritania, OCAM has continued its campaign against Nkrumah and its threats to boycott the OAU summit meeting in Accra in late 1965 have led to Ghana's clamping restrictions on dissident African groups based there. Just how much risk of destroying OAU the OCAM leaders are willing to run in order to impose their orientation upon the organization only time will tell; however, it is plain that in the political and economic realms two different concepts of identity are still competing to define the character of any future unified Africa.

VIII

BUILDING A NEW CULTURE

Political institutions, economic structures, nonalignment in international affairs, even national independence itself are only secondary aspects of the struggle of contemporary Africa for self-realization, for self-creation. African states and African socialism are important not so much in themselves but because they are considered to be the essential preconditions for restoring the dignity of Africans as Africans. Neutralism in the Cold War is an expression not just of a desire to avoid the physical and economic loss which involvement in new wars would entail, but of a desire not to be counted on in advance, not to be considered in anyone's pocket. Western and Communist nations as such (although not necessarily all Western or Communist ideas) are viewed as forces which, consciously or not, threaten the ability of Africans to be themselves in the world. By a paradox of history, the Cold War has in part made African independence (and economic development, through competitive foreign-aid programs) possible, yet the continuation of the Cold War threatens what Africans most desire, a separate identity within the human family.

The crucial question, therefore, is that of what shape the

new culture will take. Behind all the posturing and hyperbolic rhetoric of Negritude and the African Personality lies a real perception—that Africa's crisis is above all a cultural crisis. Yet Africa comes of age in world affairs at a time when the forces of modernity throughout the world are working in the direction of reducing differences among men everywhere to minor variations in marginal aspects of human life. Even the ideological and cultural superstructures which differentiate the so-called capitalist from the self-styled Communist world perch more and more precariously upon a reality in which common technological forces are creating a common human culture and destiny. Modern industrial society homogenizes nations, and the supermarket spreads behind the iron curtain as well as to the underdeveloped world, while, hopefully, the scientific discipline of objectivity does also. Even the poets of Communist and Western nations increasingly speak a common language—the language of primary human concerns—however much ideological mentors may object, for both see the real issue of the century as the preservation of the human personality and human autonomy within large-scale, technological, mass societies.

But what offers both danger and promise to the world as a whole, the advent of the age of universal culture as one aspect of the age of universal history, affects African culture in an especially poignant fashion. For, as we have seen, the older nations of the world—the United States, the European nations, Russia, even China and India—are secure in their pasts and have, however troubled their passage to the future, an acknowledged and prideful identity to fall back on. But Africa is forced to seek to restore or create its self-image at the same time that it embraces the uncharted future, to become once again African at the same time that it becomes modern. For many ordinary Africans, eager for the material benefits of the new way of life, this presents no problem, or only the problem of forsaking a tribal past for a modern present. They are only too happy to embrace cultural change for the sake of the promise of material abundance. But for the intelligentsia who guide the continent's destiny the conflict is a recognized and deeply disturbing one, and attitudes generated by this conflict are often the source of African approaches toward both domestic and world politics.

The conflict over the meaning of being African runs through all of African life today—religion, the arts, popular culture and education—so that it is in these areas that many of the crucial struggles over Africa's future role in the world are being decided.

When it comes to religious values, contemporary Africa is the battleground of four contending forces: traditional religion, Christianity, Islam and religiously indifferent materialism. The traditional religions are everywhere in decline. Revivalistic cults such as that of priestess Alice Lenshina, whose Lumpa church caused recent disorders in Zambia, and the reversion to so-called primitivism in the Mau Mau disorders and the Congo rebellion are actually evidences of the decline of traditional religion. Such responses to current pressures are heavily infused with borrowings from Christianity or represent a conscious perversion of traditional values, as in the infamous Mau Mau oath. They are typical last-ditch reactions to the decay of traditional ideas, analogues for which can be found in Melanesian "cargo cults" and the "Ghost Dance" movement of American Indians of the nineteenth century. Nowhere in Africa is there anything parallel to the organized pressures for a return to Hindu theocracy found in India or even to the politicization of certain types of Buddhism apparent in Southeast Asia. Attempts have been made to organize the Ifa cult along modern lines in Nigeria, and throughout the continent politicians take part in traditional religious rituals such as blood sacrifice of animals and ritual libations, but these are minor and superficial bows in the direction of the old ways.

Superstition and witchcraft are rampant, and they continue to influence even many of the political elite, but, as was true of their upsurge in Renaissance Europe, they are symptoms of transition rather than of continuity with the past. The basic world view implicit in traditional African religions and philosophies may long remain an important factor in the African cultural subconscious or in shaping characterological structures, but despite academic attempts to rationalize them as forms of explicit belief the traditional religions are doomed, doomed by modernity. For in Africa progress is identified with literacy, and the traditional faiths are not embodied in literary cultures. Islam and Christianity by contrast are religions of the book; so too is the demi-religion of modern science. Preliterate value systems thus suffer a fatal disadvantage. It is not the rate of conversions to Islam or Christianity (however lasting they may or may not be) that is the crucial token of religious change, but the inability of traditional systems to come to terms with modern technological society.

Christianity has been at home in Africa since its beginning; nonetheless, it is increasingly regarded by nationalists throughout the continent as a "non-African" religion. But Christ spent his boyhood in Egyptian exile, and North Africa was Christian before it was Muslim. St. Augustine was an Algerian Berber educated at Carthage. And Alexandria (in tradition the See of St. Mark) was probably the most important intellectual center of early Christianity. At one time Christian culture apparently prevailed at least as far south and west as the environs of Lake Chad. But only Ethiopia, frozen in its mountain retreat, still bears witness to this era. To most Africans Christianity is a religion connected with colonialism.

The first Christian missionaries to come to Africa in modern times accompanied the Portuguese. They converted much of the ancient kingdom of the Congo, and a son of the king became a Catholic bishop in the fifteenth century, but their work, like so much else, was destroyed by the slave trade. It was only in the nineteenth century that missionary activity revived on a major scale. The drives of British Protestantism to abolish the slave trade and to Christianize Africa were merged from the outset. The special appeal of the legend of David Livingstone lay in his embodiment of both of these impulses. Though the Boers played a separate role of their own in the South, English and Scottish Protestant missionaries were the major forces for evangelization in the British territories. The French brought Catholicism to their territories and to Uganda, but they, like the British in Northern Nigeria, were often brought up short by the power of an already entrenched Islam. Anticlericalism in republican France was also a factor in inhibiting Catholic activity in French Africa. The Belgians sought with considerable success to plant Christianity in the Congo after 1908 and in what are now Rwanda and Burundi. German missionaries of both Catholic and Protestant persuasion provided a bright spot in an otherwise dark German record in Africa. The Dutch and later the Irish were also active, and American Protestants—including American Negro churches—made a significant contribution, especially in Central Africa. Eastern Orthodox groups have been active in East Africa in recent decades.

The attitudes of the colonial powers toward missionary activities varied. In certain periods, especially in the earliest eras, they regarded them with hostility, as did most slavers and traders. Some officials felt that by changing native ways the missionaries disrupted society and made administration more difficult; others deemed them a force for progress or docility. In time the range of mission activity became largely internationalized, but the missionaries continued to reflect in large measure the dominant orientation, whether Catholic or Protestant, of the particular colonial power in whose territories they operated.

At the beginning the missionaries devoted themselves almost exclusively to the conversion of Africans to Christianity. But almost from the first the Protestants especially ventured into education. Literacy was a necessary tool for reading the Bible, and local collaborators had to be trained. Herein lies the key to the present position of Christianity in Africa. Education was eagerly sought by Africans, especially by the lower orders of traditional society, and this was more and more true as time passed. Africans saw in literacy the key to the "white man's magic." If education included or required conversion few objected. Since generally the colonial governments were not eager to bear the expenses of educational activity, the role of the missions was all-important in this field. Hence the fact that the great majority of prominent African nationalists have been trained in mission schools at some point in their education (Nkrumah, educated in Catholic schools, even once thought of becoming a Jesuit); many have taught in them, and Christians are still disproportionately represented in the political and social elite.

The role of the missions in African nationalism is, therefore, a paradoxical one. The education they provided made nationalism possible as did their iteration of the idea of fundamental human equality. Yet Christianity is generally viewed by Africans as not indigenously African, but rather a white man's religion, because, as in other "pagan" areas of the world, Christian missionaries often opposed or denigrated traditional local customs and institutions: veneration of ancestors, traditional tribal ceremonies and authority systems, and polygamy. In many cases the opposition between Christianity and traditional beliefs and practices was inherent and unavoidable; in other cases it stemmed from misplaced zeal and even ethnocentrism. In recent years such conflicts have been diminishing. Many Christian churches have been rapidly Africanizing their clergy and hierarchy (although the continuing rapid expansion of Christian churches still requires the importation of religious workers from abroad) and also incorporating traditional African musical and artistic forms into their services and religious edifices. But, overall, Christianity's image in Africa is still that of a de-Africanizing institution, whose educational and proselytizing practices lead to the adoption of an alien culture and a turning away from African roots.

Christiantity is still growing rapidly in Africa. New adherents are flocking to Christian churches to a degree unparalleled in modern times anywhere in the world, and over 20 percent of the population is nominally Christian. Yet Christianity seems to be losing out among the educated youth in relative if not absolute terms. As the importance of state schools increases in relation to church schools in the overall educational pattern, a greater proportion of the educated than in the past are Muslims or otherwise non-Christian. Even among Christians the attempt is increasingly made to shed some of the external features which have differentiated Christians from their fellows; dropping Christian names such as John or Peter for traditional first names is common. Above all there is the tendency of African nationalism itself to become a kind of religious faith.

Church leaders recognize this and have sought to minimize points of conflict between Christianity and nationalism and, by political neutrality, to reduce accusations that Christianity is divisive, a prime sin in the African nationalists' book. Yet possibilities of church-state conflict are omnipresent in a situaton in which socialist or quasi-socialist states seek to monopolize or control public activities while churches are deeply involved in education, medical care, social work and organized women's and youth activities. For the most part African governments have appreciated the real technical assistance given in the past and present by and through Christian agencies, but tensions and conflict persist, especially in such ardently socialist states as Guinea and Tanzania. Elsewhere, as in the Sudan, predominantly Islamic states have looked upon Christian missions as a directly divisive force. The fact that here as in other similar situations in Africa Christianity has gained most of its adherents among particular tribal groups in particular areas leads to a coincidence of Christian strength with other politically relevant divisive factors and aggravates the inherent potential for conflict.

Christian leaders are also aware that, although many African Christians are as intellectually sophisticated as Christians anywhere (men such as Senghor, Prime Minister Kaunda of Zambia and Chief Luthuli of South Africa's African National Congress have been deeply influenced by their beliefs), there has in general been a failure to acquaint African Christians with the social implications of their faith and that, just as many American Christians are likely to accept dominant community standards rather than Christian principles as the norm for their attitudes in, say, race relations, so in Africa also many Christians are loath to take stands counter to local public opinion in ethically sensitive matters. Thus how potent a force Christianity will be in the life of the new Africa is still in question, for, as in the nineteenth- and twentieth-century Western world, the pulls of nationalistic and materialistic values are strong indeed.

But while nationalism does act as a counter ideology to Christianity in some respects, there is little tendency in the new states to choose an indigenous traditional religion in preference to it on nationalistic grounds. Assuming that church-state conflict can be reduced to a manageable level, organized Christianity will continue to provide one important African window on the larger world. The churches of Europe and America are still important sources of educational and other forms of assistance. African voices are increasingly heard in international Christian bodies, and at the Second Vatican Council the African bloc (of blacks and whites) was an important force for liberalization of Catholic church practices. As political ties between Europe and Africa diminish, religious ties may well gain rather than lose significance.

The role of Islam in Africa is complex and controversial. North Africa, of course, became Islamized in the seventh century, during the first Muslim upsurge. In the sixty years following Muhammed's death the Prophet's followers conquered the whole of North Africa. Over the succeeding centuries Islam penetrated south by conquest, organized missionary activity, and the influence of Muslim traders. Generally it did not, save in coastal East Africa, gain dominance below the line of 10 percent north latitude, what used to be called the "Muslim line." The Arabs and other Islamized peoples were primarily horsemen and pastoralists, and the rain forests further south in

West and Central Africa inhibited the movement of large animals while the tsetse fly made their survival difficult.

Paradoxically, Islam enjoyed a renewed expansion under European colonization. Improved transportation facilities and assured internal peace abetted the activities of Muslim traders, who acted as grass-roots missionaries for their faith. The worship of literacy that was triggered by colonialism, and the loss of confidence in traditional creeds made Africans eager to become members of a respectable religion, a religion of the Book, whose Koranic schools usually involved training in literacy, in Arabic. At the same time Islam made fewer demands on its converts than Christianity, and conversion was an easy process, requiring only a simple profession of faith and acceptance of a few ritual observances, and under Islam traditional African polygamy could continue to be practiced. Besides, those who brought Islam to Africa were not Europeans but recognizably fellow Africans; adherence to their religion could not be construed as knuckling under to the colonial power.

As a result of these advantages Islam has spread with explosive force, at a rate even greater than that of the Christian growth, remarkable enough in itself, and it continues to expand, reaching higher up the social ladder as the political benefits of Christian membership decrease with the demise of colonialism. Not only North Africa, the Sudan, Somalia, and Mauritania but such black African states as Senegal, Mali, Guinea, Volta, Niger and Chad are overwhelmingly Muslim. Muslims are the largest religious group in Nigeria and an important element throughout West and East Africa. Yet the black African Muslim states have so far resisted the temptation to identify Islam and the nation, to become a religious polity, as is done further north.

There is a general tendency to exaggerate the rate, significance and future of the spread of Islam in Africa, not least among African Christians. As in the case of Christianity, many conversions are skin deep and statistics largely meaningless. As the white man disappears from the scene, Arab relations with the black African states may worsen. The current struggle in the Sudan, where ethnic and religious elements combine to divide the south from the north, may yet damage Islamic prestige and political attractiveness in parts of the rest of the continent. In the past Arabs often came as slavers to Africa, and Premier Tshombe has tried to stimulate public support by identifying the UAR and the Sudan—friendly to his enemies—with the hated memory of the Arab slave trade. In addition, the black Muslim states are grateful for the aid they have received from Israel, and have generally been unwilling to be drawn into the politics of the Arab world.

Nevertheless Islam does offer Africans membership in an international community in which, unlike Christianity, the dominant accents are not those of Europe and America, and in which race does not seem to be important—a new bridge between Africa and the world, on which Africans can pass as equals. But even leaving aside revival of the slavery issue and particular disputes between Muslim and non-Muslim groups, Islam may yet come to suffer from some of the same disabilities as Christianity in the eyes of the nationalist. Islam may be considered less foreign to Africa than Christianity (albeit on dubious historical grounds) but it is not specifically African. Blacks may be equally Muslims with nonblacks, but to be a Muslim is not by definition to be an African. The drive for a specifically African identity could become so intense and particularistic that the current bonds between North and sub-Saharan Africa might disintegrate under the pressure of a nationalism specifically and exclusively racial in content.

But the real crisis of values in Africa today is not a directly religious one. Virtually all Africans, whether nominally traditional, Christian or Muslim, are seized by a new faith, worldwide in scope—belief in the primacy of material progress and in the efficacy and sufficiency of a rationalistic, manipulative attitude toward life. This belief is often found in Africa in a more pure and overt form than elsewhere because the impact of modern industrial civilization is so recent and sharp and coincides with an upheaval in economic, political and social life. The real African faith is in the "revolution of rising expectations." It is to this that the new-educated elites who manage governments and the bewildered immigrants from the villages who huddle in the shanty towns give their prime allegiance. Everywhere in the world, not excluding Europe and America, the spread of economic prosperity and mass production has made people members of a mass culture which is universal and based upon the lowest common denominator of mass-produced consumption goods, including motion pictures, television and newspapers. The citizen of Nigeria watching reruns of *Gunsmoke* on television and using popular American or British soaps to prevent offending while he makes plans to get ahead in that nation's money and prestige-driven society has already chosen his way of life. Differences of dress, customs and ideas are being obliterated throughout the world despite the efforts of intelligentsias seeking to defend or create other standards.

The struggle to hold back the tide of vulgar modernity and to create an African culture which is viable in the modern world is being waged under serious disadvantages. Colonialism did much to destroy traditional culture, but it did little to create an audience for cultural activities of any other kind. Whatever his other merits, the colonial administrator, trader or missionary was unlikely to have sophisticated tastes in music, art, or literature—especially in English-speaking areas. In this the new intelligentsia conform to the model of the old colonial rulers. As a result the cultural level of most African cities approximates that of a Texas oil town or an army post. Even the university graduate is likely to have little interest in the nonmaterial aspects of Western culture while remaining highly ambivalent toward traditional African culture; and the pressure for producing desperately needed administrators and technicians will tend to rule out much emphasis on nonpractical subjects for a long time to come. The fact that, as Ezekiel

Mphalele has noted, the dominant art forms of the modern world—the novel, "serious" music and painting—are themselves nonindigenous to Africa increases the difficulty of using them as vehicles for expressing essentially African motifs. It is in poetry, sculpture and popular music that Africans have made their major contributions to date to the creation of a new culture, and it seems at least possible that the motion picture will increasingly come to serve as a medium of African expression.

Despite the odds, the advocates of Negritude and others who seek to create a culture African in tone and content but modern and sophisticated in form continue to wage their uphill struggle. In French-speaking areas French culture predominates and the local French cultural center is the focus of literary and artistic activity. Paradoxically it is in these areas that the concept of Negritude has flourished. The word, significantly, was coined by a West Indian, the poet Aimé Césaire, who today represents Martinique in the French National Assembly. English-speaking Africans have commented that the positive emphasis given to a vague "blackness" or Africanness by Francophone Africans is primarily a reaction to the fact that French African intellectuals were so much more assimilated to European culture than other Africans. Negritude's dependence on Gallicized Africans is illustrated by the fact that one of its principal monuments—poet-statesman Senghor's *Anthologie de la nouvelle poésie nègre et malgache* (1948)—contained poems by only three poets writing on African soil, all of them Senegalese.

The Nigerian poet and playwright Wole Soyinka sardonically questions the need of a tiger having to proclaim its "tigretude," and South Africans such as Mphalele, confident of their own Africanness, insist that the future lies in modern industrial society and that "to us in the multiracial communities . . . Negritude is so much intellectual talk, a cult." Negritude is certainly highly theoretical, and in a sense artificial. One of its principal prophets has been the French intellectual Jean-Paul Sartre, who in his influential book *Black Orpheus* spoke of Negro poetry as "the true revolutionary poetry of our time," illustrating the tendentious quality the concept often assumes. Despite this declaration Negritude has had to struggle with Marxism for the hearts of even French-speaking African intellectuals. The leading African Marxist thinker, Frantz Fanon, though early associated with Negritude in his native Martinique, has rejected it as a misplaced emphasis on color, and the concept early fell out of favor in Touré's Guinea.

Recently the critics Ulli Beier and Gerald Moore have stated their belief that the "wellspring of Negritude is running dry." Nevertheless it was a valuable impulse while it lasted. It inspired not only poets but such historians as Fily-Dobo Sissoko, Cheik Anta Diop and Joseph Ki-Zerbo. It led to the first Congress of Black Writers and Artists held in Paris in 1956, which in turn generated the Société Africaine de Culture and its American affiliate, the American Society of African Culture, and the important political and cultural force, the journal *Présence Africaine.*

While Negritude may have reached its peak in French-speaking Africa, African culture continues to advance in English-speaking areas as well, albeit less self-consciously. Older poets such as John Pepper Clark have been succeeded by a new generation. The university at Ibadan has been a special stimulus in Nigeria as has the magazine *Black Orpheus,* edited by the German-born aficionado of African culture, Ulli Beier. The Nigerian novelists Chinua Achebe and Amos Tutuola are world famous. The literature of West Africa with its relaxed descriptions of traditional life and its realistic appraisal of not always happy contemporary trends contrasts with that of East Africa, which is still primarily a literature of social protest, conditioned by the struggle against settler racism. But even here the existence of journals such as *Transition,* published in Uganda and often highly critical of what it regards as the backward-looking and overblown concepts of Negritude and the African Personality, bespeaks the emergence of a new generation seeking to come to grips with the future in a realistic and confident manner.

South African literature has had a long history. The newspaper *Imvo Zabantsundu* (*Negro Opinion*) was founded in 1882 and from an early date included poetry and fiction. Many nonwhite South African novelists have written in vernacular tongues as well as in English (Thomas Mofolo in Sotho and Sol T. Plaatze in Tswana for instance) in a tradition that goes back to the turn of the century. But as the best known nonwhite South African writer, Peter Abrahams, now living in Jamaica, has noted, the dominant influence has been the American Negro tradition of social protest literature.

But everywhere in black Africa its writers suffer under a handicap. Lack of education and interest in literature among the rank and file of the population forces them to depend upon non-Africans, primarily in Europe and the United States, for the larger part of their audience. It is almost unknown for an African writer to make his living by means of literature, at least as an independent professional. Some are journalists, but most work for the government—for radio and television systems, in public relations or education, or even in technical or administrative fields far removed from literature. This has forced upon them a certain amount of huddling together for intellectual sustenance and encouragement. Organized writers' clubs exist in several Nigerian cities and in East Africa.

African nations are gradually turning toward government sponsorship of the creation and study of African culture. Ghana has pioneered in setting up a government bureau devoted to African culture and an Institute of African Studies at the University of Ghana, the latter headed by a Briton, Thomas Hodgkin. Ironically, the leading Ghanaian sociologist, K. A. Busia, who was a leader of the political opposition, now lives in exile, while J. B. Danquah, one of the first and perhaps the leading Ghanaian Africanist scholar—Nkrumah's boss in the UGCC and the man who first suggested that the Gold Coast call itself Ghana—who was the opposition candidate for president against Nkrumah in Ghana's last free election, was imprisoned by Nkrumah under the preventive detention law and died there, allegedly of mistreatment. Nigeria has developed African Studies in several institutions, most notably at the university in Ibadan under the distinguished historian K. O. Dike. Tanzania has a government body devoted to African culture and in East Africa, as elsewhere throughout the continent, African studies centers are being established at the new universities.

The plastic and decorative arts have probably done somewhat better in French-speaking areas than elsewhere. The influence of African sculpture on such modern artistic movements as cubism and surrealism was most evident in France, and even the French public came to appreciate African art and its values. The more matter-of-fact British attitude toward the world, with its generally lower level of aesthetic interest, has been reflected in English-speaking Africa as well. Wood carving is done mostly for the tourist trade, but government and missionaries have also been occasional sources of commissions and Africa's most distinguished sculptor, Ben Enwonwu, is a Nigerian. But the decay of traditional art is universal. There is room for argument over the extent to which African art was exclusively a means of expressing religious and social beliefs rather than arising from what Westerners would call "aesthetic" concerns, but there is no question that the decay of traditional society and traditional values has deprived African art of most of its meaning and vitality. Nationalists and intellectuals are justly proud of Africa's traditional art and music, but here as in other areas of life they face the dilemma of how to modernize their societies so as to increase African prestige, power and prosperity without at the same time destroying the cultural bases of Africanness.

Most Africans are little aware of such dilemmas, however, and care even less. Their culture is popular, modern and technologically conditioned. The oppressed urban blacks in South Africa have created a vigorous proletarian culture with its locus in the street and the "shebeens" (the African speakeasy).

Its most important formal expression has been the interracial folk opera *King Kong*, with music by a black African and choreography by a white. Strangely *King Kong* met with official approval; indeed, many forms of African culture are sponsored by the white Nationalist government. Perhaps the most vigorous expression of urban South African culture was the weekly picture magazine *Drum*—an at once more relaxed and more dynamic *Ebony*. At its height it had readers throughout much of Africa, but has recently suspended publication as a result of enervation caused by the constant and varied pressures resulting from apartheid.

Throughout Africa the mass media disseminate material which is non-African in content as well as form. The movies which the masses favor are Hollywood Westerns and lengthy epics produced in India. One African movie critic recently expressed his belief that both types were socially desirable: the Western implanted the belief that virtue triumphs and the Indian films stressed loyalty to family and community. Aside from a few "experimental" films and documentaries, some of which have won high critical acclaim abroad, film production is as yet negligible. The same cost factors that inhibit local film production affect production for television also. Having a TV station is a major status symbol in independent Africa today, but save for local news and public events most presentations are of foreign, usually American, origin. This is a major reason why the Verwoerd government has, despite public pressure, refused to allow television in the Republic. It claims to fear the influence of immoral programs, but in effect this really means programs that will give nonwhites ideas about equality or will Americanize Afrikaners.

The press consists largely of a few reviews of limited circulation and highly political content, some innocuous French-language papers, a popular English-language press approaching the worst of Britain's mass circulation papers, and some government propaganda bulletins. Virtually all the important papers are either foreign owned or owned by African political parties. North Africa has a vigorous Arab-language press but the elite still read *Le Monde* and similar Paris papers, which arrive the same day they are published. East Africa has a press which reflects settler interests and may not survive their increasing departure, and some papers owned by the Aga Khan, which are trying to shift from a purely Asian clientele to a largely African one. Only South Africa has a real press by American standards; most of it is English rather than Afrikaans and is hostile to the Nationalist government.

Whether the near future will see a press owned and staffed by Africans which provides a clear picture of Africa and the world is still an open question. Traditionally close economic relationships with particular European powers and the lack of a corps of trained, well-paid and independent journalists has meant that residents of Africa, even to some extent the elite, get more hard news about what happens abroad than about events at home. This is changing as news of inter-African political events comes to the fore, but it is changing slowly. Throughout the continent the infancy of advertising and mass merchandising acts as a brake upon the expansion of press facilities.

The logic of the one-party state has led many African nations to seek to monopolize the dissemination of information and several have turned to the Communist world for help in setting up news agencies and training journalists. Everywhere the development of journalism as an independent profession is an uphill fight.

In an era of mass illiteracy combined with hunger for information, radio is the single most important mass communications medium and is a major force for political change as well as indoctrination by the government. Relatively low production costs make it the foremost medium for spreading local news and information and providing an outlet for indigenous languages and music. Following the BBC and French precedents radio, and television as well, are government monopolies. But radio's political impact reaches across national boundaries, and the wave lengths used in Africa facilitate long-range reception.

President Kasavubu of the Congo was able to win his struggle with Premier Lumumba for popular support because at a critical moment the United Nations forces denied Lumumba access to Radio Léopoldville while Kasavubu's fellow Bakongo and personal friend, Abbé Youlou, allowed him to use the high-powered transmitter the French had designed as a political weapon and sited in neighboring Brazzaville.

Many African states regularly transmit programs designed to influence opinion in neighboring countries, programs sometimes violently hostile to their governments. Ghana and the United Arab Republic are leaders in this field. Such major world powers as Great Britain, the United States, the Soviet Union, and Communist China (French efforts have, curiously, been tapering off lately) broadcast programs beamed at Africa in a variety of African and world languages.

The popular culture is thus a mélange of the traditions of the past and the lowest common denominator of modernity. Save in South Africa's slums a genuine mass culture hardly exists. Throughout independent Africa the new elite either, as in Mali, seeks to emulate the austerity of early Communism or, as in much of Nigeria, apes the manners of the worst of the white colonialists, even to their contempt for the lesser members of African society. Africa has to a large degree lost its past without finding its future.

It is in the realm of education that the African passion for development, the drive for self-identity, and the nationalist drive for political mobilization most openly and consciously coincide, and it is in the classroom that the new Africa will go farthest toward finding its identity. Education is the fetish of modern Africa; having been to school bestows the charisma which marks the leader. Education is the fulcrum by means of which leaders expect to create the new Africa, as well as the focus of the humble villager hoping for a better life for his children.

In the old Africa, as in preliterate societies throughout the world, the young learned by doing, growing up eventually to increased responsibilities, a process usually marked by an initiation ceremony of some kind. In some areas tribal traditions, including the duties of warriors and spouses, were systematically taught in "bush schools" run by secret societies, which still exist in a truncated form today. In Ethiopia the Coptic church maintained schools of a sort, teaching the rudiments of Christianity and Ethiopian culture, though then as now the Coptic clergy was as generally illiterate as that of Czarist Russia. In Islamized areas of Africa, Koranic schools taught Arabic and Muslim law, though their rote learning and insularity were a far cry from the era when the university in Timbuktu exchanged professors with the Muslim universities of Morocco and Egypt.

Europeans came to Africa not to learn but to teach, to teach the languages and skills not of Africa but of Europe. Above all they came to bring the religion which they believe to be for all men but which they inevitably couched in European terms. The first Portuguese efforts to combine general education with missionary evangelization were feeble and short-lived and only revived, even on a small scale, in recent years. But the Bible-haunted Protestants with their need for a literate flock early emphasized education. The Dutch began a mission school at Christiansborg in 1722, the English at Cape Coast in 1766, and by 1881 there were 139 mission schools in what is now Ghana. Throughout British and French Africa education spread in direct ratio to the degree of "Westernization," of which it was perhaps the best index. For the most part education was in mission hands, though as time went on governments, particularly in British territories, subsidized mission schools and began schools of their own. In the more affluent areas of West Africa especially, proprietary schools arose in response to local hunger for education. Where Europeans settled, as in East and South Africa, well-supported educational facilities were set up for their children, some scraps thrown to the Asians, and some bones to the local Africans. The Belgians set up the most extensive system of primary schools with the aim of producing a docile, economically useful, black lower middle class.

Throughout the continent the new schooling presented problems of content and method which plague African education to this day. The schools not only stressed white values at the expense of directly or indirectly African ones but—partially through design and partially through lack of knowledge and of teaching materials—unfitted Africans for life in their own country. The botany texts discussed not native but European plants; the poetry praised June days and new fallen snow; and there is the classic case of the history textbook used throughout the French colonies which began "Notres ancêtres les gauls." Emphasis was on verbal skills which led to a kind of rote learning hostile to original thinking, and this plagues African education to this day. The primarily literary education meant that students were launched on paths leading to the ministry, law or, more likely, clerical position. A few became physicians, but preparation for agriculture or for the other technical specialties so desperately needed was lacking.

In part this European emphasis was welcomed by Africans. They were suspicious, as nonwhites in South Africa justifiably are today, that special "Africanized" curricula would mean a second-class education designed to keep them in their place. They wanted equality of standards—a matter also of practical importance since, at a time when Africa lacked university facilities, equivalence of secondary-school diplomas or examinations was the only guarantee of being admitted to higher institutions abroad.

Today Africans are for the most part eagerly embracing Africanization of education. Joseph Ki-Zerbo of the Voltaic Republic, a UNESCO consultant on education, has said that "for the African personality to assert itself, it is necessary to rediscover the African cultural heritage, and to this an important place should be allocated in education." (Ironically, his statement has been eagerly seized upon by South African proponents of the "separate development" of African education.)

But the practical problems involved in implementing such aims are legion. New textbooks, using African data and examples, must be written. Teachers must be trained, and as long as Africa depends heavily on teachers from abroad, as it must if it is to continue to increase school enrollment, their teaching must somehow be Africanized.

Language presents a major educational problem. Should teaching be in the vernacular or in the official, normally European, language? If education is in a European language students face an additional problem of adjustment to school, but otherwise time must be spent teaching French or English as a foreign language while arithmetic and reading are taught in the vernacular. If a vernacular language is used, which is it to be? The dominant tongue of the region may not be the child's cradle tongue. If education is to be in a vernacular tongue then there is not only the problem of choosing the language but of finding teachers and materials, while the student seeking higher education—which is exclusively in English, French, Portuguese or Arabic—will sooner or later have to learn a foreign language well.

The present situation in most former British territories, which generally use local languages in the early grades, satisfies no one, and complaints are often heard that students end up being badly trained in several languages. Language training in French-speaking areas is on the whole superior to that in former British areas, but this is largely a reflection of the fact that fewer have been educated to date beyond an elementary level and that stress is placed on having language instruction given by Frenchmen and others whose mother tongue is French. In English-speaking areas there is the problem of teachers teaching English who have been taught English by other teachers to whom English was a foreign tongue, and the corruption is compounded to the point where the English of some classrooms can be virtually incomprehensible to listeners from Britain or the United States. There is increasing pressure for the promotion of Pan-African unity through making the teaching of

English universal in French-speaking countries and French in English-speaking ones. This simply compounds the language difficulties of students and schools.

Perhaps no aspect of culture is more important in shaping the future of Africa than education. It is virtually the only road to higher income, social status and political power. The schoolmaster, however ill paid he may be in relation to higher civil servants, is a figure of power; he controls students' futures, he is the visible representative of the party, the state, indeed of African nationalism and of social progress. What the schools teach, indirectly as well as by precept, will largely determine what the future Africa is like. If the schools continue to be vehicles for mechanically transmitting modern and above all European values, despite bows in the direction of native history and tradition, then the Africans of tomorrow will be subject to the same internal conflicts as most Africans of today. If the school succeeds in synthesizing the old and the new, the universal and the uniquely African, the Africans of tomorrow will be able to live as confident members of the world community.

IX

AFRICA IN DOUBT: THE CONGO

Between independent Africa and the as yet unredeemed South lies a vast nation whose very Africanness is today in question. Disagreements over the meaning of events in the Congo offer a key of sorts to disagreements over what being African means.

In 1960 when nineteen African states became free it seemed as though the promised land of continental freedom and unity could now be seen by any who had eyes to see. But it was not to be. That year marked a turning point in African history but a turning not wholly for the better. Not only did the tortuous problems of Portuguese, white settler and Afrikaner Africa still lie ahead, but in a very real sense the cause of African freedom was about to encounter a setback. Critics of the new Africa could point to uncertainty, stagnation, political conflict and repression in many parts of independent Africa, but these problems could be and were largely hidden from the eyes of the international public; besides, it was easy to entertain hopes for their ready solution. The Congo broke down in full view of the world, mocking African claims of readiness for self-rule, and stirring in many African hearts those self-doubts that are the progenitors of rigidity and aggression.

Africa in Doubt: the Congo

The Congo is important for many reasons. Second only to the Sudan in area, it borders nine other countries and is a link between the Atlantic and Indian Ocean states, between the Muslim North and the white-dominated South. Only Nigeria, the UAR, Ethiopia and South Africa have larger populations, and its literacy rate has been among Africa's highest. In the Katanga it possesses one of Africa's largest industrial complexes and much skilled African manpower.

But even more important than geographic, demographic or economic factors are the psychological ones. For the Congo has long been a symbol of Africa. The very word "Congo" has resonance for the many Americans who never heard of most of the African states which quietly reached independence and unobtrusively went about their business. Motion pictures of Pygmies and Watutsi dancers (whom most Americans wrongly identify with the Congo), the poems of Vachel Lindsay and the storytelling of Joseph Conrad had made the Congo the symbol of a primitive, savage Africa. Here if anywhere was the "heart of darkness." This image of Africa had faded into the background of Western consciousness before a confused montage of skyscrapers and steam shovels, luxury hotels and scrubbed schoolchildren, and hardworking, earnest UN delegates. But now tales of bloodshed and terror, magnified by the devices of modern journalism, poured forth from the troubled Congo. A kind of psychological atavism asserted that here indeed was the real Africa.

Africans knew better—not only about their land as a whole but about the unhappy Congo as well. Nonetheless, increasingly the Congo became a symbol not only of bloodshed but of frustration. Before Conor Cruise O'Brien went to the Congo as United Nations political representative he was briefed by his predecessor's aide, Gustavo Duran, a former Spanish Loyalist general and a man of strong nerves: "The Congolese? You will hate them all—all without exception. Mobutu, Gizenga, Munongo, left, right, blacks, whites, all horrible. . . . There is nothing like the Congo. You will thank God for that."

Africans had an explanation for the situation in the Congo in decades of Belgian mismanagement, but this was not enough. For had not all of Africa been to some extent mismanaged under colonial rule? A more proximate cause for civil war and misery must be found than lack of trained leadership and tribalism, both of which were endemic throughout Africa. Neo-colonialism was the natural villain, Patrice Lumumba the fortuitous hero.

There is no need to recite here the whole tragic history of the Congo. But so often have the facts been obscured (not least by their very profusion) that events must be put into perspective in order to make the problems of the present meaningful.

The Congo was a land of legendary horror under Léopold's reign as sovereign of the Congo Free State. The gathering of ivory and wild rubber required the virtual enslavement and not infrequent torture of millions of Congolese. How widespread the resulting depopulation was can never be known, since adequate population figures for the period prior to the European conquest are lacking. Even the extent of economic exploitation is impossible to estimate, since the Free States's records were destroyed at its demise. But the cloud of misery and repression that hung over the land was visible to the naked eye. Once it was exposed to the world, the Free State had to be jettisoned. The new Belgian regime was put on its best behavior in the Congo; it adopted a policy of showy and by no means fictitious paternalism from the day it took over control. But the ghost of a Congo political entity which was a mask for foreign economic exploitation of Africans was born at the Free State's demise. Many of the most bitter opponents of Tshombe feel that his Katanga and, later, his Congo are the Free State formula all over again, a sham sovereignty masking rapacious white corporate interests.

During the colonial era the Congo was ruled by a coalition of the Belgian government, big business and the Catholic church. In Belgium political debate tended to stop at the water's edge as far as the Congo was concerned. Until shortly before the end, colonial policy was isolated from the currents of Belgian politics; anticlerical liberals and proletarian socialists as well as the religiously oriented center party knew a good thing when they saw it. Though lacking clear direction and any really developed colonial philosophy, Belgian administration was based on several working principles. Colonial policymakers were determined to avoid what they considered to be the errors of their British and French counterparts. There would be no creation of a class of rootless intellectuals to spur nationalism. Education was designed to create a black petty bourgeoisie—through elementary education on a large scale and limited, largely technical secondary education. No one would be educated unless he could be fitted into the economic machine in the proper slot. Higher education was not available in the Congo until the founding of Lovanium University in 1954, and Congolese were not allowed to go to Belgium for higher studies.

Yet the picture of a Congo with only a handful of university graduates at the time of independence is overdrawn. Over a thousand Congolese were serving as Catholic or Protestant clergy and an even greater number had had some seminary training, President Kasavubu among their number. Their essentially classical education, though not fitting them directly for leadership in a developing nation, was only marginally different from the literary training of French lycées or most British secondary schools in Africa. Other Congolese had secondary-level or advanced technical education or had been to teacher-training institutes. The Congo on independence had a pool of educated leadership of roughly the same magnitude as French West Africa. In any event the extent of its educated elite was a secondary factor in the Congo's internal difficulties, since those who had formal university training did not exercise (as Congolese students today do not) any appreciable political leadership.

Though Belgian policy was to keep Congolese not needed in the modern economy in as primitive a state as possible (acculturation to Western ways of life, like everything else, was to be carefully managed) the Free State had long ago bypassed the traditional chiefs by putting authority in the hands of *capitas*, local straw bosses often drawn from the dregs of tribal society, whose most important qualification was their ability to produce for their white masters. After 1908 the Belgian administration attempted to work through traditional local authority (although continuing to undercut it through overcentralization) but no tribal authority was restored which could stand alone once Belgian rule was removed. Tribalism in the sense of continued intense and bitter ethnic parochialism and rivalry remained strong, but effective tribal leadership was virtually nonexistent. The end product was a combination of tribal hatreds and semimodern anomic societies—the worst of both worlds.

It was Belgian policy in the Congo to minimize white-black rivalry. In the Congo whites as well as blacks lacked political freedom. The Congo was run like an isolated company town or a ship at sea, with all power in the hands of an elite representing Belgian interests. There was to be no racial rivalry on the economic plane either. The Belgians hoped to slowly raise African economic standards by preventing the growth of a competing class of poor whites. No one could come to the Congo except as a government, mission or corporation employee unless he had substantial financial resources. Whites would provide technicians and executives, blacks skilled labor. Unlike the situation in many areas, wives and families of black workers were encouraged and subsidized to live with their men in the industrial areas, where children were given schooling and wives taught modern family care and domestic skills. The Congo in time came to possess a large black working class exercising skills which in South Africa or the Rhodesias nonwhites were not allowed to aspire to. But when and to the extent that Belgian supervisors fled the country, the Congo was left like a body without a head, which could only thrash about in impotent fury.

There was to be no racism in the Congo. Whites would have

certain jobs and status, Congolese others; but distinctions were in theory based solely on skill, education and income. Since blacks were limited in their acquisition of these, no distinction could arise which was overtly based on race as such. Many people, including the Belgians, believed that racial discrimination did not in fact exist, and that therefore race relations were no problem. But this of course was nonsense. The whites had virtually all the money (Tshombe was one of the few African businessmen of substance) and, save within the Catholic clergy, all the power. The fact that the cities were divided into luxurious white quarters and often neat and respectable but much less handsome native areas was clearly visible, and black faces in hotels and restaurants, except as servants, were almost as rare as in the American South of a few years ago. Obviously, the Congolese saw and resented the superior wealth and status of the whites.

Their resentment, which could find few legitimate outlets, vented itself in quasi-religious revolts such as Kmbanguism, which were brutally crushed by the Force Publique. Officered exclusively by Belgians, the Force Publique was composed of Africans who, as a matter of policy, ordinarily did not serve in the areas of their ethnic origin, so that they would have little in common with and little sympathy for their victims. They have aptly been described as an army of occupation in their own country, since they were trained not to fight other military forces but to repress civilians. Most of the savagery, military incompetence and lack of national spirit this group (since renamed the Congolese National Army) has manifested since independence is clearly traceable to the form given it by the Belgians.

Belgians subconsciously felt and reciprocated Congolese hostility. Congolese were "*les noirs*" or quite often "*mekaks*" —monkeys. When on Independence Day Patrice Lumumba told King Baudouin of Belgium in public, "We are not your monkeys any more," he spoke for all Congolese. The reality behind the façade of Belgian racial tolerance became evident in the events of the immediate post-independence period. If relations between Belgians and Congolese had been all that had been claimed, Belgians in the Congo would hardly have been so terror-stricken at the first hint that order was breaking down in remote areas. They would not have been fleeing from friends. Nor would the Congolese have been so wrathful and terrified at the return of Belgian paratroops to restore order. The atrocities committed against whites—even against missionaries—during the disorder were an index of the quality of black-white relations. What happened in Stanleyville in 1964–65 was only an extreme manifestation of attitudes clearly evident elsewhere in the Congo in 1960. Whatever the causes, history's verdict on the success of Belgian interracialism is suggested by the simple fact that in no British or French colony freed to date, not even Guinea, have similar purely racial clashes ever occurred.

The events leading up to Congolese independence were swift and somewhat mystifying. Pressures within Belgium helped speed the breakdown of what had seemed permanent. Once Belgian clericals and anticlericals began quarreling over schools in the Congo in the late 1950's, the Congolese saw that they could play the Belgians off against each other. Once the monolith of Belgian solidarity in regard to Congo policy was broken the Congo could never be the same again. World War II had already begun the disruption of the neat Belgian system. White ingress into the Congo became impossible to control and at the same time poor unemployed blacks were increasingly moving into the cities. Racial tensions mounted as the Flemish, who seemed to get along especially poorly with the Congolese, began appearing in the Congo in larger numbers. Later, whites in the Congo agitated for and received some degree of local self-government and the Congolese naturally sought to follow their example.

External pressures also played an important role. The anomaly of the Congo regime in the rapidly changing Africa of the late fifties became evident to the whole world. Events across the river in Brazzaville, where De Gaulle's promise of self-determination for French Africa was being fulfilled, stirred imaginations and desires. The Belgians were forced to make some concessions to changed conditions. They began by reversing the whole drift of their policy. More higher education and opportunity for local political activity would be provided, timetables would be set for hitherto unthinkable independence.

Once they abandoned their completely rigid attitude toward change in the Congo, Belgian policy seemed to fall apart, and Belgian actions and reactions appeared to lack any coherent rationale or purpose. Some African leaders, including Patrice Lumumba, had been allowed to attend the All-African Peoples Congress in Accra in 1958, where they immediately established ties with such African nationalists as Nkrumah. Disorders, led by the followers of Joseph Kasavubu though not under his direction, broke out in Léopoldville in late 1959. Kasavubu's Abako party was really a tribal organization of the Bakongo people of the lower Congo. To political grievances against Belgian autocracy had been added unemployment (falling world mineral prices were having a drastic effect on the whole Congolese economy) and resentment of "tribal strangers" in Léopoldville. Significantly, large numbers of whites were killed in the riots. The Belgian government temporized and planned new local elections in the Congo and new concessions to African sentiment. A Round Table Conference in Brussels was called for January, 1960. The Belgians were surprised to find the Congolese leaders unanimous for immediate independence. To everyone's amazement the Belgians agreed. The Congo would hold elections for a national parliament and would become free under this new government on July 1. A new era was at hand.

Why did Belgium yield? The obvious answer is pressure—pressure from spreading disorder in the Congo and from sentiment in Africa and elsewhere. But this is too simple. Pressure could have been resisted if necessary and a reasonable timetable for evolution provided. There was no inherent reason why the untried African leaders' maximum demands should be granted immediately. The Congo was not yet a nation, and had never even been partially governed as a national unit by Africans. It is impossible not to suspect an ulterior motive. Once again the Belgians were going to show how much wiser they were than the other colonial powers. There would be no protracted, bitter nationalist struggle exacerbating relations with the motherland. It was thought that, like an adhesive bandage, colonialism could be most painlessly removed all at once. Of course if the Congo was not yet ready to go it alone without Belgian technical, administrative and financial assistance so much the better. To gratitude would be added dependence as motive for maintaining close ties. From the outset the Congo would be accustomed to the idea of combining national sovereignty with strong Belgian control of much of the government and the economy. Belgium would shed responsibility but would continue to exercise effective control and to reap its profits. The results of this Belgian gift of independence were to be both profound and paradoxical.

Despite its size and tribal diversity the Congo was potentially just as much a nation as any other African state. Congolese spoke many African tongues but Lingala and Swahili were widespread. All educated Congolese—the so-called *évolués*—spoke and wrote French, most of the educated were Roman Catholics: yet such factors were not enough to make a nation. What was needed was common experiences and perceived bonds. The Belgians had divided in order to rule. All the trans-Congo institutions and experience were Belgian. Congolese leaders hardly even knew each other; many met for the first time at the Congo pavilion of the 1958 Brussels World's Fair. They had not had a chance to work together, take each other's measure, prove to each other what they could or could not do. The Congolese army was too powerful to be ignored but unlike that of Algeria it had never fought for its country—on the contrary—and could not serve as a unifying bond. No Congolese had ever participated in a national government in any capacity. There was no national party system. Lumumba's Mouvement National Congolais styled itself a national party in its platform and its propaganda and claimed most of the demi-educated, who had been the backbone of nationalism elsewhere in Africa, as its followers, but in essence it was a coalition of tribes which were in a minority in particular areas. Kasavubu's Abako was clearly a tribal party, other important groups only slightly less so. In the key Katanga province, generator of most of the Congo's international assets, Baluba and Lulua tribesmen were bitter enemies, with Tshombe's Conakat party representing the latter and enjoying white support.

Above all, the Congo in 1960 was not a nation because in Africa nations are created not alone by colonial boundaries or institutions or influences but by nationalist movements. The Congo lacked a real nationalist movement because Belgian policy changed so quickly from repression to withdrawal that none had had a chance to grow. More than a score of small splinter groups contested the pre-independence election; none could claim to have had any important role in bringing about independence. The Congolese experience proved that while too much resistance may destroy a nationalist movement too little can do so as well. A nationalist movement needs something to contend against so that it can harden and shape itself and, in the process, create a public opinion identifying with it and with the nation it is creating. The Congolese were nationalist enough to detest the Belgians, but they had no consciousness of being Congolese.

The Congo was and is being forced to create itself as a nation not before but after independence. Mistakes of judgment which bring political problems to aspiring nationalist leaders elsewhere bring disaster in the Congo, for the Congo's leaders are not seeking or preparing to exercise power, they are already wielding it. There is no common colonialist enemy to force rivals to compromise, and all disputes must be conducted in public with an interested Africa and the rest of the world looking on. What would be minor political skirmishes within a developing nationalist movement elsewhere not only shed real blood in the Congo but are ridiculously counted as victories or defeats in the Cold War by the major world powers. The margin for error, the possibilities of compromise have been reduced to the vanishing point because every action has been invested with the power and prestige of powerful outsiders.

The first crisis of the Congo was the predictable political breakdown in the national elections. No party could win anything approaching a majority. When the postelection maneuvering ended the flamboyant Lumumba was prime minister and the crafty Kasavubu president. On the heels of their inauguration, the Force Publique celebrated independence by revolting against their white officers. Belgium in panic intervened and Kasavubu and Lumumba jointly appealed for United Nations protection against the Belgians. The Congo was suddenly a world problem.

But what was the nature of this problem? The reintroduction of Belgian troops to restore general order and to protect Belgian lives and property, or the internal quarrels among the Congolese themselves? The second problem succeeded the first almost immediately, for, at the same time that the central government's authority was giving way to indiscipline and anarchy elsewhere, Premier Moise Tshombe of the Katanga province decided to make his bid to undo the strongly centralized government provided for in the Congolese constitution. With some covert Belgian support he declared Katanga an independent state.

The United Nations reacted in a predictable welter of confusion and national self-seeking, and here began the real agony of the Congo. Now that through the UN action the Congo had been delivered up to them, the nations of Africa and the great powers sought to use it as a means of realizing their own varied political objectives.

The original appeal to the UN by the Congolese leaders on July 12 not only asked that Belgian troops be removed because they had committed an act of aggression against the Congo but claimed that this aggression was inseparably tied in with the internal question of Katanga's secession, that the Belgians were responsible for that secession and were now intervening to secure it. Though subsequent Congolese requests modified this appeal, the two issues of Belgian intervention and Katangese secession had become inextricably confused from the beginning, and the mandate of the UN forces remained permanently confused also.

The United Nations acted. The Security Council requested the Belgians to withdraw to their bases, and sent in UN troops from various nations to keep order until a new Congolese army could be created. But what constituted a restoration of order? To some in the UN (including Secretary General Hammarskjold) it meant preventing armed conflict. But if Katanga was to be again brought under central government control armed conflict would be necessary. The UN therefore must either underwrite Katanga's secession or conquer it itself.

But even before this issue could be fully joined within the UN, a struggle broke out between Kasavubu and Lumumba. Since the UN was not acting fast enough to restore order—that is, to return Katanga to central government control—Lumumba turned to the Soviet bloc for help. In so doing he had the support of Ghana and the other Casablanca powers. The Soviets leapt at this chance to increase their influence in the heart of Africa. Both they and the radical African nationalists looked upon Katangese secession as a neo-colonialist plot. Both groups also—even before Kasavubu rejected Soviet intervention—looked upon Lumumba as the more congenial of the Congo's rulers. Though never a Communist (Lumumba's political thought was eclectic at best and his major "Appeal to the Belgians" for Congolese freedom quotes extensively not from Marx but from the neo-Thomist French philosopher Jacques Maritain), Lumumba favored a strong centralized government for the Congo, as the Belgians also originally had. He appealed to the left because he sought to build this unity upon a mass party, and to create in the Congo something which could easily have been the precursor of an African socialist regime.

Kasavubu not only objected to Lumumba's appeal to the

Communists, he dismissed him from office. Lumumba in turn declared that Kasavubu was no longer president. An obscure army officer named Joseph Mobutu, a high-level clerk who had risen from corporal to colonel within the year, was moved by the resulting confusion (and some say by the prompting of the American Central Intelligence Agency) to overthrow both factions and to rule himself. Eventually he and Kasavubu came to terms and Lumumba was forced into opposition and arrested. But Lumumba's followers continued to regard him as the legal ruler of the Congo.

The United Nations on two occasions managed, to the dismay of many Africans, to involve itself in this internal struggle for power in Léopoldville, on the side of Kasavubu: once when the UN command forbade Lumumba the use of Radio Léopoldville to rally support while Kasavubu was permitted to use the facilities of Radio Brazzaville across the river; again when the UN chose to accept a Kasavubu delegation seeking to represent the Congo in the UN rather than a delegation of Lumumba supporters. This issue found the United States on Kasavubu's side against a coalition of the Casablanca powers and the Soviet bloc—and, though temporarily patched over, this rift was a forerunner of things to come.

The imprisoned Lumumba was eventually turned over by Kasavubu to the still dissident Tshombe on the grounds that he could be more securely detained in Katanga. Then he was killed. Though the circumstances of his death are still obscure, its political meaning is obvious. In death Lumumba gave the Congolese a symbol of national unity which he had never been able to create in life. Throughout Africa, the Communist world, parts of Asia and among Africans overseas he represented African nationalism murdered by neo-colonialism—by the unholy alliance of Kasavubu, Tshombe, Belgium and the United States. His wife and children were greeted with asylum and subsidy by the United Arab Republic, where they still reside. Moscow renamed its foreign-student university for him and scores of institutions throughout Africa and elsewhere similarly honored him. Children are named for him and poems and plays celebrate his memory throughout Africa. In the long history of African nationalism he is not only its foremost but, except for nameless men in Algeria and Portuguese Africa, one of its few authentic martyrs. Moise Tshombe has said, "The fuss over this evil man will soon die down. The people have no memories here. *C'est fini.*" But though he protests his innocence and lays wreaths at monuments of Lumumba on occasion, he is likely to find that Lumumba's ghost is the one thing which can keep him from becoming and being acknowledged as a major African leader.

Lumumba's death was only a symbol, however potent. But his supporter Vice Premier Antoine Gizenga, who claimed to be Lumumba's successor and thus the legitimate ruler of the Congo, set up a regime in Stanleyville which was recognized as the nation's legitimate government by the Soviet Union and by leading African states which had supported Lumumba. Thus two governments, neither with much effective authority, were recognized by different UN members, while the Tshombe regime, which effectively governed the southern portion of Katanga (the mines hardly lost a day's production throughout the Congo's vicissitudes) was recognized by no one, not even the Belgians.

Diplomacy found a compromise, and the first major breach between the United States and the leading African nationalist states was healed. A new government was set up in mid-1961 of which Cyrille Adoula was premier. Gizenga abandoned his Stanleyville regime and joined the Adoula government as vice premier. The new government announced as the first order of business the suppression of Katangese secession. In effect what had happened was that, in return for accepting a primarily non-Lumumbist government nationally, the supporters of Lumumbism were given UN and American backing for the pursuit of the foremost Lumumbist aim, the forcible reconquest of Katanga.

It was obvious from the outset that the United Nations

would have to play a direct role in the reconquest of Katanga, since the Léopoldville regime's Congolese National Army could not hope to conquer Katanga alone. The United States like Western Europe was reluctant to act, though it recognized the anomaly of Katanga's position. Hammarskjold too was reluctant since he shrank from the idea of UN troops shedding blood except in self-defense and saw the threat such action would necessarily pose to the UN. But nations such as Ghana considered this the price of abandoning the Stanleyville regime. The United States was fearful of being again at odds with these nations while the Communists reaped political profit by supporting them. When a suitable occasion arose in December, 1962, Katanga was occupied by UN troops. Tshombe had hoped to hold out long enough to bankrupt the UN but did not quite make it.

The real issue in the Congo was never the substantive question of Katangese independence. It is clear that Tshombe did not want permanent independence but was holding out for a satisfactory distribution of revenues and political power within the Congo. It is also obvious that no Congo could possibly survive without a major share of Katangese mining revenues, a share to which it is in some sense morally entitled because of the Belgian policy of concentrating on the development of Katanga at the expense of the Congo as a whole. It should also be clear that Tshombe was not a stooge of the Belgians, as most of the world's leftists believed, nor was he championing Western civilization against Communism, as the American and European right wing loudly proclaimed. He was and is an African politician of above average political and organizational talents but of minimal ability to move men's minds or to mobilize their emotions. Like most politicians, African or otherwise, he is a consummate opportunist. He could never have created a national movement and a nation as Nkrumah did, nor become an African spokesman like Senghor, but he could make a good Tubman or Houphouët-Boigny. The Congo's tragedy is that it needs more; it needs a combination of the talents of a Lumumba and of a Tshombe: someone to excite the masses and someone to direct them in their tasks. But Lumumba is dead and Tshombe killed him, and, contrary to Tshombe's beliefs, Lumumba's death will not soon be forgotten.

The events in the Congo since July, 1964, bear a ghastly similarity to those immediately after independence. This time it was not the Belgians but the whole world, represented by the United Nations, that walked out on the Congo, and with far more reason to believe that chaos would follow. The UN had kept the Russians out of the Congo and settled the false problem of Katangese secession, but after four years of UN activity the Congo, despite heroic efforts by UN personnel on the scene, was politically and economically as badly off as at independence. Above all, the UN had obviously failed in its mission of training a Congolese army capable of holding the nation together.

But the United Nations' withdrawal, for financial reasons, was no surprise to anyone concerned. How did the parties involved prepare for the inevitable result of this withdrawal? The United States had no plan for helping the floundering new government. Africans, who had insistently claimed that they could solve Africa's problems themselves, had no plans. Even the Communists were obviously improvising. France had temporarily given up its campaign to lure the Congo into its economic and political orbit. Belgium had a clear field. Belgian administrators and technicians had been moving back into the Congo, with ebbs and flows, throughout the period of UN activity. Almost as soon as the last UN soldier left—left without even a formal goodby from the hostile Léopoldville regime—the government of Adoula fell. To the surprise and shock of the American State Department and even more of the nations of Africa, President Kasavubu named Moise Tshombe, in semi-exile in Europe, to return to the Congo to become its premier.

There is no need to look upon Tshombe's return as a deep-dyed plot. Kasavubu and the Belgian influences in the Congo were simply looking for someone adroit enough to keep the

Congo afloat. Tshombe was greeted with some warmth by many Congolese looking for stability, and was able to elicit some economic concessions from the Belgian business-government combine which runs the Congo's economic life—concessions necessary to the nation's economy and to his political prestige. But Tshombe's promise to solve the nation's problems in three months proved vain. Gizenga, Lumumba's heir, was induced to return as part of the new Tshombe regime but was soon under house arrest. Rebellion broke out in the old Lumumbist stronghold of the northeast. The Congo was again in flames.

What was the revolt about? It was compounded of many things: the revival of tribal warfare, bitterness over the economic misery resulting from the earlier civil war, disgust with government inefficiency and corruption, and the ambitions of politicians for whom Tshombe had failed to find an adequate place in his regime. To some extent it was simply an atavistic reaction to general disorder and misery, a massive act of political delinquency. It was not an ideological struggle. The rebels were not organized enough politically or intellectually to be Communists or anything else. Their political center of gravity was an extreme form of the rhetoric of African nationalism and African socialism, but all they claimed to be fighting for, before discipline broke down entirely, was a unified government responsive to popular needs. They identified with Lumumba—whose martyr's halo was burnished by the failures of his successors—and they hated Tshombe. Since they identified whites, above all Belgians and Americans, with Tshombe, they hated them too. But to speak of the rebellion as Communist in its inspiration is nonsense.

Unfortunately everyone outside the Congo behaved in predictable fashion. The Chinese Communists, seeking chaos in Africa as a means to general revolutionary upheaval, did what they could to keep the pot boiling, but not for any reasons more directly ideological than motivated them to support the monarchist and aristocratic Watutsi refugees against their more proletarian Bahutu oppressors in Rwanda. They wanted trouble for its own sake.

The United States, having swallowed its pride in dealing with Tshombe, now saw everything as part of a hypothetical Communist plot to conquer Africa and intervened. American logistic support was given Tshombe and anti-Castro Cuban pilots supplied for the Congo air force, apparently via the ubiquitous CIA. As usual the American support was enough to involve America politically and prestige-wise, but not enough to do the job militarily. Tshombe had to look elsewhere for additional help. The United States, belatedly realizing the dangers of overcommitment, counseled him to turn to the independent African states, as Nyerere and Kenyatta had done after the British had put down revolt in their nations. Now it was Africa's turn to show its ineffectualness.

In theory an African peace force for the Congo would squeeze out non-African meddlers and demonstrate that Africans could run their own affairs, free of Cold War involvements. But an African peace force, like the earlier UN force, must either support the status quo, that is, strengthen Tshombe against the "Lumumbists," or change it. Tshombe did not really want an African peace-keeping force since he knew any change would be against his interests. The Africans would not send one because they could not bring themselves to support Tshombe against forces they found more ideologically congenial. While Tshombe and the OAU leadership parried and thrust over this issue, Tshombe and his friends in Europe and elsewhere were not idle. They knew they could not afford to wait for nonforthcoming African help, so they recruited white mercenaries to fight their enemies. To add insult to injury as far as African nationalists were concerned, the mercenaries were largely white South Africans and Rhodesians. Certain African states had already been giving moral support to the rebels; now these states—Ghana, the Sudan and, above all, Algeria and the UAR—intensified this assistance on the grounds that Tshombe had again shown his neo-colonialist stripes by his actions, above all in using mercenaries.

The tragic dénouement came in December of 1964. The rebels were being pushed back against the borders of friendly Sudan and Uganda by mercenary columns. They took as hostages several hundred whites (including Belgian and American missionaries in the area) and some Indians as well. A conference was held at Nairobi under OAU auspices. Kenyatta sought to mediate, with Thomas Kanza, a gifted political leader who had failed to find a place in the new Tshombe regime, representing the rebels and William Attwood, American ambassador to Kenya representing the United States. In the background was the OAU position that there must be a cease-fire and a conference between rebels and government forces to settle the political future of the Congo; indeed, an OAU delegation was en route to Washington to press for this. The rebels demanded that the mercenaries cease advancing, threatening otherwise to kill the hostages. The United States refused to discuss a cease-fire on the grounds that taking hostages is a violation of international law.

Washington and Léopoldville alike were united in being unwilling to deal with the rebels as political equals, which is what the pro-rebel African bloc wanted and what the taking of hostages was designed to force. Washington was also wary of the rebel leaders' abilities to control their followers, as well they might have been. Therefore, the United States acted, though not without forewarning the rebels. Belgian paratroops were airlifted by United States planes to British-owned Ascension Island. The next day they landed in Stanleyville in order to free the hostages, and took two other towns as well. In an outburst of panic and hatred the rebels murdered over a hundred hostages almost under the eyes of the advancing Belgians. Mercenary and Congolese troops moved into Stanleyville on the paratroops' heels, vying with each other and the rebels in savagery and looting. Organized rebel rule was at an end, though the leaders slipped across to Uganda and the Sudan, and semi-organized rebel forces, continuing to fight, melted back into the bush. The government had been saved, at least temporarily.

But a new era had dawned in Africa's relations with the world. While the Western press regaled their readers with stories of black brutality and interpretations which were generalized to indict Africa as a whole (*Time* spoke of Africans' "alleged readiness for self-government"), Africa exploded. The OAU peace plan had been discredited, the delegates sent to the United States had been rebuffed and sent home on the next plane. Kenyatta had lost sorely needed prestige in internally unstable Kenya. Africa had proven unable (or had not been allowed) to solve the problem of the Congo rebellion. Instead white troops had shot down blacks in order to save white hostages. What America regarded as a mission of mercy against savagery most of Africa regarded as a racialist attack. Africans brought the matter to the UN; speaker after speaker representing "moderate" as well as "radical" nations attacked white "brutality." Belgium and Britain now had to yield the position of prime villain to the United States. That the attack had been personally approved and supervised by President Johnson confirmed a popular African belief that the martyred President Kennedy had been their friend, but that American policy had turned against them with his death. Demonstrators mobbed American embassies throughout the world and the Communists happily watched and abetted them.

If the American action at Stanleyville had struck a raw nerve in Africa, the African outbursts against the United States were the culmination of a long process of disenchantment and exacerbation. The United States, for its part, had been restraining itself for years and not responding verbally to frustrations in its dealings with Africa and the underdeveloped world generally. But this was too much. In a dramatic UN speech American delegate Adlai Stevenson accused the Africans of racism in reverse, of doctrinaire antiwhite suspicions, and of disgracing international comity by their outbursts. The American public and (more privately) much of official Washington sighed in catharsis.

The long-run impact of Stanleyville upon American-African relations must be assessed in a broader context, but Stanleyville was not a real turning point in the Congo itself, for that labyrinthine land tortures the world with its lack of decisive turning points. Tshombe, temporarily saved, still was faced with a pacification hardly completed. He could not complete it without massive economic and administrative assistance from abroad; the rebels had not so much scorched the earth in the part of the Congo they held as destroyed its human resources by killing most literate persons in the large areas under their control. Not only was aid on the scale needed for real rehabilitation not even discussed but Tshombe remained dependent on mercenaries for his government's political security. The United States and Belgium, wearying of the struggle, began to press him for some concessions to his political enemies. Tshombe knew better even than they that this was the only ultimate solution, but continued to bide his time, for he was aware of the real meaning of events. What had been going on in the Congo was not Cold War Armageddon in the heart of Africa but an internal political adjustment, an extended old-fashioned African "palaver," which because of outside pressures was carried on through bloodshed and foreign interference.

In addition to feeling pressures from the United States, Belgium and the African states, Tshombe soon found himself subject to attack from former Premier Adoula, who came forward as the apostle of reconciliation. Former rebel leader Kanza began to make conciliatory noises and to be regarded in influential Belgian circles as a moderate. Tshombe's hopes for continued power rested on one thing alone, on being regarded as the legitimate, however much hated, ruler of the Congo. The rebellion died down with the drying up of outside support, in part because arms shipments through the southern Sudan were falling into the hands of the southern Sudanese rebels. The creation of a more moderate Sudanese government in 1965, following the fall of Abboud, strengthened Tshombe's hand. Simultaneously he began to move forward on two fronts. His Congolese National Convention (CONACO) won a resounding victory in the spring elections in the Congo, while in May OCAM voted to admit the Congo to full membership, and gave Tshombe a standing ovation when he appeared at their meeting in Abidjan. The one fly in the ointment was the inherent instability of Congolese politics. The new constitution gave the president increased powers vis-à-vis the prime minister. Prior to election President Kasavubu had hinted at the possibility of dropping Tshombe in the name of Congolese and African unity. Whether a legally strengthened president and a politically strengthened premier could work together was yet to be decided.

Tshombe had proclaimed himself the Congo's last hope when he took office. Although this claim is somewhat hyperbolic, it seems obvious that what the Congo most needs is to be ruled—with some efficiency, by someone, regardless of his ideological predilections or in Tshombe's case, lack of them. Tshombe's major fault is his difference in temperament from the dominant type of African nationalist leader, his phlegmatic and pragmatic manner, his disdain for ideology and public relations. Even aside from his complicity in Lumumba's murder, this would make him a marked man.

The Congo is at present a challenge to the dominant drives in Africa's search for its identity. Tshombe's use of white mercenaries is symbolic of a deeper lack of allegiance to the governing attitudes of contemporary Africa. Most African states use former expatriates in their governments, but only Tshombe has felt it necessary to reintroduce them in force. (The man responsible for the rehabilitation of ravaged Stanleyville wears the Congolese stars on his epaulettes, but for ten years he was Stanleyville's Belgian administrator; he now expects to retire in the service of the Congo Tshombe has created.) All African states lean on their former colonial masters for help to some extent, but none has the symbiotic relationship with them that the Congo has with Belgium.

Tshombe seeks to create a Congo which will not only be a continuing partnership of Africa and Europe, but one in which the European note will not be drowned out by aggressive African nationalism. As long as he and men like him control the Congo it is unlikely to be an effective staging area for ventures to upset the white-dominated status quo to the South. Tshombe's road may be the best, perhaps the only practicable road for the war-ravaged Congo, but for Africans to accept it as such requires a new approach to the whole question of Africa's identity and role in the world. It is no wonder that to most of the African political elite Tshombe is a disturbing and hated figure.

X

AFRICA SOUTH: THE UNREDEEMED LAND

If the Congo of today is a scandal to African nationalism, it is not merely because of the dubious Africanness of its regime. In time this could be overlooked, for in actuality the Tshombe regime, save in its lack of deference to the rhetoric of African nationalism and the openness of its dependence on Europe, is not so different from many other regimes in Africa, in French-speaking Africa particularly. But the Congo is not merely a scandal; it is also a problem, for it is to a considerable extent the key to Southern Africa, and it is here, in the territories still openly and legally ruled by white minorities, that the final and decisive battle to determine what kind of identity Africa forges for herself will be joined. If the white territories can peacefully become part of the new Africa, Africa will probably retain its intimate connections with the West and an openness to all the outside world. If the withdrawal of white domination can only be accomplished by bloodshed, over a long and bitter period of travail, Africa's relations with the West may become so strained as to force her to turn inward and adopt a narrow, racially chauvinistic definition of what it means to be an African.

White-led Africa is composed of three very distinct though sometimes politically allied sectors: Portuguese Africa, a traditional type of European colony despite its juridical trappings; Rhodesia, a settler-dominated territory; and South Africa, a state consisting of a black majority ruled by a minority of whites who are Africans of long standing.

Portuguese Africa

The Portuguese—the first Europeans to colonize Africa—have also been the last to maintain their holdings there, and their leadership intends them to remain and in so doing threatens the peace of Africa and perhaps of the world. In 1961, while the eyes of the world were fixed on the Congo, over 1000 whites and 50,000 Africans were dying in Angola, not only men but women and children—mutilated in their cradles or gunned down on the roads. While today an uneasy quiet lies over Portuguese Africa, pressures are mounting that threaten a tragic holocaust, as long and bloody as Algeria and as confused and indecisive as the Congo.

Portuguese Africa consists of three territories: Angola with a population of 5,000,000—including something over 200,000 white settlers and a Portuguese garrison which has included as many as 50,000 men; Mozambique, with 7,000,000 Africans and 60,000 whites, and Portuguese Guinea, with 500,000 people, a handful of them white. All have been the scene of extensive violence in recent years, and war still rages in Guinea. The end of colonial rule in all three is a priority item for African nationalism.

Portugal has been in all three territories since the end of the fifteenth century—in other words, since Columbus "discovered" America. In actual fact however, effective Portuguese occupation of much of Mozambique's interior dates only from the European scramble for Africa in the period after 1875, and Angola was not officially "pacified" until 1919, after bloody fighting.

To understand the depths of the problem one must keep in mind several factors about Portuguese policy and Portugal itself. Portugal is a poor country—its economy is fragile and in large measure dependent on profits from its African territories, especially Angola. The illiteracy rate of 97 percent in Portuguese Africa must be measured against an illiteracy rate of about 50 percent in Portugal itself. An African exile from Angola once said that he hated the Portuguese less after having been in Portugal and finding that it too was an underdeveloped country. Portugal is not only poor, it is a fascist dictatorship. After over a century of bitter and bloody political turmoil, Antonio Salazar was brought to power by the military in 1932. An austere professor of economics, he stabilized the country and balanced the budget but at a cost: absence of free elections, censorship, virtual economic and cultural stagnation, and a widening gap between rich and poor. Opposition is rising to his regime within Portugal. Whether the regime when it falls—as it must—will be replaced by a democratic or Communist government is still in doubt. Liberal opponents outnumber Communists, but the latter are better organized, and repression is an ideal diet for extremism.

The Portuguese have a romantic heritage. For a brief period they were the leaders of European colonization throughout the globe. They view their way of life, based on Latin and Catholic culture, as of universal validity regardless of race and see themselves as having a civilizing mission. The idea that culture and politics must be determined by racial and geographic considerations—the basis of the nationalism that expelled them from Goa and attacks them in Africa—is rejected by the Portuguese. They claim that despite differences in governmental structure, Portuguese Africa is as much an integral part of the Portuguese state as Hawaii and Alaska are parts of the United States. Their own poverty and present difficulties make them cling even more tenaciously to their role on the world stage and, despite liberal Portuguese rhetoric and reformist attitudes toward Africa, much of the opposition to Salazar is just as convinced that Portuguese Africa must remain tied to Portugal as are the dictatorship's supporters.

As a result of Portuguese attitudes and Portuguese poverty, her African colonies are in some respects less prepared for independence than was the Belgian Congo. Angola has more university graduates than the Congo did at independence and, like the Congo, Portuguese Africa has hundreds of African Catholic clergy. Many Africans are now undergoing advanced education in Portugal and elsewhere. But the illiteracy of the masses makes Portuguese Africa the polar opposite of the Congo in one crucial respect, and it has no modern African work force. Despite the alleged absence of racial bias, only a handful of Africans had attained the status of *assimilados* (black Portuguese citizens) before it was abolished recently in favor of a virtually meaningless bestowal of citizenship on all residents of Portuguese Africa. Substantial numbers of Africans are found in the lower ranks of the civil service, but whites dominate all levels of the economy, especially in urban areas. Save for the Liga Africana, an organization of the intelligentsia subsidized and largely, though not absolutely, controlled by the government, there are no legal organizations of Africans save for church groups. A large proportion of the population is at least nominally Christian (50 percent in Angola) and Christians are Catholics by a ratio of about three to one. Save for voting in Portuguese national elections, which are rigged by the government throughout the empire, no political experience has been available to Africans to date. Given the structure of Portuguese government generally there has been room for none.

Yet, bad as the situation has been as far as educating Africans and training them for leadership is concerned (and the Portuguese, under outside pressure are currently improving their policies in this respect), the prospects for the future, though not as favorable as they were in some parts of Africa prior to independence, would not appear noticeably worse than in the Congo were it not for recent Portuguese racial and political policy. To the overall problems of development and nation building the Portuguese, with substantial help from African nationalists, have added a legacy of hatred and division which makes the future look bleak.

There is first of all tension between the races. Prior to World War II conditions were bad enough. Portuguese policy and poverty evolved a system of forced labor, allegedly necessary to force lazy Africans to work to build up "their" country. Since building up the economy could involve working in private white enterprises as well as on public projects such as road-building, and in any event entailed physical compulsion, the system was looked upon by Africans as outright racial oppression. African farmers were discriminated against by marketing agencies on the ground that their crops were of inferior quality. The African generally was looked upon as a recalcitrant child requiring complete direction and frequent chastisement.

These conditions, serious enough in themselves, were made immeasurably worse by the Portuguese government's policy in recent decades of encouraging and subsidizing poor Portuguese to emigrate to Africa, above all of bringing Portuguese peasants to Angola. Though this may have relieved the situation at home slightly it more than canceled out such eventual reforms as the theoretical abolition of African forced labor. The poor Portuguese competed with Africans for jobs. Though they did not compete directly with Africans for land to any extent, they did compete for agricultural markets. Since they were poor and often illiterate themselves and had their own families with them they immediately infused an ugly racism into what had been prior to this time a possibly viable interracial situation. That Premier Salazar—at a time when Britain and France were striving to resolve the difficulties of decolonization where large numbers of white settlers were involved—should choose to more than double and even now continue to increase a white-settler population in Angola is but one indication of the extent to which Portuguese colonial policy is out of tune with the times.

But as if such division between the races was not sufficient the events of the rebellion and post-rebellion period have further exacerbated and complicated the situation. The origins and nature of the 1960 revolution in Angola are highly controversial, but certain things are clear. Angola could not be isolated from the nationalist ferment throughout Africa, especially in the neighboring Congo, since the population of northern Angola shares with the inhabitants of the lower Congo a common Bakongo background, and there were over half a million migrant workers from Angola seeking economic opportunities in the Congo. The Congo disorders of 1959 led to sympathetic outbreaks in Angola and Angolans began to demand political rights. The Angolan nationalists were divided politically into two basic groups—the Democratic Front for the Liberation of Angola, led by Mario de Andrade and by the Angolan poet Agostinko Neto, and the Union of the Populations of Angola (later the National Front for the Liberation of Angola) led by Holden Roberto. The former group was broadly based ethnically with some appeal to mixed-blood and white elements. It had ties to Portuguese liberals and leftists and was therefore accused of being Communist by the Portuguese. The UPA was originally a primarily Bakongo group with ties to Léopoldville and the Angolan community there. Roberto was close both to Lumumba and Kasavubu. In 1960 the Portuguese arrested Neto and many of his followers and violence ensued. New riots broke out in 1961 in the largely white capital of Luanda and in March the UPA struck in the Northern Congo.

It was in this latter rebellion that hundreds of white settlers were brutally murdered. The UPA operated in a terrorist fashion reminiscent of the Mau Mau, with hemp smoking and the incantations of witch doctors spurring the rebels on as in the eastern Congo uprisings in 1964–65. The political ideas of the rebels were hazy, and strongly resembled the pattern of much opinion in the Congo: that independence is synonymous with no more taxes or work and with possession of the white man's goods, homes and women, a kind of perversion of the cargo-cult pattern familiar to anthropologists, the reaction of a dispossessed and despairing primitive group. The Portuguese have contended that most of the terrorists were strangers who came from the Congo. Since so many Angolans were living in the Congo anyway this is a largely meaningless accusation. In any event the rebellion did not take fire throughout Angola. Virtually every African outside of the organized group in the area of immediate attack remained loyal to the government, though a few Protestant and Catholic catechists and even a few Catholic priests supported the rebels. The rebellion was soon crushed.

But at what cost? The white settlers, fearful of and hating the Africans anyway, were enraged by the atrocities and repaid them in kind by engaging in a bloodbath, indiscriminately shooting Africans, and a white terror raged even in the capital city of Luanda, until the Army finally brought it under control. The Portuguese army apparently held aloof from indiscriminate reprisals, but the settlers, having been armed for self-defense in the course of the rebellion, wreaked their revenge. The tactics of the army, however, had involved wholesale burning and bombing of villages in areas harboring rebels and included machine-gunning of refugees on the roads. The army has since tried to heal the wounds and rebuild confidence by a psychological warfare campaign patterned on that developed by the French Army in Algeria—building schools, providing medical care and so on—but like those of the French their attempts at pacification may be undone by settler racism.

Portuguese political tactics in suppressing the rebellion bode ill for the future of Angola. With some success the Portuguese set tribe against tribe and those groups which were not actually loyal to the government were at least passive, earning and reciprocating the enmity of rebel groups. Thus, although Angola has fewer basic tribal cleavages than the Congo, the political impact of these may have been intensified.

Similarly, the Portuguese government has set religion against religion. Although the Catholic hierarchy in both Angola and Mozambique has called for reforms and has criticized the government over many years, and although some Catholics supported the rebellion, the most rebellious areas happen to be those of Protestant missionary concentration. The Protestant missionaries, largely British or American, had little love for the Portuguese regime anyway. Government attempts to present the rebellion as Protestant-inspired have sown additional seeds of division for the future. Finally, as in any rebellion, those who supported the government have become the enemies of its enemies. African government workers who, together with Cape Verde Negroes and nonwhites from Goa, might have formed a link between the Portuguese and the mass of Angolans could well be in a difficult position when and if nationalism ultimately triumphs.

But these are considerations which look to the distant, independent future. In the meantime the nationalist movement itself is divided. Roberto's group (now the UPLA) did virtually all of the fighting, but as of mid-1965 the rebellion seemed to have been reduced to a few guerrilla skirmishes along the Congo border. Roberto succeeded in July, 1964, in winning general recognition for his Léopoldville government-in-exile (the GRAE) from the OAU heads of state, but lately the rival MPLA has been reviving and the OAU Committee of Liberation has hedged its bets by authorizing support to the MPLA as well. That Roberto is dependent on Léopoldville and thus indirectly on American toleration, while the MPLA operates now out of Chinese-dominated Brazzaville, means that the split within the nationalist movement inevitably has taken on Cold War overtones.

Similar splits apparently are developing in Mozambique, although the situation there is less clear. The Frente de Libertacao de Moçambique (FRELIMO) led by Eduardo Mondlane, formerly a professor of anthropology at Syracuse University, is recognized by the OAU as the official nationalist movement. Headquartered in Dar es Salaam, it receives some military aid from and through the Tanzanian government. So far Portuguese control over Mozambique has remained tight and the rebels' efforts militarily insignificant. There are much more serious potential tribal fissures in Mozambique than in Angola and no base of support such as Holden's Bakongo is currently available. Discontent is rising in African nationalist quarters outside Mozambique with Mondlane's allegedly overly moderate and inefficient leadership, and, largely depending on the drift of Tanzanian relations with the West, he may be replaced by a more extremist leader.

Only in tiny Portuguese Guinea do the rebels seem to have any real chance of military success in the near future. Here Antonio Cabral's PAIGC are in control of much of the countryside, receiving some support from neighboring Senegal and especially from neighboring Guinea.

How long can Portugal hold out? Portuguese military morale in Africa is reportedly low and the colonial war a major drain on Portuguese resources; yet these territories are of great economic value to Portugal. Recent large-scale movements of troops from Angola to Guinea indicate optimism about the situation in the former area, where the economic picture is rapidly improving. Many African and some Asian states have boycotted Portugal economically, but this is of little practical significance. The attitudes of Britain and, especially, of the United States remain ambivalent.

What hope is there for Portuguese Africa? Despite defiant rhetoric, Portuguese policy has mellowed under outside pressure. Concessions have been made: more personal rights for Africans, more education (including a university in Luanda) and a decentralization of administration from Lisbon to the colonies, which gives some leverage to local Africans. Portugal has no desire to see a settler government in Luanda or Lourenço Marques break away from Lisbon, and in fact the settlers have little direct political power. Thus, unlike the situation in Rhodesia, the way still lies open for improvement in the condition of Portuguese Africans.

It may not be too optimistic to hope that a liberal successor to Salazar (whether such a succession is possible without bloodshed in Portugal is another question) might be willing to grant a primarily African Angola and Mozambique real freedom within a Lusitanian community in which close economic and cultural ties with Portugal remained. A situation midway between the relations of certain independent African states to France and that of the Dutch Caribbean possessions to the Netherlands is not inconceivable. For this to work the constituent African societies would have to be not multiracial but interracial, that is, integrated. Such an outcome is fully in accord with proclaimed Portuguese racial policy. But could the settlers and the Africans still accept integration after the rebellion? There are important bonds uniting the races. The Portuguese suppression of African languages, religion and culture (an effort even more determined and successful than that carried on under French assimilationist policy) has been much and rightly criticized as an assault on African human dignity. But paradoxically it has given the nationalists a common bond, and both religion and language join whites, blacks and mixed bloods with one another, as well as joining Africans together.

Most African states have maintained some degree of connection with their former metropoles, including the use of European technical and administrative personnel. The Congo has shown that the greater the lack of preparation for independence, the more necessary this connection can be, despite interracial violence and bad feeling. A free Portuguese Africa would require similar ties to Portugal, supplemented perhaps by close relations with Brazil. But such ties can only be instituted if good will can be maintained on both sides.

There are two major obstacles to this. One is possibly transitory—the extent to which the Salazar government and the Verwoerd government in South Africa are forging common economic, political and even military ties in a common front against black nationalism. Overidentification of the Portuguese community in Africa with the Afrikaners could swiftly erode the remaining traces of interracial ideology and feeling on both sides in Portuguese Africa and make future reconcilation even more difficult.

But there is a more basic problem. What is sometimes confusingly called a "Brazilian" solution—independence plus membership in an international Lusitanian cultural community—would conflict with fundamental aspects of Pan-African nationalism. The very ties of culture which might bind an interracial Angola or Mozambique together and to extra-African countries would be a rejection of most of what is symbolized by Negritude and the African Personality. Independent states of black Lusitanians, states based not on traditional African cultural bonds but on a universalistic mystique, run counter to African cultural nationalism. The Gallicized nations of North and West Africa such as Tunisia and Senegal escape this in part through their Africanized Muslim heritage, but this way out would not be available to a largely Christian Angola or Mozambique. South Africans have denied the relevance of Negritude and like doctrines to their nation, holding that they are modern men who happen to live in Africa and have dark skins. But perhaps Negritude stops even further north than the Limpopo—at the Rivumo and the northern boundaries of Angola—checked not by urbanization and industrialization but by the power of the universalism of Latin civilization. African nationalists could not readily accept such a situation and Portuguese Africa could be torn apart not only by racial, social and tribal divisions but by a conflict between those seeking to reinstate purely African identifications and those opting for a nation primarily nonwhite in race but consciously Western in culture. Although throughout Africa this clash of values occurs within states and within individuals, the future of Portuguese Africa poses the question of African identity more squarely and in a more directly political fashion than has been the case in any territory liberated to date.

Rhodesia

While all the lands of southern Africa now under white rule present challenges to Africa in its search for identity, the challenges are of different kinds. The nature of the Portuguese African challenge is twofold: how colonial rule is to be terminated and what role that part of the population which consists of Africans assimilated to Portuguese culture or of Portuguese and mixed bloods willing to cast their lot with Africa might play in a future culture. The problem of Rhodesia is much simpler, for here there is no question of the existence of a multiracial society which on attaining self-determination might add a new element to African culture. Rhodesia is nothing more nor less than a settler state in which an overwhelming black majority is ruled by a small white minority who view Africans as at so low a stage of cultural development that they must be kept under tutelage for an indefinite period. Unlike their South African counterparts, the rulers of Rhodesia do not postulate a permanent separation of the races. Even the current prime minister, Ian Smith, who represents the poor white farmers, the element most hostile to Africans, says, "The ideal, as I see it, is for us to try to arrive at a position where we will accept people in this country on merit and we will not ask whether they are Africans or Coloreds or Europeans. But this will take a long time. It is an evolutionary process." Given the lack of attempts by the Rhodesian government to speed this process, their pessimism about its length is a self-fulfilling prophecy. But Africans are not disposed to wait for acceptance as equals in some far-distant, hypothetical future. The issue in Rhodesia therefore becomes increasingly the simple one not of how to fit a multiracial Rhodesia into the new Africa but how to destroy white rule.

It is less than one hundred years since the young Cecil Rhodes left England for Africa to repair his health, make his fortune, and leave his countrymen an empire—with the map of Africa red from Cape to Cairo. He is buried in a dramatically situated tomb in the hills of Rhodesia, but whether his last political monument—the embattled demi-state of Rhodesia—will survive to the centenary of his arrival in Africa in 1971 is unlikely.

Rhodesia is more than a monument to a man; it is the last vestige of a peculiar, short-lived but significant era in the history of European colonialism. After the death of the slave trade—the basic nexus between Europe and Africa—European nations extended their dominions in order to suppress slavery and to expand legitimate trade and for reasons of prestige and strategy. Rhodes had a somewhat different dream. He was, in the most fundamental sense, a racist. He believed that, while there were superior individuals in all groups, the white race—and within it the "Teutonic" race—was superior, and had a God-given mission to rule the world. The Rhodes scholarships were originally designed to train a cadre of supermen from the Teutonic powers—the British empire, the United States and Germany—for this purpose. Where inferior races already had filled the earth, as in China and India, they could only be dominated economically and politically. Elsewhere, as in much of Africa, empty lands and unused resources should be seized, occupied and exploited by the chosen people. Such an idea should not shock Americans; something like it was the unconscious and, at the last, conscious rationale for the winning of the West and Manifest Destiny. To understand Rhodesia in the mid 1960's one must visualize an independent Texas or Oklahoma run by political figures similar to the right-wing leaders such states have been known to provide but where the 200,000 whites are outnumbered 18 to 1 by a mass of largely voteless aborigines.

What for a brief period was the Central African Federation—Northern Rhodesia and Nyasaland (now the independent African-run states of Zambia and Malawi) and Southern Rhodesia (now officially styled Rhodesia)—was the result of an unplanned extension of British sovereignty into the heart of central Africa. Lobengula, the dominant African leader of the area, had been recognized as a sovereign by Queen Victoria, but Rhodes and his followers by a shrewd combination of guile and force (Lobengula once compared himself to a fly being stalked by a chameleon) undid him. Becoming a ragged and defeated guerrilla leader, he died of smallpox in 1893. The brief flurry of ideological sympathy for imperialism in late-nineteenth-century Tory England, added to a desire to keep the Germans and Portuguese out, and lubricated by bribery in London, assured British confirmation of the de facto domination of this part of Central Africa by Rhodes's United South Africa Company.

Two factors stand out in the history of Rhodesia. One is the settler mystique. The Pioneer Column which planted the Union Jack in 1890 in what became Salisbury consisted of two hundred settlers and five hundred police of Rhodes's South Africa Company. Actually the hardships of the early days were more those of a gold rush camp than of an orderly pioneer settlement, and despite talk of settler wars against the Africans the most fabled act of heroism in Rhodesian history was as trivial and militarily inept as Custer's Last Stand. But the myth remains. To ask Rhodesian settlers, except for a few clergy, to yield the Africans political primacy is like asking a right-wing member of the Dallas establishment to return Texas to the Indians or Mexicans.

Related to this pioneer mystique is the fact that from the outset Rhodesia was essentially self-governing. The settlers were on the spot, the company was in charge, the British colonial office had mainly nominal authority. Indeed, the role of the British Resident Commissioner was not unlike that played in the American West by the agents of the Bureau of Indian Affairs, largely powerless and bitterly resented by the settlers when they failed to yield to their wishes. As time went on the company became more and more dependent on settler support and good will. In 1922 the white voters of Southern Rhodesia chose to go it alone rather than become part of the Union of South Africa, and when the company's charter expired in 1923 Southern Rhodesia became legally as well as in fact a self-governing state. Britain retained certain reserved powers in regard to foreign affairs, defense and native affairs, but after a time the civil servants as well as the political leaders were Rhodesians, and from the outset the military forces had been composed of Rhodesians.

The resulting regime rested on two pillars: development of the land (Rhodesia is primarily agricultural and is the most important source of tobacco within the sterling bloc) and, above all, the maintenance of the artificially inflated standard of living of the white settlers. The Rhodesian way of life may clothe itself in a pioneer mystique but its essence is a precarious poor-white rule over potential black competitors. Most Rhodesians are either migrants from South Africa (both British and Afrikaner) or recent immigrants from Britain, who are doing better than they could ever have dreamed of doing at home. Former Southern Rhodesian Prime Minister Garfield Todd's description of his former constituents is a bitter one: "We brought out the scum of Europe, so long as their skins were a bit white, to fire engines and get drunk and keep the black man down." But leaving aside the possible hyperbole of a disappointed politician his statement makes the valid point that Rhodesia is essentially a society of people on the make, and their own personal insecurity is perhaps the major factor in barring any improvement in the status of Rhodesia's Africans. To preserve the Rhodesian way of life necessarily requires keeping the "native" in his place. Discrimination in Southern Rhodesia in the past was notoriously worse than in the Union of South Africa itself. Good land was very nearly a white monopoly, African voting rights were almost nonexistent, and above all the African was discriminated against in education, lest educated Africans threaten the precarious status of many whites.

In the 1950's a new concept had a brief flowering on the Central African scene, that of a multiracialism in which whites and blacks would work together in a common partnership for the good of all. This was the rationale of the short-lived

(1953–63) Central African Federation. Sir Roy Welensky, a former locomotive engineer, when premier of the Federation frankly and aptly characterized the situation by comparing it to the partnership of a horse and its rider. The white man of course was the rider. Although the Central African Federation made some sense economically, its primary purpose was obviously to perpetuate and rationalize white domination of the whole area: white miners in Northern Rhodesia would have the support of their more numerous white brethren to the south, the South would control the Federation since most of the whites lived in the South and its racial attitudes would dominate the rest of the Federation so that it would be secure against the development of black African states on its flanks. The meaning of all this was clear to Africans in the northern territories and they protested vigorously. But in a virtually straight party-line vote the proposal was pushed through the British House of Commons by the Conservative party: it was approved by the (white) legislative councils of Northern Rhodesia and Nyasaland and by the electorate of Southern Rhodesia, which included some 380 Africans.

There followed almost a decade of agitation. The government of Welensky and others to whom multiracial partnership was the key word were caught between the demands of the Africans and of the British, of world opinion on one side and the settler diehards on the other. Some social barriers were lifted and the Federation and its components came up with a series of fantastically complex "funny franchises," devices to bar Africans from political power by differential economic and educational requirements, multiple voter rolls and complicated constituencies, all designed to permit token African voting but to ensure continued white control. However, the system soon collapsed. Nyasaland and Northern Rhodesia, unlike Southern Rhodesia, were not autonomous states but British protectorates even after the establishment of the Federation. Following a series of disturbances in 1959, British authorities hearkened to what Prime Minister Macmillan was to call the "winds of change" sweeping Africa, and began to move these areas toward independence under black rule. Nyasaland, with ten thousand whites out of a population of three and one half million, became free in 1963 under the leadership of American-educated Dr. Hastings Banda. A poor and overpopulated country, it faces grave economic problems complicated by political disputes between Banda and subordinate nationalist leaders who actually brought him to power and who resent what they consider to be his one-man rule. Called Malawi, after an ancient African kingdom of the region, it has clearly chosen the identity of a purely black African state.

Northern Rhodesia, which became independent as Zambia in 1964, offers many contrasts. Its three million plus African population shares the nation with seventy-six thousand whites, mostly miners, technicians and administrators. Its mineral wealth provides one of the highest per-capita incomes of any black state in Africa. Its premier, Kenneth Kaunda, holds virtually unchallengeable political authority though Zambia is still a two-party state. Kaunda, a moderate in personality and policy, while eschewing multiracialism as a doctrine (though Europeans still hold ten reserved seats in a seventy-five-seat parliament) is on good terms with the white community. Since independence industry, primarily copper mining, has shown its confidence in Zambia by moving from the former Federation capital of Salisbury to more convenient Lusaka, and general prosperity should ease lingering resentment at superior white living standards.

The rise of African power in the rest of the Federation, which led to its dissolution, was accompanied by an increase in white extremism in the South. Welensky's compromise, even aside from its inequity, was simply not working. In December, 1962, when for the first time the Africans were assigned fifteen of sixty-five legislative seats, the African nationalists enforced an almost complete boycott of the elections, while most whites gave their support to Winston Field and his Rhodesian Front. Field was replaced in 1964 by the even more extreme Ian

Smith, who contended that Rhodesia should be prepared to "go it alone" and unilaterally declare its independence if Britain would not grant it without a Rhodesian guarantee of greater political power for the Africans.

By 1965 Rhodesia stood virtually alone in the world. Britain was pushing for measures which would eventually lead to a government based on one man, one vote—the rallying cry of Africans against European minorities elsewhere. So too the United Nations, with American approval, was pressing for freedom for imprisoned Rhodesian African nationalist leaders and eventual majority rule. But Britain was in an impossible position. Rhodesia was de facto an independent state, although Britain retained ultimate legal control. One could hardly imagine Britain dropping paratroops on Salisbury, even if it wished to reverse the trend of Rhodesia's constitutional history and take away rights once granted without the consent of those concerned (this had been done recently in emergencies such as that in British Guinea, but only as a temporary expedient after outbreaks of violence). Yet what had almost happened in Kenya had happened in Rhodesia—the white-settler minority government was allowed to evolve toward independence to the point where turning back seemed impossible. Rhodesians control their own state and man the guns of their own army and air force. Their officers have sworn loyalty to the Crown, but who they would follow if a Rhodesian government should declare itself independent and Britain held this to be rebellion against the Queen is far from certain.

Yet African states, unable to put pressure on a not yet sovereign Rhodesia, have been pressuring Britain, which in turn can only try to pressure the Rhodesians. To the stick of nonrecognition and loss of her vital Commonwealth markets in case of UDI (unilateral declaration of independence) Britain can add the carrot of minor economic concessions if Rhodesia does enough for the Africans to satisfy world opinion and the British left. The United States is in a difficult position with regard to Rhodesia since it does not wish to embarrass its

British allies to no avail but is condemned by Africans and others for not doing so. The impasse is aggravated by the breakdown of the nationalist movement in Rhodesia itself. So dominated have Africans been economically and politically by the settlers for so long that African nationalism has never been strong in Southern Rhodesia despite the smallness of the white minority. Most of Rhodesia's two hundred thousand or so whites are women and children and the number of whites is yearly decreasing as a result of emigration, so that the few white males would be hard put to run a government and economy and fight off a determined nationalist military onslaught at the same time. Rhodesia has only about nine thousand men in its combined army and police. Both of these are half African, although the Air Force is all white, and Rhodesia, like Portugal, counts on the loyalty of armed Africans in an emergency.

The nationalist movement is sorely divided between the Peoples Caretaker Council led by the somewhat indecisive Josiah Nkomo and the African Peoples Union led by a Protestant cleric, the Reverend Ndabaningi Sithole. Sithole though a moderate is a more effective leader and enjoys support from Zambia and Malawi. But the division between the two factions runs deep, and the on and off incarceration or restriction of their leaders makes organization difficult. As elsewhere in white-dominated southern Africa, the government has convinced many—in this case most—chiefs and tribal elders that they will be better off collaborating with the government, either because of fear of whites, bribery or fear of losing power to young upstart nationalist leaders. White Rhodesians try to convince themselves and others that the attitudes of these chiefs indicate that Africans generally support the status quo and that their loyalty can be counted on in time of crisis with Britain or other African states. Surrounded as it is by white-controlled territories and cautious, if hostile, Zambia, Rhodesia is not under direct military pressure at present.

But there is another factor which affects Rhodesia's future

and its role in Africa, and that is economic. Indeed all of southern Africa has economic ties which directly influence its role in a future Africa and must in turn influence the character of such an Africa. One of the reasons why Banda is as moderate as he is in his foreign policy is that Malawi men must work in white territories, including Rhodesia and South Africa. Prime Minister Smith has threatened that if Britain embargoes Rhodesian goods after unilateral independence he will be forced to deport over half a million Malawi laborers, to the economic peril of their homeland. Similarly Zambia holds the whip hand over Rhodesia in some respects while being at a disadvantage in others. Together Zambia and Malawi provide important markets for Rhodesia's growing consumer-goods industries. Zambia's greater ability to attract foreign investment because of its less uncertain political future is a factor of strength. But, despite plans for new rail links in the future, Zambia's exports are now dependent on rail connections through Rhodesia and Mozambique. The giant Kariba Dam, a joint project of the former Federation, is situated on the border of Zambia and Rhodesia and joins the two nations in lingering fiscal and economic ties. Rhodesians have threatened to cut off power from Kariba, which they are in a physical position to do, if Zambia is hostile in any emergency, but this would be so unfavorable to British-owned industry in Zambia it is hardly likely to meet with the toleration of the British government. Indeed, so closely are all the territories of southern Africa, the industrial heart of the continent, linked to one another that even a temporary sundering along racial lines, much less a protracted conflict leading to loss of most white skills and capital, would be a disaster for all concerned.

Rhodesia, given the nature and traditions of its white community, holds out virtually no hope of becoming a multiracial state. Indeed whether such a thing, as distinguished from an interracial one, which is still a possibility in Angola or Mozambique, is really possible when the minority is economically dominant is highly doubtful. An equally important factor with economics in making multiracialism a dubious proposition is the psychology of African nationalism. Nationalists in Tanganyika, debating granting citizenship to whites, have said that before one can become a Tanganyikan one must be willing to become an African. Many whites are proud of being Rhodesians, but though they claim the continent as their home they draw the line at thinking of themselves as Africans. The nationalist movement has already given the cue to its ultimate attitudes by referring to Rhodesia as Zimbabwe, after the ancient kingdom whose ruins white men long denied could possibly have been the works of black hands.

South Africa has sought to bolster Rhodesia's economic position with loans and tariff concessions. But much as it appreciates having a white rather than a black state north of the Limpopo, the Republic is unlikely to take real risks in order to maintain white supremacy in Salisbury. The Republic's leaders have a keen sense of geopolitical and military realities, and it has already drawn the boundaries of its *laager* (the traditional circle of wagons which Boers—like American pioneers—used as a defensive formation against aboriginal attacks) further south. Rhodesia is on its own. Politicians may strike attitudes but the continued emigration of whites from the country—something the government would desperately like to minimize and conceal—shows that the settler regime is slowly being abandoned by its own people as well as its white neighbors. Irrationality and desperation are not unknown ingredients in human affairs, and the Smith government might follow through with its threat to declare independence, probably after the 1965 tobacco crop is sold, in hope that by the time the next one is ready for market Britain will have accepted a *fait accompli*. But such an action would be considered by African nationalists within and without the country as depriving the government of the last shred of legitimacy it now possesses, and it would become an open target for a mounting campaign of subversion. Rather than precipitate a race war it knows it cannot win, Rhodesia will probably make concessions leading to majority rule within a few years.

Should black rule triumph in Rhodesia some white technicians may remain (as virtually all have in Zambia) but most farmers would probably leave in the face of pressure from African hunger for land. The process of dissolving the present society and regime could be slow and relatively painless if a direct confrontation of force could be avoided, but in time Zimbabwe will become as much a black state as Malawi or Tanzania. The name of Rhodes will disappear from the national map of Africa. What, one wonders, will the new Africa do with his tomb?

XI

AFRICA SOUTH: THE ULTIMATE CHALLENGE

South Africa is sometimes thought of as a "problem area" for Africa and the world or as a last piece of "unfinished business" in the sweep of nationalism over the continent. But this understates the significance of the future of the area in Africa's search for itself. The resolution—for good or ill—of the future status of South Africa will not only be the final act in the drama of nationalism's sweep across the continent, but could become the climax of Africa's search for identity. All the dominant questions—the nature of the African Personality, continental integration, the clash of political and economic systems, the place of nonblacks in Africa, and the image and role of Africa in world civilization and politics—are deeply dependent upon the future course of events in South Africa, and the answers the whole continent gives to these questions will be in large measure determined by what happens there.

South Africa is unique in many ways. Not only does it contain the only real nation of European ethnic origin which claims Africa as its home, it also includes the largest African population to have become thoroughly acculturated to modern industrial civilization. Though millions of Africans still live on tribal reserves, millions more are as much a part of the new universal civilization as is the American Negro. Indeed, detribalized "Westernized" Africans outnumber whites in the Republic of South Africa. They are part of modern industrial civilization in that they are involved in its processes and accept its norms, though, like the American Negro, they lack political and economic equality. South Africa boasts several thousand African university graduates, a figure which all the rest of sub-Saharan Africa combined is only now surpassing, and its pool of African skills in many other respects is of the same order. Equally important, South Africa possesses the largest and most prosperous industrial complex on the continent. Its gross national product is more than double that of bustling Nigeria, a nation several times larger. Though South Africa's trade with other African nations is still a small portion of its total trade, its economy is already closely linked with those of neighboring territories. The Republic of South Africa could become the powerhouse of an economically integrated continent and the fulcrum by which much of Africa could lift itself into modern technological society.

Thus the stakes in the current bitter struggle over South Africa's future are more than the lives and futures of its three and a half million white inhabitants and its more than thirteen million Africans, Colored and Asians. A peaceful and constructive solution of South Africa's racial problems could mean a revitalized Africa; a violent and destructive one would have unforeseeable consequences for Africa's relations with the world. That is why, despite the protests of the South African government that apartheid (the policy of "separate development") is an internal matter, whatever happens in that nation is of deep concern to all mankind.

The simple facts of the racial relationships which underlie South Africa's problem are these. There are something over three and one-half million white inhabitants of whom over two million are of Afrikaner origin, that is, descendants of the Boers. It also contains one and a half million Colored (persons of mixed racial ancestry, usually Afrikanaans-speaking) whose origin goes back to the earliest days of South African history. Concentrated in Cape province and occupying a subordinate place in society to whites, they have in the past identified with the whites. Now that government policy is to force them downward socially, they are confused and resentful. Politically they are impotent as a separate group, and more and more they are throwing in their lot with black nationalism. The half million Indians, mainly resident in Natal, have been discriminated against by whites, but are envied and resented by Africans. They too are being brutally despoiled of their social and economic position by apartheid but are unsure of their standing with the blacks; hundreds of Indians suffered in the bitter race riots of 1962. Finally there are thirteen and a half million Africans, somewhat more than half of whom are urbanized and "Westernized," and somewhat less than half of whom live under tribal conditions on inadequate lands allocated to them by the government. The African majority is still divided on many fundamental issues: Shall they opt for modernization or seek to preserve traditional ways? Shall they seek justice in collaboration with whites and Indians or alone? Shall they seek it violently or nonviolently? There is also the continuing clash, as in any oppressed population, between those who are willing to choose the easier road of acceptance or collaboration with the dominant power in society and those who strive to fight back as best they can.

Despite tremendous disparities in living standards between whites and blacks (white miners receive seventeen times the wages of blacks, while black infant mortality is almost eight times that of whites), African living standards in South Africa compare favorably with those of Africans in the independent nations in most respects, and are constantly improving. White leadership relies on this relative economic well-being to maintain African acquiescence to the present system, heedless of the truth that man does not live by bread alone.

What kind of people are the white minority who rule the

nation? To think of them as settlers only confuses the issue. Most Afrikaners belong to families which have lived in Africa for hundreds of years. They look upon Africa as their homeland as much as Americans whose ancestors fought in the Revolutionary War look upon North America as theirs; indeed, the official myth is that most of the blacks living in the Republic did not arrive there until after initial white occupation. White Afrikaner nationalism is just as much an authentic national movement as any other in Europe or Africa. A group of people bound together by a common language and religion, culture and history, with a deep and tightly knit self-identity, have freed themselves from foreign rule (that of the British) and created an authentic national destiny. With the advent to power of the Afrikaner-based Nationalist party, the Boer War has been refought peacefully, and this time won. The other struggle of the Afrikaner nation, that for survival against the horde of aborigines, still goes on. The Afrikaners are not a recently arrived group of individual sojourners in Africa who look upon another country as their real home. They are no more settlers in Africa than Americans or Brazilians are settlers in the New World. They are a real nation forged in Africa, a white nation.

Gradually the English-speaking whites are becoming part of this nation and are being assimilated to Afrikanerdom. For years not only their superior numbers (now reversed by the higher Afrikaner birth rate) but their greater economic strength (they receive almost three-quarters of the national income) enabled them to live distinctly and apart, and to look down upon the Afrikaans-speaking farmer or worker. But numerical superiority has meant political power for the Afrikaner, and that in turn has meant increasing economic strength and, especially, increasing cultural domination, a lesson white South Africans recall when they think about the growing black majority around them. Although in the past the English-speaking whites have feared the African a bit less than has the Afrikaner because with better housing and jobs they were in less direct competition with him, today the English-speaking increasingly accept the Afrikaner state and the Nationalist party as a necessary bulwark against black domination. The Republic was proclaimed in 1961 and left the Commonwealth soon thereafter under pressure from nonwhite Commonwealth members, though economic ties with the Commonwealth remain close. Gradually English-speaking South Africans are coming to realize that the Republic is the only motherland they know. The Nationalists dramatically increased their vote in English-speaking areas in the 1965 local elections, something which the government trumpeted as a drawing together of white South Africa in response to outside misrepresentation and pressure.

This white South African nation, born in Africa, must live or die there. There is no place to which it can retreat. Though there are moderate strains within the Afrikaner community, especially among the clergy and intellectuals (Afrikaners are not simply rednecks or poor white trash) all are faced with the same problem of survival in an increasingly hostile continent. The system of apartheid to which so much attention is justifiably given is primarily a warped attempt to answer the two basic questions upon which the future of South Africa rests, questions arising out of the problem of national survival.

The first question is this: Is Africa a black man's continent, and if so what does this mean? African unity, we have seen, is based upon the combined ties of common race and a common experience of colonial oppression. Does "Africa for the Africans" include white Africans or must all of the sub-Saharan continent be under black control for Africa to be free and therefore at ease with itself and the world? Most African nationalists, both within and without the Republic, and their non-African sympathizers as well, have held that no one save unrepresentative extremists wants to drive all whites from South Africa; the whites are free to share the country on the basis of individual equality. Minority rights, they say, would be respected by any future black African government.

Such statements while sincere do not address the real problem. One might as well have told the Irish in the pre-1919 United Kingdom or the Poles in the Austro-Hungarian empire or the Muslims in pre-partition India that as individuals they would have equal rights with members of the majority or controlling groups in the state. Even when such pledges are reliable this kind of equality is not what nationalists seek, so that its concession solves nothing. Nationalism must in part mean that national groups will have political entities of their own within which they can express their national cultures. One cannot be a nationalist as an individual. Juridical halfway houses tend to be unstable (witness pre-independence Ireland or contemporary Quebec). Individuals may continue to take pride in being Scotsmen or sons of Dixie, but one cannot have a nation without a territory, however small, in which its nationals have political primacy. A South Africa based on "one man, one vote" would mean the end of the Afrikaner nation as much as a greater Israel with an Arab majority, however humane and liberal, would mean the end of the Jewish nation. This has nothing to do with individual rights or humane treatment of minorities; it is a question of the very definition of national existence. An Africa which defines itself as a collection or unity of nonwhite states (at least south of the Sahara) can have no place for the one white nation which claims to be not only in but of Africa.

But even if by some miracle no one tomorrow any longer cared about the Afrikaner nation, even if all white South Africans were content to think of English as their mother tongue and were to identify simultaneously with Zulu and Xhosa traditions, even if they came to look upon the Battle of Blood River and the Boer War as unfortunate and disgraceful incidents, and upon the moving anthem "*Die Stem*" as something which should join the "*Horst Wessel Lied*" in the dustbin of history, there would still exist in South Africa a problem of mutual adjustment unique in modern history. Democratic nations may be multiracial or integrated, but almost necessarily it is the racial minority which is or comes to be at the bottom socially, economically and politically. In Southeast Asia the position of the still economically dominant Chinese minorities becomes more precarious each year, and is maintained only by the shadow of nearby Chinese Communist power. In some nations of Latin America there is enough social mobility combined with enough racial mixture to provide a cushion between the dominant minority of "pure" whites and the majority of their countrymen. But, although such a situation could conceivably come to pass in Angola, a primarily colored South Africa is hardly in the immediate offing. All modern nations, capitalist and Communist alike, are ruled by small power elites, but in no place where the majority have political power is this favored few easily distinguishable by its skin color from its fellow citizens. The present leading position of the whites in South Africa would not survive the first election in a unified democratic national state.

But what difference should this make to anyone who believes in democratic or egalitarian values? Why should whites expect to continue to occupy a favored position? Is it not enough for each individual to be treated like everyone else, with race an irrelevant consideration? If the nationalist leaders such as those of the multiracial African National Congress are sincere—which they are—and if they can control their own followers, more racialist groups like the Pan-Africanist Congress and extremist terrorist groups such as the Spear of the Nation—something which the experience of Nyerere in Tanzania and Kenyatta in Kenya suggests may be difficult—why should whites fear discrimination and oppression?

Some have suggested that things have gone so far that a catharsis is necessary, in which some of the white oppression of blacks is reciprocated in kind. Patrick Van Rensburg, a leading white South African liberal, has even held, with some logic, that only violence and antiwhite repression can assure South African blacks that South Africa is really their country and can free their energies for building it themselves. But even if one does not assume that control of South Africa by the black majority would mean outright oppression of whites, a problem would still exist, for political equality would directly imperil the white standard of living.

Laws designed to promote equality, even if race was not mentioned, would still bear most heavily on whatever racial group had been better off. Given the tremendous advantages whites enjoy in the present economy, equalization would involve massive transfer payments from the white economy to the rest of the population. Equality would mean an increase of social welfare activities directed toward a nonwhite clientele, and the consequent increased taxes would necessarily bear more heavily on the white community than on the black (nonwhites now pay a disproportionate share of taxes in relation to their incomes). Greater equality of schooling, employment opportunities and wages would mean the transfer of skilled and professional jobs from whites to blacks. Equality of wage levels would deprive whites of cheap farm and domestic labor.

Any sharp and rapid diminution of white living standards would imperil political order and stability, since it would almost inevitably result in many of the white population trying to reassert their position through illegal means, or else losing confidence in the society and emigrating in large numbers. Conditions tempting whites to rebellion or exodus would in turn lead to a loss of foreign confidence, investment and trade.

The only hope for avoiding the conflicts inherent in drastically reducing the minority's standards of living while increasing that of the majority would lie in rapidly increasing the size of the economic assets and rewards to be divided, while muting pressures for immediate division of the white share among the blacks. This has been the path which Kenya and Tanzania have hoped to follow in order to keep economically useful white farmers producing. But in these countries economic growth has been slow while black resentment and land hunger have grown rapidly. In South Africa increasing general economic standards would be possible but extremely difficult, since unfortunately much of the South African development boom of recent years has had its source in the artificially cheap labor supply created by racist legislation. To hold back majority pressure for immediate leveling measures during a transition period would require a tough one-party state in which cries to share the wealth were held ruthlessly in check in order to prevent the inevitable white reaction to loss of economic as well as political status.

Given the improbable death of Afrikaner nationalism, given a peaceful transfer of power, and given political skill and patience on each side and some good luck economically, a future multiracial South Africa is possible, though it might be a tense and unstable polity for generations to come. But under what conditions might such a transfer of power as postulated occur? It is hard to imagine the whites yielding to pressures for such an alternative without first being confronted by overwhelming physical or economic force. South Africa has a small but efficient military establishment, and paramilitary training of both sexes and almost all ages is increasingly widespread. The present regime is capable of maintaining domestic physical control short of a prolonged, universal and highly disciplined general strike, which seems unlikely. It is sufficiently compact and industrialized for guerrilla warfare to be difficult, and so far the secret police have effectively penetrated African nationalist organizations. South Africa seems capable of fighting off any attack that could be mounted by other African powers unless the attackers had extracontinental assistance.

Any use of force carries the danger that the struggle will go beyond a testing of wills and become a full-fledged civil war. In the course of such a war two things would almost certainly occur: the destruction of much of the economic infrastructure on which the future of any South Africa, white or black dominated, depends, and also the destruction of any possibility of the different races' working together in a common political community. Any transition to a multiracial South Africa could not be more than marginally violent without destroying its own possibility.

What of economic sanctions imposed by the outside world?

Could the South African government be brought to its knees by such action? There are actually three different and difficult questions involved here. One concerns the theoretical possibility of sanctions' succeeding, the second the practical political possibility of their being imposed, and the third the effects of such sanctions.

Theoretically speaking, economic sanctions against South Africa could probably succeed in destroying the present regime. South Africa's economy is booming. Not only has it never been healthier, it has reached a stage of self-sustaining growth where further expansion can be financed domestically, and the importance of continued gold exports to international economic stability—particularly to the fiscal stability of the United States—gives the country a significant advantage. But if nations were willing to make the effort, they could do without South African gold by turning to alternative higher-priced sources or perhaps through an overdue readjustment of the prevailing international monetary mechanisms. Though South Africa could if necessary withstand a great deal of economic pressure from outside, even from the crucial nations involved, Britain and the United States, it has one major vulnerability, its need of large quantities of imported oil to maintain both its economy and its whole modern way of life.

As a practical measure can sanctions be instituted? So far the sanctions campaign has met with limited success. Virtually all African states are officially eschewing any economic relations with South Africa, but a certain amount of South African trade even with OAU members goes on clandestinely or indirectly. Loss of air routes has meant only minor adjustments. Loss of trade with various hostile nations has been compensated for by increased trade with others, including Japan, Communist China and the European Communist powers. The success of any sanctions against South Africa depends almost entirely on her two major trading partners, Britain and the United States. Both have large investments in South Africa which sanctions would injure, and strong domestic pressure groups which would oppose such sanctions. Almost certainly the United States would not institute sanctions without the approval of Britain, which has even more to lose. It is hard to visualize either nation's acting except in response to some dramatic incident or drastic change in the prevailing situation, occasions which the South African government is determined to prevent.

To eliminate the possibility of large-scale smuggling, sanctions would almost necessarily require a blockade backed ultimately by military force. The task of coordinating the economic, diplomatic and military aspects of such a compaign would be horrendous. Though African nationalist leaders have sometimes, especially in the past, talked of their desire for sanctions, the fact remains that the effect of sanctions would fall most heavily and first on the poorest, on the black African population. Humanitarian concerns together with the inherent difficulty of coordinating policy would make it difficult if not impossible to maintain sanctions in the face of any apparent concession from the South African government. Once such a concession was made, even if it turned out to be illusory, reinstituting sanctions would prove even more difficult than initiating them.

This of course raises the third question: What would the real aim of sanctions be? What is at issue in the present debates over South Africa in the United Nations and in the Western democracies is not the future of democracy in South Africa but usually only apartheid itself—the policy of deliberate, open, legalized racial segregation on the grand scale, the separation of the races with the loss of previously existing social, economic and in some cases political rights on the part of non-whites. This is something which, especially given the manner of its implementation and its side effects, rightly engages the conscience of mankind. While theoretical discussions about the Bantustan problem occupy both proponents and critics, live individual human beings are losing jobs, status, homes, even, in some cases of racial reclassification, families as well. Resentment of such action within South Africa causes agitation which the government must repress, destroying in the process the civil liberties of Africans and whites alike. The whole world is aware of, and all the humane world deplores, this policy and its consequences. Yet it does not act. Why?

In large part of course it does not act because of timidity, apathy, inertia and the pressures of national and group special interests. Yet to some degree it does not act for a deeper and better reason, the largely inchoate realization on the part of most British and American leaders at least that apartheid is not the real issue. Suppose that sanctions were instituted, and were effective, or that, as many proponents hope, white South African public opinion once faced with the certainty of the imposition of sanctions forced its government to announce it was abandoning apartheid. What then? Suppose that tomorrow, even without the threat or imposition of sanctions, the Nationalists—or the opposition United party—were to abandon the tragic farce of apartheid. Suppose that Africans were free to travel internally, to seek work in a free market economy, attend white theaters, to live wherever they could afford to and wherever anyone would rent or sell to them—residential segregation on the American and British pattern. Suppose they were even to have restored to them the token representation they once enjoyed in South Africa or to have representation on the Rhodesian model. Africans would still be at the bottom of the ladder, the African infant mortality and tuberculosis rates would still be many times those of whites, and African nationalists inside and outside of South Africa would still be bitterly dissatisfied, would still be crying for a political system based on "one man, one vote," and seeking extra-African support for pressures designed to move South Africa toward such a system. In such a situation things would not be basically different from before.

It is clear therefore that sanctions simply to end apartheid are meaningless and would not be worth the effort involved. They would not strike at the root of the problem, since what is really at issue is the question of who shall rule in South Africa.

Sanctions would be a politically rational act only if the participants had an aim beyond ending apartheid as such, only if they were intending actually to undermine the present government of South Africa to the point where it would lose control within the country. Some proponents of sanctions, such as Colin Legum, have suggested that the aim be to force the South African government to call a national convention which would write a new constitution for the nation based on human equality. How successful such a convention could be in such circumstances is dubious. The widespread suffering, dislocations and interracial bitterness caused by effective sanctions, plus the discrediting of the authority of the regime, would necessarily create a revolutionary situation. Many, indeed probably most, African nationalists would not shy away from such a possibility, but clearly British and American leaders, especially after the Congo, are not interested in such an outcome, for they fear that overthrow of the present government, however deplorable it may be, will create a power vacuum from which a worse government might emerge. Sanctions therefore are not in the cards.

But, leaving aside the question of what Western governments will or should do about it, if one concludes that the policy of apartheid is of such little intrinsic importance in determining the conditions of life of blacks in South Africa, why do South Africans cling to it when it so exacerbates their relations with the rest of the world and threatens them with the possibility, however remote, of worldwide action to overthrow their government? Is it that they are so afraid of living near blacks or so insecure in their control of the mechanisms of public order that they must hold potential enemies at arm's length? No, apartheid survives, despite its many inconsistencies and failures and the inconveniences it causes even whites, because many South Africans, especially the Afrikaners, see in it the only long-term solution to their problem of how to maintain white identity on a black continent. Some South Africans may be influenced by irrational fear of pollution arising from interracial contacts, while many more see apartheid as a device to keep the "kaffir" in his place, to maintain "baaskop"—the "boss rule" of the whites over the Africans. But others have a more humane and idealistic rationale. Paradoxically, these are usually the extremists among the ideologists of apartheid. They believe, however erroneously, that only complete separation of the races in South Africa is compatible with the full cultural and political development of either. It is from this group that the plans for the Bantustans have come. Under this system certain areas are reserved for white settlement and others (a mere 14 percent of the total area of South Africa) will become native homelands which will be the basis of eventual black "nations." Whites would control the white areas, blacks the black areas. In some future time a kind of independence, at least within a South African confederation, would be permitted the black components, which apologists speak of as the "Bantu" nations.

Though superficially attractive, the objections both theoretical and practical to this scheme are obvious and legion. Separate but equal facilities are as unlikely in Africa as in the United States. Those who decree the separation always end up with the better part. The Nationalist government's own Tomlinson Commission Report of 1955 outlined the vast amount of money it would take to bring living standards in the Bantustans up to a reasonably adequate level. It advocated the expenditure of over $280 million in the period 1955–65 alone. The South African economy could not afford it and the government has not tried to implement the report's general recommendations, though it has done enough so that some of its own backbenchers and the United party opposition accuse it of coddling the Africans economically. The economic boom in South Africa has meant that more and more black labor is coming to the cities and taking jobs reserved in theory for whites. This is winked at through a process whereby employers receive waivers of regulations and skilled jobs are reclassified downward so that Africans can fill them at lower wages than would be paid whites for doing the same work. Under a fully implemented Bantustan system the millions of Africans still living or working in white areas would not vote there but in their "homelands" (where their families would normally have to reside). They would still have no control over their daily lives and they would still be subject to all the everyday restrictions of "small" or social apartheid. The Bantustans would in effect be colonies of white South Africa which would supply it with cheap migrant labor. For, despite talk of eventual independence of the Bantustans with their own flags and national anthems, not only the foreign policy and defense but the finances and economic life of the Bantustans would be controlled by the white South African government.

Yet there is a slight ray of hope in the Bantustan system, indicated by the difficulties to date of the Transkei, the first black nation to begin operation. Last year local self-government was, after much disorder and repression, instituted in the Transkei, a native reserve of one and a half million people. Most Africans within and outside the Republic were bitterly opposed to its creation in principle. In the elections held to form a Transkeian government, anti-apartheid forces won despite government pressures, and only the votes of chiefs nominated to the legislative assembly by the South African government enabled Chief Kaizer Matanzima, a supporter of apartheid, to become head of state. Yet Matanzima was not expected to be just a puppet of the government and has not been. He has pressured the government for more schools and economic development and a timetable for real independence, and has recently demanded greater rights for Africans living in white areas. The ambiguous significance of the Transkei is symbolized by the fact that the national anthem is "*Nkose Sikelee' i-Afrika*" (God Save Africa), the African nationalist hymn and the nearest South African equivalent of "We Shall Overcome." The Transkei's existence and activities could accelerate rather than retard government response to African needs and demands.

What future makes sense for South Africa? Is there still any alternative to the bloody holocaust so often predicted as inevitable? If, as most observers assume, "one man, one vote" democracy in a unitary state run by a black majority (a state which Africans increasingly project as "nonracial" rather than "multiracial," implying the elimination of the minority community as such) will not be accepted by the whites without massive bloodshed, and if apartheid or some less-open form of white suppression of the majority cannot continue indefinitely without bloodshed either, what alternative can there be? The only way out, the only solution giving some consideration to all established interests, would seem to be some form of partition in which both the major races in South Africa would be able to maintain their political and cultural identity within a framework of economic integration and on the basis of equal personal rights.

Indeed, the Nationalist government has given some indication of moving in this direction, using the Bantustan system as a base, but moving covertly so as not to alarm the electorate. Under various plans put forth by different individuals and groups in and out of government, South Africa would be carved up into a mosaic of white and black, with several black states eventually eligible for membership in the United Nations if their size and resources warranted. But such plans have two basic flaws.

The most obvious practical objection is the difficulty of carving up the nation equitably or in a fashion that makes economic and geographic sense. But an equally basic objection is the fact that even under real political partition and independence the same problems of economic relationships would exist as under apartheid and the Bantustan system. Since white South Africa would never voluntarily turn the country's major industrial areas over to wholly black rule, stranding their white inhabitants in black areas, most Africans would still be working in white-run areas, and all would be dependent on the white economy. The same kind of exploitation that now exists would become sources of international friction. For the sake of equity some way would still have to be found for giving black workers some power over their living and working conditions in white industry, regardless of the fact that the areas in which they worked were not their domiciles for political purposes.

The only way of meeting the difficulties inherent in partition would therefore appear to be through the establishment of a confederation in which ordinary administrative control of the individual member states would be in the hands of local black or white majorities, but a central political organ (representing members of all races equally but with strongly entrenched minority rights) would have sufficient power to ensure that economic relations were as minimally exploitative as possible, given economic realities, and that the legal basis of social segregation throughout the confederation was abolished. The objectives of this plan are the same as those embodied in proposals informally put forth by Scandinavian members of the United Nations in 1964, but instead of trying, as in the Scandinavian plan, to entrench minority rights in the constitution of a unitary, majority-run state, the entrenchment would be fortified by the existence of a federal system. Such a solution would have the merit and appeal of not disrupting the real economic and cultural integration still taking place, regardless of government policy, throughout South Africa as a whole, while at the same time allowing the minority nationality a homeland of its own in which it could have some feeling of security and some control over its own communal life.

Confederation could also help solve the problems inherent in the relations of South Africa with its nearest neighbors. For the overall future of South Africa is complicated by the likely future independence of four black African states bordering on it and closely bound to it economically. One of these, South-West Africa, is currently administered as part of the Republic. It has a population of 600,000 Africans and 73,000 whites and is a bitter bone of contention between the United Nations, which is trying to enforce South Africa's legal obligation to make it a UN trust territory, and the South African government, which claims that it has no obligations to the UN regarding the territory, a claim qualified by South Africa's admission of UN observation teams. Mineral resources might someday make South-West Africa self-sufficient economically but it lacks adequate leadership cadres at present, and its major port, Walvis Bay, is legally part of the Republic. A South-West Africa which would be an independent black member of a South African confederation makes more sense than would an orphan state which in the short run at least would be dependent on a hostile neighbor.

The other areas closely tied to the future of South Africa are the three British High Commission Territories of Bechuanaland, Basutoland and Swaziland. These areas, administered directly by Great Britain, have long been claimed by the Republic. They are economically dependent upon it as a market for their goods and for their surplus labor. Basutoland, with its 800,000 people, is completely surrounded by South Africa; Swaziland, with a population of 200,000, is surrounded by South Africa and Mozambique. The vast, largely desert Bechuanaland, with 340,000 inhabitants, is bordered by South Africa, South-West Africa and Rhodesia. Swaziland is currently ruled by a conservative coalition of white settlers and tribal chiefs. Basutoland and Bechuanaland will soon become independent states under black nationalist governments pledged to multiracialism and bitterly opposed to apartheid and union with South Africa. But both of their leaders, Seretse Khama of Bechuanaland and the recently elected Chief Jonathan of Basutoland (to become independent under the name Losotho) publicly recognize the economic necessity of amicable relations with South Africa for the immediate future. All of the High Commission Territories (like South-West Africa) could conceivably become units of a greater multiracial confederation. Actually it would improve their position by giving them a more direct voice in the industrial economy to which they are inevitably tributary.

Such a confederal multiracial system as proposed herein for South Africa would please no one perfectly, and some not at all. The white racialists would have to give up the concept of a great South African empire based on the permanent subordination and exploitation of the "sons of Ham." Black nationalists would be asked to reconcile themselves to the permanent existence of enclaves in Africa politically dominated by whites of European origin.

Would leaders of other African states accept a compromise which granted political equality to black Africans as individuals while permitting the continued existence of a rump white state? Just as Arabs are coming to recognize in practice that Israel exists and will continue to do so short of a major war in which non-Near Eastern powers are involved, so Africans may come to accept a white South African state, albeit a truncated and transformed one, as a permanent feature of the landscape. This would be simply giving priority, in Max Beloff's words, to the "continuities of history" over the "contiguities of geography." Africans despite their political rhetoric are realists where economic self-interest is concerned. The relationship of Tshombe's Congo to South Africa is a special case, but even today some African states maintain de facto ties with South Africa because of the close economic links among all the states in southern Africa. A solution of the South African problem on the compromise basis suggested here could be made even more palatable by South Africa's becoming a source of capital investment and technical assistance throughout Africa, as well as an employer and trading partner.

How could such a solution, assuming its equity, be brought about? It would be utopian to postulate some sudden formal and peaceful agreement which would create such an arrangement. But events have a logic of their own. The Bantustan system could evolve into a network of meaningful entities, especially if the Western nations judiciously applied economic and political pressures upon the South African government while providing it with positive incentives to live up to some of its wilder promises. Curtailment of Western investment could also make it more profitable for South Africa to recognize the logic of its increasingly interdependent modern industrial system and gradually abolish impracticable and costly forms of racial separation. Britain and the United States could give large scale economic aid to the former High Commission Territories and assist them diplomatically so as to increase their bargaining power in their necessarily intimate future relations with South Africa.

If the South African government showed signs of willingness to yield to reason to any extent, British and American diplomatic efforts would have to seek quietly, subtly and persistently to induce South Africa and the African states opposed to the present regime to make mutual concessions on a quid pro quo basis, concessions which would have to be made in such a fashion as not to alarm extremists on either side. If all this was done while continuing economic growth brought more and more Africans into the city and into industry, and if white South Africans were successful in reversing the trend toward measures restricting their political and cultural freedom and racial policies which cause them economic and personal inconvenience, then in the course of time a confederal and multiracial society could grow up throughout southern Africa in all but name—created by the slow, glacial pressure of a thousand small concessions and undramatic events—until all that remained would be to recognize its existence in fact. Given the existing clashes of interests and the bitterness of racial feelings, coexistence in southern Africa seems as remote and unlikely as coexistence between East and West appears to many on both sides, but the consequences of the alternatives force rational men to do what they can to avoid them.

That the acceptance of some part of the South as permanently white would revolutionize Africa's sense of identity is obvious. The issue which most divides Africa today is essentially the argument between those who would make a doctrinaire, anti-Western, anticapitalist stance the touchstone of African personality and those who do not find retention of economic and cultural ties with the Western nations inconsistent with being African. The development of a southern African community of nations based on interracial cooperation, with a white capitalist element as its economic nucleus, politically dominated by black Africans who on the whole reject Negritude and traditionalism in all their forms and accept the ideal of racial partnership in a modern technological society, would necessarily greatly affect Africa's sense of self. Africa could not become a monolithic, inward-looking community based on uniquely African, primarily racial, values. The new Africa would be one which was national but also international, in which groups and even nations were not ashamed to admit that they had, in certain respects, closer ties to outside forces—the Commonwealth, the community of French culture, the Islamic world, the New World—than they had to many of their African neighbors.

At first glance such an Africa might seem like a negation of all that African nationalists have striven for throughout this century. Yet a new cosmopolitan Africa, open to the winds of change from all sides, would be a more authentic revival of the old Africa than any closed continent cut off from non-African forces and stimuli. The old Africa was not monolithic, the new need not be. Our examination of African history has shown us an Africa that was deeply affected by events in Europe, Asia and the Americas and that influenced these areas in turn. Like other continents and cultures it has been formed by the ebb and flow of worldwide movements. An Africa without European or American or Asian ties makes no more sense than a New World exclusively Amerindian, or, more pointedly, a Europe that had never known a Roman or Byzantine intercontinental empire, the "imported" religions of Judaism, Islam or Christianity, the science of the Arabs or the culture of the Moors. The choice between a narrow, inward-turning African identity and one open to the world could well be made in South Africa.

XII

WHAT AFRICA SEEKS

African nations share with all nations certain aims which they seek to realize through their foreign policy: security, the preservation of independence, peace, power, prestige and prosperity. But African nations in common with other underdeveloped or "new" nations have certain special characteristics that qualify the meanings they give these common aims and determine the policies and instruments by which they seek them. In addition, factors unique to the African situation further modify these goals and the means available for attaining them.

National security, for instance, means something special to Africans. Nations have traditionally sought security by means of their own military power, by association with the power of others or by isolation from major political conflicts. For the developing nations, and for Africa especially, none of these means to security seems satisfactory. In a nuclear age one can argue whether any nation-state, even the most powerful, can through its own military strength find security as traditionally understood. Is even the United States or the Soviet Union secure today, to say nothing of Britain or France? No African nation or group of nations can hope to build up a military force sufficient to guarantee its security against aggression from any but the weakest of foes. Though the shadow of an arms race provoked by local quarrels hangs over Africa, its nations have never hoped to find general security through their own armed might.

What of a policy of alliance? Here too there seems little to be gained. African nations have had military arrangements of various sorts with the former colonial powers. But these have increasingly come under fire and been abandoned. It is assumed that in case of outright aggression traditional friends will come to the aid of Commonwealth or former French territories even without an alliance. Alliances would add little to the power available to defend African states and could make them the target of enemies who might not otherwise attack them. In addition alliances, even if freely entered into, seem to Africans to imply a loss of independence. Therefore the key words guiding policy have been neutralism and nonalignment. Soon after independence even the Nigerian government was forced by public opinion to revise its military arrangements with Britain. France, primarily for its own reasons, is progressively reducing its garrisons in friendly African states. Anything smacking of African involvement in Western alliance systems would make impossible its self-chosen role as an independent mediator and balance wheel in the world's politics. For all of these reasons alliances are not a feasible means of guaranteeing security.

Yet the policy of nonalignment also rules out traditional isolation and neutrality. In part the neutral position of European states such as Sweden and Switzerland was and is based on their geographic position and military strength, but it is also based on their willingness to remain more or less aloof from European politics. African states do not wish to isolate themselves from the world's affairs, however. To them their "nonalignment" is "positive" and only means that they do not wish to join any contending bloc in world politics; it does not mean aloofness. Indeed it implies taking a stand on many issues. For instance the idea of a nuclear-free zone in Africa is only part of the broader African push toward nuclear disarmament. Indeed

African states, within the United Nations and elsewhere, have shown a proclivity for stating opinions on a wide variety of extra-African issues, often to the dismay of non-African and especially Western statesmen.

One can argue how consistent such behavior is with the oft-made analogy between the neutralism of contemporary, newly independent Africa and that of the United States in the era following the American Revolution. The Monroe doctrine, after all, pledged the United States to keep out of European quarrels, as well as enjoining European nonactivity in the Americas. On the other hand, Americans who fault the Africans on the score of meddling often forget that, Monroe Doctrine or no, Americans offered a steady stream of gratuitous advice to the world, bitterly criticized the established monarchical order in Europe, and welcomed to our shores partisans of revolutionary change in Germany, Hungary, Ireland and elsewhere. Perhaps the controlling difference between the old American neutrality and contemporary African neutralism is that the nineteenth century lacked a United Nations, the existence of which makes it almost mandatory for every nation to have an officially registered opinion about everyone else's affairs, even if, as is sometimes the case, it might prefer to remain silent.

Finding themselves unable to seek security through their own military strength, alliance with others or political isolation, African states have sought it in a universal and internationally guaranteed state of peace. The African concept of peace, like that of many Asians, differs from that of Western advocates of collective security. For the latter, peace means eschewing force as an instrument for social and international change regardless of the merits of the particular case at issue. Africans generally argue, not without some merit, that this freezes the existing situation; therefore, they would exempt from their general antipathy to war actions aimed at reducing what they regard as colonial oppression. African nations—though still retaining a theoretical preference for nonviolence—increasingly regard the overthrow of white power in Rhodesia, South Africa and Portuguese Africa as desirable even if force is necessary. Consistently with this attitude most Africans applauded India's forcible seizure of Goa and accepted the Indian defense of its essentially peaceable nature. Peace for Africans means peace between the major nuclear powers, an absence of global nuclear war. Wars of "national liberation" are not breaches of the peace. Anyone who has followed recent shifts in the Soviet line on coexistence and national liberation will recognize the convergence between the African and contemporary Soviet positions on this issue.

Cardinal among African concerns in the field of international politics is independence and its corollary, sovereignty. But are not all the new African states by definition independent? Can there be any question of the legal sovereignty of member states of the United Nations—which they all are? Many outside observers are wont to characterize the constant African outcries against outside interference and so-called neo-colonialism as simply a psychological hangover of the drive for national independence, deplorable though perhaps understandable, but in any event destined to be short-lived. But the facts are somewhat more complex.

Actually there are circumstances, however inevitable and unsinister, which give rise to African suspicions of neo-colonialism. History has served the new Africa badly in that Africa has come to political independence (an independence which must serve as the major expression of its new-found racial pride and identity) at a time when the limits of independence are slowly being recognized by nations, small and large, throughout the world. Without perhaps realizing it, Africans are bound to feel somewhat cheated, having striven so hard for a prize that has lost much of its value. The fact that the international economic and cultural interdependence which marks the modern world generally has in Africa been introduced through the institutions and relationships of the colonial era lends a special bite to African frustrations. And no matter how much the ideological inclinations of African nations or their desire to strike a balance between East and West in order to demonstrate the reality of their independence leads them to turn to the Communist nations for aid, their natural partnership is still with the West. The frank realization of this fact on the part of many former French colonies has caused other African states to attack them as European satellites, yet they all continue to accept substantial economic, educational and even military aid from the Western powers, and for most of them aid and trade relationships are primarily with the West.

Such aid naturally creates situations which can be regarded as interference in African affairs on a national or continental basis. Disputes are bound to arise over the extent to which aid-giving nations have the right to stipulate the ends for which and the conditions under which their aid may be used; indeed, most grants are necessarily for specific purposes. No nation can feel at ease with large numbers of foreign nationals—especially employees of foreign governments—within its borders, intimately involved in its education system, its governmental administrative agencies, and its economy. Transfer of aid activities from bilateral to multilateral agencies even if this were feasible on a large scale would mitigate but not solve the problems posed by national sensitivity to outside interference. Given the extent of overseas activity in Africa and the new-found pride of the recently freed African states, friction between Africans and aid agencies is inevitable. Economic development is a prime requisite for whatever eventual independence is possible for African states in the contemporary world, but in the short run the means necessary to obtain economic development may seem to compromise independence. This paradox lies at the root of much of the hostility of these states toward their benefactors evident in African talk of neo-colonialism.

Closely related to the question of sovereignty is that of national territorial integrity. Herein also lies a paradox. During the colonial era and the early years of the surge toward independence the cry was often raised by nationalists that colonial rule, especially in West Africa, had done great harm to Africa by setting up arbitrary and artificial frontiers which did violence to African life, cutting across natural ethnic and economic groupings. Also the right of self-determination was often a major cry raised against the colonial powers.

But self-determination is now anathema insofar as it applies to situations within independent African states. Ghana has used the cry of Ewe reunification as a weapon against Togo, and the Somalis have pressed irridentist claims against their neighbors. But such claims, like the struggle of the black southern Sudan against domination by the Arab north, have received little support from opinion elsewhere in the continent. African leaders are too busy trying to unify the nations they have inherited to be interested in continuing to promulgate a principle which if applied could threaten the stability of virtually every state on the continent. The Liberian delegate to the United Nations spoke for virtually every African statesman when he said several years ago:

> We know that brothers and sisters were separated mutually by boundaries imposed to meet the requirements of the colonial powers. Much as we deplore those arbitrary acts, those boundaries have been fixed after a period of time and form all boundaries of the independent African states. What chaos, what confusion, what hatred could be engendered by each of the new African countries against each other were those boundaries to be changed or readjusted. My advice . . . is to let sleeping dogs lie.

The acceptance given Africa's colonial frontiers was vividly illustrated during the Congo crisis when some Western supporters of Tshombe chided other Africans for refusing to allow self-determination to the Katangese. Without even raising the issue of whether the Katangese did in fact want self-determination, Jaja Wachuku of Nigeria, a noted moderate among African foreign ministers, replied by asking, "How would you as an American like it if the State of New York or the State of California were to be cut off from the United States because the people wanted self-determination?" For virtually all Africans ethnic self-determination is synonymous with tribalism. Tribalism is a relic of the past, and any cries for self-determination are held to stem from machinations of neo-colonialists seeking to divide and conquer.

African aims in world politics are an interrelated whole, given the premises of nationalist thinking. Africans seek security, independence and economic development through a policy of nonalignment. It is the Cold War which threatens peace and so threatens them physically, it is the Cold War which threatens to stifle their economic development by encouraging the world to waste its resources on armaments, and it is the Cold War which threatens their independence by making Africa a potential scene of international rivalry and conflict. By keeping the Cold War—whatever name or form it may take in the future—out of Africa they can reduce world tensions and aid the cause of peace generally. Nonalignment is therefore a positive policy. It not only helps preserve African independence and prosperity but promotes the interests of the world at large, which lie in the reduction of East-West tensions.

But it is impossible adequately to assess the role of Africa in world politics solely in abstract or general terms. One must also examine its differing and constantly changing relations with each part of the world in detail in order to understand what, beneath the rhetoric of East, West and Africans alike, this role has been and may become.

XIII

AFRICA AND EUROPE

The nations of Africa attained their independence with a speed which caught both Africans and non-Africans by surprise. But to many observers even more startling has been the rapidity with which even extralegal ties have been broken and the new states have struck out on their own. Kwame Nkrumah envisioned Ghanaian independence as the beginning of the creation of a Pan-African state which would be a completely self-sufficient entity in short order, but most others in British Africa assumed before independence that ties with Britain would remain closer than those which have in fact been maintained, while leaders of the French colonies such as Houphouët-Boigny anticipated and advocated, as some less openly still do, a Franco-African partnership, with France as the senior partner. Not only have overt political bonds such as the British Commonwealth and the French Community come to mean little, but the speed with which both the administrative personnel and the political institutions inherited from the colonial period have been replaced has been much more rapid than anticipated.

In some respects the former French territories have moved less far from France than the former British territories have moved from Great Britain. Soon after Guinea's rejection of French overlordship, all its fellow colonies in black Africa achieved their sovereignty by negotiation with France. Yet important economic and military ties between France and these new states still exist, and with them political influence. All of the former French colonies save Guinea and Mali have remained in the franc zone, so that their fiscal affairs are ultimately under French control and their fiscal soundness dependent upon that of a happily thriving France. France claims that through FIDES (Fonds d'Investissement pour le Développement Economique et Sociale) it has been devoting a higher proportion of its national income to foreign aid than any other nation. Although this is basically true, hidden economic advantages accrue to France in its relations with Africa, and the French government collects enormous sums in taxes on African products sold to French consumers. FIDES as a cardinal principle seeks to integrate the economies of the territories aided with each other and with metropolitan France. In terms of planning France itself under De Gaulle has become a semisocialist economy and this principle has been extended to Africa. All of the usual types of economic aid projects are found in the package, but although industrialization is included emphasis is on agricultural production, including the processing of agricultural products. The complaint is sometimes made that in the interest of efficiency too much emphasis is placed on the use of French administrators and technicians and not enough is done to train and use Africans in these capacities, but the plan works and under it such nations as the Ivory Coast have made great economic strides. Besides providing aid for development, France has even subsidized the regular budgets of some French-speaking states.

Although former Italian and Belgian territories are associate members, and Nigeria has recently attained this status, the impact of the European Economic Community upon Africa has been mainly an extension and modification of Franco-African economic and political relationships. Most of the eighteen associate members of the EEC are former French colonies: all former French territories except Guinea, Mali and the North African states belong to EEC. The existence and growth of

EEC has had an ambivalent effect upon these nations' relations with Europe. Their relations with France will become somewhat less intimate economically as the French tariff wall becomes a European one, while their relations with Europe as a whole will become closer. In time EEC aims at a common external tariff which will not treat the products of its associate members in a radically different way from those of other tropical countries (though in the meantime the differences can be crucial). But benefits will continue to accrue to African member states, since the pill of the loss of protected markets will be sweetened by a major EEC-sponsored aid program for Africa, which Africans themselves will have a role in administering. Thus France will gradually transfer some of her residual responsibilities in Africa to Western Europe as a whole.

In addition to direct economic aid, France provides its former territories with important forms of cultural aid. Thousands of French teachers paid for by the French government are working in sub-Saharan Africa. They teach many subjects, but they concentrate on maintaining the purity of the French language, and their influence permeates education and culture in former French Africa at all levels. In addition to French citizens working as technicians on aid projects or as teachers, many still help staff the civil services of African nations, and some of them are of high, even subcabinet rank. The rationale for such a situation has been stated by Houphouët-Boigny, who has rejected demands for immediate Africanization on the grounds that the development of the Ivory Coast will be best served if jobs are held by competent Frenchmen rather than by incompetent Africans. As a result some African states boast more French residents, even more French government servants, now than before independence, and the central districts of French African capitals have the ambiance of French provincial cities with an overlay of Mediterranean-African adjustments to the tropical climate.

It is only in the past two or three years that French African states have begun to develop their own armies. Prior to this time they were garrisoned by African troops in French units. France has recently withdrawn from most of its African bases, but retains those in Abidjan, Fort Lamy and Madagascar for strategic reasons. The result has been African distress not only at the loss of cheap protection but at the economic losses resulting from the closures. The abandonment of the French base at Dakar, a city already in economic difficulties since it is overgrown for the hinterland it now serves, was expected to result in a 10 percent reduction in Senegalese government revenues.

North Africa is a special case in French-African relations. Though not associate members of EEC, the Maghrib nations still enjoy certain tariff concessions in France. France has been generous with both economic and cultural aid, despite temporary rifts with Bourguiba of Tunisia over such issues as the French naval base at Bizerte and expropriation of French-owned land. Tunisia has always been highly Gallicized, and thinks of itself as a Mediteranean as well as an Arab or African nation. Both Tunisia and Morocco have sought to retain ties with France, but found themselves in frequent conflict with her because of their support of their Muslim brethren in the Algerian war. Once Gaullist diplomacy ended the war, old relationships began to be revived.

Strangely enough, De Gaulle went out of his way to cultivate Ben Bella's Algeria. Most of the cost of compensating displaced *colons* was subsidized by French economic aid, and despite continued confiscation of French assets De Gaulle has remained patient. Over twelve thousand French teachers are in Algeria under French sponsorship. The French and Algerians share the profits of a growing oil industry in the Sahara, and its existence within the franc zone is a major asset to France's balance-of-payments position. Ben Bella, despite his strident anti-imperialism and nonalignment, continued to allow the French to test atomic devices in the Sahara. The basic reason for Franco-Algerian amity, however, is politics on the broadest level. In large part De Gaulle's claim to leadership of the *tiers monde* turns on his relationship with Algeria; here he can build a reputation as the one Western leader who understands the unaligned and is magnanimous to them. Franco-Algerian partnership still flourishes under Ben Bella's successor, Colonel Boumedienne, who has proclaimed Algeria's continued dedication to socialism.

France's virtual withdrawal from NATO and SEATO and its economic eclecticism give states closely related to it a large degree of freedom for maneuver. African nationalists can hardly complain that it is the Quai d'Orsay that is preventing their governments from recognizing Communist China. Paris has no phobia against socialism and works with leaders of all economic proclivities throughout the world who will play its subtle game.

More difficult to assess than the degree to which former French territories are at one with France in international politics is the question of the degree to which their domestic institutions still reflect French tutelage. As in Africa generally, one-party systems are virtually universal. Yet this may not represent as much of a departure from the French heritage as at first appears. Many of the leaders of Francophone Africa had direct contact with French parliamentary institutions under the Fourth Republic and may be pardoned a jaundiced view of them. The presidential quasi-dictatorship of the generally admired De Gaulle not only seems to African states an appropriate model for developing nations under severe external and internal stress but also a proved and preferred alternative to the instability and *immobilisme* of French democracy. The Africans have simply paid their mentor the tribute of going him one better by formally institutionalizing rule by a leader heading a national front above all parties.

The close relationship of France and her former colonies has not been without its critics, not only among other Africans who look upon it as a form of neo-colonialism but among dissidents within these states. Africans seeking more rapid personal advancement regard the presence of French in key posts with antipathy. Nationalist and youth groups object in principle, and look upon French influence as the reason that these nations, save for Guinea and Mali, whose political relations with France are less close, are not in the forefront of radical African nationalism. But so far the leaders of the former French-controlled territories have kept their dissidents in line by force, persuasion or the demi-bribery of jobs and emoluments, and can point to relative political stability and economic progress as the justification of their policies.

Even in France itself the close relationship with former French Africa is not universally approved. Led by men such as the journalist Raymond Cartier, proponents of Cartierisme contend that money which could be better spent in developing France itself is being squandered for dubious political returns and a fictitious *gloire* and that aid should be drastically curtailed. Recently there has in fact been some diminution in French aid. But as long as De Gaulle remains in power and as long as he continues to seek recognition as the leader of a semineutralist Third Force, the present relationship between France and Africa seems likely to remain essentially unchanged.

The relationship between former British territories and Great Britain is more complex than that between France and Africa, but one thing seems clear. Compared to the role many envisioned for it as late as the 1950's, the British Commonwealth of Nations is almost as much a ghostly relic of the past as the French Community. South Africa has of course departed the Commonwealth but even so the differences in outlook between the older white states and the newer Asian and African members is so profound as to make the old intimacy and trust more and more a memory. This is not merely a question of Ghana, Nigeria, Tanzania, Kenya and Uganda having become republics (following the lead of India and Pakistan), a step considered necessary in order to focus all of the psychological force of the veneration of leadership upon African political leaders who need all the strength they can muster. Nor is it purely a matter of race. It stems basically from the fact that Britain is fading from the scene as a major world power. Her growing industrial handicaps and her small population have forced her to renounce effective nuclear armament and she is now torn between eventual European union and going it alone without the increasingly insupportable responsibilities of Commonwealth leadership. Smaller African nations such as the Gambia or Sierra Leone may retain close ties to Britain, which still has worldwide economic and political interests, but Britain is no longer able to serve as the linchpin of a multiracial Pax Britannica.

This is not to say that the Commonwealth is already dead. Economic and cultural ties still make it a convenient vehicle for the exchange of goods and ideas. Commonwealth prime ministers still meet and Commonwealth educators, jurists, military men and parliamentarians still maintain close associations. Indeed, Ghanaian President Nkrumah, though an ardent neutralist as well as an aspirant for the leadership of a tightly unified and nationalistic Africa, has been pressing, with some success, for a renovation of the Commonwealth relationship, specifically for the creation of a strong and well-endowed Secretariat.

Britain extends some financial assistance to former colonies through the Commonwealth Development Fund, and British teachers and technicians still work in English-speaking Africa in large numbers. But by virtually every measure Britain has departed Africa faster and more completely than France, save for her residual commitments in Rhodesia and the High Commission Territories of South Africa. Britain provides less aid than France, its aid is a smaller portion of the total aid supplied the recipient nations, and the aid is less coordinated on an overall Eurafrican basis. Large numbers of Britons remain in Africa, and in some West African nations there are more Britons today than before independence. But Africanization of the civil service, especially in less-prepared East Africa, has proceeded more swiftly, not to say precipitously, than anyone in Britain could have imagined. On the whole, the remaining British have less political influence than their French counterparts.

Other Commonwealth countries such as Canada have stepped in to offer small but significant aid in the postcolonial period, which to some extent reinforces the basic tie to Britain, but because of language affinities and the absence of discouragement from the former colonial power, the United States has done more to take up the task of providing foreign assistance to former British Africa than to former French Africa, and is necessarily therefore more of a competitor for political and cultural influence. British military withdrawal took place earlier than French, and is now virtually complete. Individual British officers on loan to African governments serve almost solely as teachers and advisers, and attempts at military alliance, such as the British-Nigerian pact, have had to be abandoned. British military disengagement from Africa is of course just one aspect of the rapid contraction of British land power (never very great in Africa in any event) throughout the world.

Political events in the world at large have also played a part in making it more embarrassing for Britain's former colonies to retain their close political ties with her. Britain is tied to NATO and the United States more closely than is Gaullist France, to put it mildly. Britain has obvious financial ties with South Africa and the Conservative government leaned toward support of Tshombe's rule in Katanga even when the United States was hostile and France aloof. Despite French atomic testing in Africa, and the hard French line on Berlin, African states may feel freer in following the quasi-neutralism of De Gaulle than the Anglo-American alignment of a Britain which has supported the American position in Vietnam and, tacitly, in the Dominican Republic, and has fifty thousand troops defending Malaysia against Indonesia. Yet one should not be too hasty in generalizing: French flirtation with Peking upsets many African leaders who are more anti-Communist in this regard than De Gaulle, and not all of Francophone Africa has chosen Peking over Taipei, while English-speaking African leaders still care about their Commonwealth past and perhaps secretly desire British approval and support of their actions. The speed and ease with which the rulers of East Africa called on British troops to quell mutinies of their military forces, and the degree to which their citizens accepted these actions, show that old habits of dependence and mutual trust are far from dead.

The relations of Africa with European nations other than Britain and France are still tentative and limited. The cases of the relationship of Belgium and Portugal to Africa are unique and require special treatment, and it is still too early to see what if any the long-range effect of EEC will be on non-economic aspects of African life. Italy still has important financial interests in Somalia and the Eritrean region of Ethiopia. The Italians have made economic and technical contributions in many African nations and are politically and socially unobtrusive. Who fears Italy? West Germany fills a similar role. Despite the fact that its major interests are in former German colonies and despite the generally bad record of German colonization in Africa, Germany is not today thought of as a colonial power, but as a quasi-neutral like Italy. It continues to expand its commercial and cultural ties with the new African states, although the Hallstein doctrine—that recognition of East Germany means a breaking of relations with Bonn—has caused difficulties in Tanzania. The Swiss support a modest but gradually expanding aid program which concentrates on providing technical training, both in Switzerland and in Africa, and on assisting the smallest African nations. Yugoslavia plays a curious role as a kind of Communist version of Israel—another model of how one developing nation can help others to do what it has modestly done itself. The Yugoslavs seek three things in Africa: trade, reputation as a force to be reckoned with in world affairs, and the advance of their brand of Communism. In line with their recent rapprochement with Russia, they have joined it in warning the Africans of the danger of Communism à la Chinoise. In general, Yugoslav aid activity, though minor, is effective and well received, more so than that of the Soviets and their European partners.

Most curious of all perhaps is the role of Franco Spain. Dreaming his own dreams of grandeur and recalling Spain's Moorish past, Franco has sought friendship with Africa and influence in the Arab world by playing a kind of pseudo-neutralist role on the model later perfected by De Gaulle. Spain quietly withdrew from Morocco, save for a few tiny enclaves which have recently become a source of discord. She still rules a wasteland in the western Sahara (the misnamed Río de Oro) and the important island of Fernando Po, as well as its mainland tributary Río Muni. Life seems placid in Spanish Africa; Spain has to date reorganized government there ahead of effective nationalist demands and has talked of eventual autonomy. Though liberation movements exist in Spanish Africa they have until recently excited little interest among African nationalists elsewhere, who almost never attack Spanish colonialism either in public or in private. It is almost as if her presence in Africa were forgotten. Undoubtedly African nationalists have more urgent things on their agenda and expect that in due time the Spanish anachronisms will fall like overripe fruit. But in an era of violent anticolonial polemic and counter-polemic the Spanish position remains a curious footnote to history.

XIV

AFRICA AND THE UNDERDEVELOPED WORLD

Africa is not only a significant part of what has come to be known as the "underdeveloped world," it is for some purposes the most important part. Though its population is slightly less than that of Latin America and a fraction that of Asia, the conditions of political fragmentation imposed by colonialism have meant that as African states became independent they soon became numerically the most important bloc among the underdeveloped states in the United Nations. Only six African states attended the Bandung conference in 1955. By 1965 there were thirty-five African votes in the UN as against nineteen Asian and twenty-three Latin American.

The dramatic rise in the sheer number of its states has meant a profound change in Africa's world position. Once the object of solicitude by Arab and Asian states, it has in many ways now become the center of gravity of the non-Western world, and for many Westerners is the archetype and symbol of underdevelopment. In the early years of Africa's postcolonial period it accepted the leadership of the Arab states and of such giants as India. The Afro-Asian bloc was in reality an Arab-Asian bloc with African trimmings. Today the Afro-Asian bloc hardly exists in the UN. Africa still participates in international gatherings of non-Western nations, such as the second Bandung conference in the spring of 1965, in order to work for a common neutralist front, but it also has particular relations with particular non-African, non-Western nations which deserve comment. Beneath the surface of common underdevelopment and non-whiteness exist special approaches and problems.

Africa's relations with the nations of the Near East are especially complex since they involve not only intercontinental but intra-African politics. Six North African nations are members of the Arab League, and the United Arab Republic is an African power which has intermittently sought a special African role and even African leadership. The degree to which the North African states will seek their destiny as Arabs rather than as Africans poses again the question of Africa's self-definition, of its creating a viable identity.

So far a major bar to complete solidarity between Arab and black Africa has been their differing attitudes toward Israel. Though Asian by geographic location Israel has had to struggle to retain membership in the ideologically rather than geographically defined camp of Asian nations, a problem aggravated by its financial and military ties to the West. Until now it has enjoyed, and fought hard to attain, an important role in Africa. It has had surplus technical personnel and even, for certain purposes, capital with which to aid the development of fledgling African nations.

Many things about Israel make it especially appealing to African nations as a source of external assistance. It is a socialist state; it understands the techniques and necessity of social mobilization as a tool for national development. It has faced and conquered problems of economic development on a scale comparable to those of most African nations. Africans are wont to say that if they have irrigation problems the United States sends them blueprints of Hoover Dam while Israel sends a three-man team to show them how to dig wells. The contrast is overdrawn, but there is no question as to Israel's often greater ability to render the kind of assistance needed by most of the new Africa.

At the same time that Israel is economically and technically more advanced than Africa it is too small to be viewed as an imperialist menace. Yet Arab states regard Israel as an outpost of Western colonialism, a view reinforced by Israel's role in the Suez crisis. The Arabs are seeking with increasing success to implant this image in the minds of other Africans. African states generally have accepted without question the pressures exerted against Jewish minorities in the Maghrib which have caused most North African Jews to migrate to Israel or France. The extent to which the Arab bloc succeeds in turning Africa against Israel will ultimately depend on how much practical good African statesmen are willing to sacrifice for the sake of solidarity with the Near East, which is another way of measuring self-interest against ideological abstractions. To date black Africans have preferred to echo the slogans of their Arab friends but continue to accept Israeli technicians, scholarships and money. Israel itself has gone so far as to withdraw its ambassador to South Africa as a protest against apartheid despite the pressures this puts upon South Africa's large, wealthy and strongly Zionist Jewish community. But the tide appears to be slowly turning against Israel, particularly in those states most involved in the North African-led anti-Tshombe activities.

African relations with Latin America are virtually nonexistent, despite a past when so many sons and daughters of Africa were transported there as slaves and when not a few returned, especially to Nigeria, bringing with them New World arts and ideas. Haiti, despite the activities of some Haitians in early Pan-Africanism, is too horrible a portent of one possible political future for the Africans to wish to identify with it, though many Haitians, most of them in flight from the terror in their homeland, are now serving in Africa in various capacities. Recently leaders from Jamaica and Trinidad, largely Negro states which are geographically if not culturally Latin American, have visited Africa and been well received, but these nations, so poor and so dependent on Britain as well as so Anglicized culturally, play a limited role in the United Nations, and their recent contacts with Africa seem rather like those of long-lost brothers who on reunion find they really have nothing to talk about. Generally speaking, Latin American nations have voted the cautious anti-colonial line advocated by the United States in the United Nations, and have only recently gone beyond U.S. policy in dealing with colonial questions. But two nations of Latin America deserve special mention—Cuba and Brazil.

The Castro revolutionary mystique, in which higher status for Cuban Negroes was an important element, has gained a hold upon some of the more radical anticolonial and antiwhite elements in Africa. Castro's successful defiance of the United States and his willingness to take up the cause of extremist Negro groups such as the Black Liberation Front in the American civil rights struggle (a Radio Free Dixie broadcasts to the American South from Havana) have appealed to many Africans, as has his eclectic Marxism-Leninism with its playing of Russia and China off against each other and the West. Though Cuban influence in the revolt in Zanzibar was greatly exaggerated, Havana has become a haven and military training ground for some African exiles, both from black states and from South Africa.

Brazil represents a more solid contender for future influence in Africa. Her African heritage has been recognized in the establishment of a center of African Studies at the University of Bahia and she has long flirted with the notion of a supra-political, multiracial Lusitanian world community. Future political developments in Brazil are as unpredictable as those in Portugal or in Africa itself, but should conditions change rapidly in Portuguese Africa Brazil could play a major role since it shares with this area a language not in wide use elsewhere. If law and order should break down in Angola and Mozambique as they did in the Congo, Brazil could be a major source of troops and technicians; if they achieved a viable independence, Brazil would be an obvious alternative to Portugal as a source of guidance and assistance.

Apart from Communist China, two Asian nations are especially active in Africa. One is the Chinese Nationalist government on Taiwan. Itself recently graduated from underdeveloped status, Taiwan occupies a position curiously similar to that of Israel. Sufficiently far away and weak so as not to pose a threat to African independence, it needs African friends in the United Nations and has been willing to pay for them by a major effort in grass-roots and highly effective technical assistance. Nationalist embassies are for political reasons established wherever they are accepted. Nationalist technicians show Africans how to grow rice and set up small industries with semiskilled labor, and scholarships are offered to African students. In many French-speaking nations especially relations with Taiwan are good and may, especially given current African fear of Communist subversion, survive De Gaulle's *haute politique* in Asia.

Japan's role in Africa is a strange one. An unknown quantity to Africans, with no historic associations there, it is an anomaly. A major world industrial power, actually a developed nation, less Asian than Western in many respects, it treads softly in the United Nations and elsewhere, with a military and political role incommensurate with its vast economic and demographic strength. Japan seeks no political dominion or even influence in Africa. It seeks and desperately needs only trade. A major trading partner of such nations as Nigeria, it is hurt by its inability to buy as much as it sells. Africa needs its cheap industrial goods more than Japan needs African products. It has lately, but slowly and slightly, sought to broaden its role in Africa by scholarships and technical assistance. But it has a possibly fatal handicap. Its need for markets makes it a major trading partner of the despised Republic of South Africa (where Japanese are considered whites, a status reminiscent of their position as "honorary Aryans" in Hitler's Germany). Japan has sought to evade choosing between white and black African friendship by remaining as unobtrusive as possible, but this may not be enough for long.

The real touchstone of Africa's relations with the underdeveloped world, however, is India, once Africa's patron, now increasingly a potential political foe. India was a lodestar for African nationalism because it provided a model of a dark-skinned nation which had overthrown colonial rule. The non-violence of Gandhi and the eclectic socialism of Nehru appealed to African ideologists. So also did and does India's role within first the Commonwealth and now the United Nations in protesting South African treatment of Indian and other non-white citizens. (After all, it was in the struggle against discrimination in South Africa that the young African-born lawyer Mohandas Gandhi earned his political spurs and formulated his political philosophy.) Today South African treatment of Indians as well as Africans is increasingly harsh, yet Indian prestige in Africa continues to drop. Why?

The reason lies in the fact that South Africa is not the only African nation with an Indian minority. If one for the sake of convenience counts Indians and Pakistanis together there are about 60,000 in Uganda, 170,000 in Kenya, and 107,000 in Tanzania in addition to the half million Indians in South Africa and the 15,000 Goans in Mozambique. They bulk large in these countries not only because of their numbers but because of their economic strength. Though discriminated against by European governments, save in Mozambique where they are an important element in the Portuguese administration, they have done better than the Africans economically, educationally and politically. Clannish for religious and racial reasons, they sometimes sought and found European favor, not only becoming dominant in the retail trade but forming a layer of junior civil servants, teachers, and noncommissioned military and police officers interposed between whites and Africans. Often their position has forced them to be the actual implementers of discrimination against Africans.

Africans generally hate the Indians and view them as an obstacle to national unity and to their upward social mobility. Settler propaganda sought with some success to play off Indians against Africans in the past, alleging that the former might be a future fifth column for an Indian imperialism seeking to dump its surplus masses in underpopulated East Africa. Indeed, the first British government statements that Kenya was a "black man's country" were, ironically, inspired by white settlers who were seeking to reduce Indian economic influence. There was bloody African rioting against Indians in Durban, South Africa, in 1949 and bitter and bloody boycotts of Indian stores in Uganda in 1961. Leaders of antigovernment forces in South Africa have sought to lessen African hostility against Indians in order to promote their common struggle against white racism; the Verwoerd government's policies may yet create a common bond of misery between the nonwhite races there. Indians in East Africa have, as have Europeans, been offered local citizenship should they choose to stay on now that independence has arrived, and many are accepting. But many second-echelon members of the East African political elite privately express the desire to drive them into the sea. The potential for future conflict is great, with India cast in the role of a major power protecting unwanted "nonindigenous" settlers against African governments.

India has done surprisingly little to maintain its position in Africa in recent years. Though there is an African studies center at one Indian university and African students are welcomed in India, claims of racial discrimination against students have been made similar to, though milder than, the complaints of Africans in the Communist nations. India has become more moderate in its anticolonial positions as time has passed, often voting contrary to African wishes on such disputed issues as the admission of the Cameroun to the United Nations under a government which Africans charged had been elected by French influence. Africans applauded India's invasion of Goa but were lukewarm in response to her border difficulties with China. In an era of increasing Indian-Chinese hostility the Chinese seem to have the greater appeal to many Africans as a result of being more "revolutionary." India's diplomatic representation in Africa is sparse and poor.

Should renewed violence and possible mass deportations of Indians occur in East Africa more than African-Indian relations would suffer. Africa would have elected a new role in world affairs, not as just another nonwhite victim of colonialism but as a racially chauvinistic black power.

XV

AFRICA AND WORLD ORGANIZATION

In the world of traditional power politics, where strength is reckoned in terms of gross national product, military technology and population, Africa would count for little, even as a whole. But in the second half of the twentieth century, diplomacy and international relations generally have taken on a new cast. Bilateral international relations and the multilateralism of treaties and traditional international law constitute only part of contemporary international intercourse. An increasing role is being played by international organization.

Despite her potential, Africa is a relatively weak continent economically, militarily and even demographically. But international organizations, by emphasizing the principle of sovereignty, bestow power in international affairs on the weak as well as the strong by giving each an equal voice in parts of their machinery. Both the League of Nations and the United Nations have included leading organs in which the great powers have had permanent representation, but both have also had assemblies in which each power has had an equal voice. In such assemblies the weakest African nation is formally the equal of any great power. The implications of this principle for Africa's role in world affairs is plain enough (though Africans have not always been aware of them): whatever strengthens world organization as a means of solving world problems strengthens Africa's voice in solving these problems; whatever weakens world organization weakens its influence on world affairs.

The League of Nations had little impact on Africa, and Africans virtually none on it. Only four states—Egypt, Liberia, Ethiopia and the Union of South Africa—were members. The League investigated slavery and international debt problems in Liberia in 1931–34 and almost succeeded in placing that country under international trusteeship. In 1936 the League failed spectacularly to protect Ethiopia against invasion and occupation by Italy.

Nor did the League have much influence on colonialism. None of the Class A mandates (territories to be moved toward independence as soon as possible) were in Africa, and African territories in mandate status, the former German colonies of Togo, the Camerouns, Tanganyika and Rwanda-Urundi, were little affected by the fact of being mandates.

The role of the UN in Africa and of Africa in the UN has been an entirely different story. Today approximately one third of all United Nations members are African states—a factor in encouraging and perpetuating the balkanization of Africa, since more unification would mean less UN voting strength—and much of the UN's attention is devoted to African matters. Indeed, in 1965 the United Nations was on the verge of collapse over controversies springing directly from the Congo intervention. What had killed Secretary General Dag Hammarskjold threatened to cripple the organization for which he had died.

Yet not only has Africa had a profound effect upon the United Nations; the reverse has also been true. In many ways the UN acted as midwife for the coming into being of the new African states, and admission into the UN became the hallmark of their sovereignty. But above all the UN has provided an arena in which Africa could seek to find and express itself in the world—

a stage on which the African Personality could be proclaimed and developed.

The entry of the African nations into the UN occurred at a time when the UN itself was changing internally, and the African states accelerated and influenced the direction of that change. As the United Nations Charter clearly indicates, the UN was designed as a means by which the victors of World War II could avoid repeating the mistakes of the victors of World War I in allowing their vanquished foes to again threaten world peace and security. The Security Council—with each of the five permanent members the possessor of a veto—was designed to ensure that collective security would prevail against disturbers of the status quo. The UN was not set up to settle disputes among the major powers. The veto power was intended to ensure that no action would be taken unless all the great powers agreed; thus any action voted for could be implemented, for an overwhelming preponderance of world power would coincide with the voting strength required for any Security Council decision.

The United Nations was paralyzed in its early days by the discovery that the real conflicts of the postwar period were between the Soviet Union and its erstwhile Western allies. Yet the UN could act only if the Soviet Union was willing to let it act. A turning point came in 1950 with the invasion of South Korea. Only the Russian "walkout" made Security Council action possible. In order to avoid a situation in the future in which Soviet negation would prevent desired action, the United States introduced and secured the passage of the "Uniting for Peace" resolution, according to which the General Assembly could itself recommend action in case the Security Council was deadlocked, thus shifting the balance of power from the Security Council to the Assembly. But the resolution was designed not to give power to the small nations as such but to give it to a bloc led by the United States. The Soviet Union objected but acquiesced. It was only later, with the gaining of independence by a myriad of new—especially African—nations, that the

United States realized the implications of its action. The nonaligned nations were not interested in the Assembly as a device by which the United States could bypass a Security Council which the USSR could deadlock. They wanted the Assembly to wield power in its own right.

In the fifties and early sixties this evolution toward a strong General Assembly continued. Since the Assembly was too unwieldy to act rapidly on a day-to-day basis, its power and prestige gravitated into the hands of the Secretary General, and in this role Dag Hammarskjold did all he could do to increase that power, although he remained to his death cautious and wary of its practical limitations. The United States usually, as in the Suez crisis, was on the same side as a majority of the nonaligned nations, so it encouraged the development of the power of the Secretary General. More and more the small powers came to feel the equal of the great within the United Nations, if not collectively their superiors.

During all this time the influence of the African nations within the UN was growing along with their number. The elected, nonpermanent members of the Security Council (seats originally divided up according to a gentlemen's agreement which had the effect of excluding Africa) now included representatives of nonaligned and African nations.

Largely as a corollary of this increasing African influence the UN had an important direct impact upon Africa. Through its Trusteeship Council it did much to speed the trust territories (the UN successors to League mandates) to independence at a rapid rate, and the requirement of giving the Trusteeship Council reports on non-self-governing territories ameliorated conditions and accelerated political development throughout colonial Africa, even in colonies which were not trust territories.

The United Nations also became an important forum for debating issues related to African independence. The Arab states fought to put Morocco on the agenda in 1951, and Tunisia on in 1952. The Algerian problem was called to the attention of the Security Council by Saudi Arabia in 1955 and in that year it made the General Assembly's agenda. Though the outcome of events in North Africa was not determined in the United Nations, the French were forced on the defensive before world public opinion, and other nations required to take stands. UN pressures were increasingly brought against South Africa because of its apartheid policies and its continued control of South-West Africa, against Portugal and against Great Britain in regard to the Central African Federation. For the Africans a major, perhaps the most important, role of the UN was as a weapon against colonialism. As long as they had the votes in the Assembly they could move events in the direction they wished, even though this involved disturbing the status quo. The Soviet bloc, increasingly committed to an active as well as a doctrinaire anticolonialism, encouraged them, and the United States, embarrassed, ordinarily acquiesced, seeking however to make the outcome of UN action as palatable to its NATO allies and its own views of the interests of the African populations involved as possible.

The African nations also enjoyed the role of debating non-African questions. Some of them added to the increasing strength of the forces supporting the admission of mainland China to the UN, though American and at one time French suasion helped keep their number down. Fearful of nuclear war, they pressed for its abolition, thus usually voting closer to the positions of the Soviet Union than of the United States, whose acceptance of nuclear disarmament was hedged by considerations relating to inspection and simultaneous conventional disarmament.

Yet there was a certain illusoriness to all this. Despite the African claim to be exercising the role of a third force, and the even less valid claim of many of their critics that Africans slavishly followed the Communist line, the Africans have had less importance in shaping events in the United Nations than might be expected, largely as a result of their own indecisiveness. In most cases their votes have been for measures which were overwhelmingly supported by the Assembly with only token opposition by the USSR or the United States. When those powers were really bitterly at odds, the Africans, like the nonaligned nations generally, tended to leave the scene of battle, that is, to abstain from voting. Abstentions ran high on such issues as Hungary and Tibet, and in 1961 Togo alone abstained thirty-four times. This is hardly playing a balance-of-power role. Concurrently also, the United Nations—perhaps because of the shift of power to the Assembly and the small nations' role in it—did not become the real deciding force in world conflict. The Suez crisis was settled because the United States and the Soviet Union stood together, but nothing came of UN resolutions on Hungary or Tibet. The Cuban missile crisis of 1962, like the Berlin crisis of 1948, was settled outside the United Nations. When the great powers really wanted to do business they shut the door against outsiders, including Africans.

But paradoxically the financial crisis which threatened to destroy the United Nations in 1964–65 was African not only in its direct cause but in part in its basic source as well. After much maneuvering—and the timely assassination of Lumumba—American and African positions on the Congo coincided, and Britain, France and the Soviet Union had to yield. But the Soviets never forgave Hammarskjold for his successful defiance of them and became weary of an Assembly which could take action that the USSR could not control. Unable to advocate outright destruction of Assembly power by returning exclusive jurisdiction over world crises to the Security Council where Russia had a veto, they took another tack. In the famous "troika" plan of 1961 they attempted to incorporate the veto into the office of the Secretary General itself, by suggesting a tripartitite secretaryship—in which one person would represent the West, one the Communist bloc, and a third the nonaligned nations. Since cooperation of all three would be necessary for effective action, the presence of a Communist member would effectively prevent action inimical to Soviet interests.

The African and other nonaligned states who were supposed

to be flattered by this arrangement saw through the maneuver. Even the Casablanca powers—then at odds with Hammarskjold—denounced it, and the Russians quietly withdrew the plan. Africans had realized that the strongest expression of African ideals and power could come through a Secretary General acting on behalf of an Assembly in which the large number of African states each had an equal voice with the great world powers and collectively outnumbered them.

But the relevance of all this to the financial crisis of 1964–65 was obscured by events in Africa. The Soviets were refusing to pay their assessments—as were the French—on the grounds that the expenditures incurred in the Congo action were illegal because they were outside the powers of the Assembly to authorize. The United States, largely for propaganda reasons, made the issue one of Soviet bad faith and lack of general cooperation despite its own growing disenchantment with Assembly equality, evidenced in some "trial balloon" speeches by United States officials on the possibility of weighted voting. The Africans did not see, or chose to ignore, the implications for their position in the UN and in the world if the USSR was allowed to substitute a financial veto for a legal one and bring the United Nations close to bankruptcy by refusing to pay for actions of which it did not approve. The Africans, despite the presence as General Assembly president (by acclamation since formal votes could not be taken) of the first Negro to hold that post, Alex Quaison-Sackey of Ghana, chose to regard the struggle as a purely Russian-American one. Bitter over American support of Tshombe and the Stanleyville paratroop drop of November, 1964, they generally were not anxious to isolate the Russians and hoped, in the event correctly, that the United States would eventually back down.

From an objective point of view the African attitude seems irrational. Virtually every proposal for achieving the prime objectives—liberation of Rhodesia, South-West Africa, South Africa and Portuguese Africa—involves, explicitly or implicitly, eventual internationalization of the problem. Local revolutions or invasion by outside African forces could not realistically hope to do more (the spectre of great-power armed intervention aside) than create a situation in which a body such as the UN might step in. But a UN brought to the verge of bankruptcy and disorganization by the Congo crisis was already becoming hesitant about involvement in possible new Congos. A United Nations in which the Assembly could not call on members for economic support of its actions could become a mere debating society.

What is at stake in the question of African support for a strong UN is not merely the future of a hypothetical United Nations Expeditionary Force in Southern Africa but something even more basic. To date the African voice in the UN has been increasing in volume and authority as African independence and unity have advanced. If Africans should lose faith in the UN as the result of pique with the Western Powers and this should result in a loss of the UN's ability to act decisively, it would not only diminish African power in the world; it would also destroy a shield which has done much to keep the great powers from intervening in their continent.

It is of course possible that the Organization of African Unity, despite its vicissitudes, might gain power and support from African states to the point where it could become an alternative to the UN in Africa, one based on an African desire to keep others out of their affairs. They have already hinted at a desire to reduce UN power in Africa. Prior to the creation of the OAU they had pushed for restricting UN troops in the Congo to African units operating under UN aegis. Similar in intent have been some suggestions that the future might see an OAU-sponsored liberation of South-West Africa undertaken with UN sanction. The role of the Organization of American States in the Dominican Republic helps set a precedent for such international action on a continental basis, with the UN restricted to a bystander's role.

The same motivations that underlie the temptation to turn from a less powerful or less trusted UN to a regional organization can be seen at work in the recent history of trade unionism in Africa. Originally many African unions were members of the World Federation of Trade Unions. The increasingly open Communist domination of the WFTU on a world scale led to the formation of the International Confederation of Free Trade Unions, to which many African unions adhered. Tom Mboya of Kenya was a notable leader among Africans supporting the ICFTU, which received much of its financial support from the AFL-CIO, something which led some Africans to charge that Mboya was in effect an American agent. In 1957 Sékou Touré founded an all-African organization, the Union Générale des Travailleurs de l'Afrique Noire (UGTAN) which has since been succeeded by the All African Trades Union Congress (AATUC) organized at Tunis by the Casablanca powers. This latter organization has great appeal for many reasons. One is its chauvinism—it is exclusively African in membership, directed by Africans and theoretically above the East-West struggle. One can become an African patriot by leading unions to desert the WFTU (largely dead in Africa, since Communist-leaning groups have ardently imbraced the AATUC), the CATC (Confédération Africaine des Travailleurs Croyants), considered religiously divisive and European tainted because of its ties to Christian Democratic organizations in Europe, and the ICFTU, largely staffed by non-Africans even in Africa.

Another motivation for membership in an exclusively African group is the present African trend to political control of unions. Save in a few nations such as Nigeria—whose trade-union movement is seriously split—African unions are government controlled, part of the apparatus of one-party mobilization regimes. The less international influence upon them the better from the point of view of their political mentors. Already, therefore, African unionism presents a picture of an Africa whose national self-assertion is not a bridge to the rest of the world but a wall against it. Retreat from the UN, Africa's most important voice in the world, would similarly mean that African attention would necessarily turn inward, to the impoverishment of both Africa and the world.

XVI

AFRICA AND COMMUNISM

The Communist powers are newcomers to African affairs and as such they enjoy all the advantages of novelty. Unidentified with the colonialism of the past and preaching a revolutionary ideology similar in many respects to that of African nationalism, the Communists, even the white-skinned Russians, appear as natural allies. Yet despite parallelism of revolutionary aims, Communism has not fared well in Africa. The heavy-handedness of much Russian activity and Russian lack of empathy with Africa have added to suspicion of the obviously ulterior motives of the Communist powers and minimized the effect of many initial Communist advantages. The involvement of China—just beginning—is a story whose outlines are only now becoming clear.

Russian interest in Africa antedates Communism. As the motherland of Orthodox Christianity and the religious as well as geopolitical enemy of the Ottomans, the Czarist state early showed an interest in the Christian kingdom of Ethiopia, so conveniently poised on the Turks' flank; Amharic was part of the curriculum at Kharkov University at the beginning of the nineteenth century. The Russians gave medical aid to Ethiopia during the Italian invasion of 1896, and followed this up with construction of a major hospital in Addis Ababa that makes friends for Russia even today. But real Russian interest in Africa had to await not only Communism but further development of Marxist theory.

For orthodox Marxism, revolution was to come first in the most highly developed nations, where capitalism had reached its fullest growth. Nationalism was a weapon which the imperialists used to divide the working class. Therefore, even though Lenin's *Imperialism* postulated that capitalism was worldwide and transnational and might therefore break at its weakest link (an argument designed primarily to justify the imminent outbreak of revolution in Russia, the most backward nation in Europe) nationalist revolution in the colonies was frowned upon. The colonies, not being industrialized, could only produce bourgeois nationalist movements which were intrinsically dangerous. The road to their freedom was through successful proletarian revolution in the colonial powers themselves, as the Comintern manifesto of 1919 expressly stated.

This doctrinal formulation was altered and re-altered in subsequent years, but prior to Stalin's death the substance was maintained so that the world Communist movement had little motivation for or interest in organizing in Africa, even had this been practicable. In the 1920's, though national liberation was subordinated to proletarian revolution, the Communists flirted with the nationalist bourgeoisie in China, hoping thereby to speed Chinese development through capitalism into readiness for socialism and also, more importantly, to secure an ally in Asia. Their fingers were burnt by Chiang Kai-shek's unilateral, armed breakup of the alliance and from 1928 onward there was to be little collaboration with bourgeois nationalists.

During the period from 1934 to 1939 the Communists were utilizing the tactics of the Popular Front, attempting to secure the support of the non-Communist forces in the Western nations against Hitler and fascism. They could hardly preach a common alliance against fascism while advocating revolution in the British and French empires, so that anticolonial nationalism had to be subordinated even further than purely theoretical considerations demanded. When the party line shifted during the period of Soviet collaboration with the Axis from 1939 to 1941, Communists branded the Allied effort as an imperialist war and Communists in colonial areas were free to sabotage it, but the German invasion of Russia in 1941 reversed the party line once again. The anti-Nazi war effort was to be supported and anticolonialism and social revolution everywhere in the world subordinated to it.

Actually none of these events had much direct impact on Africa; except for South Africa, Northern Rhodesia and the Belgian Congo, there was little in the way of an industrial proletariat. South Africa had a Communist party but it was intertwined politically with South African trade unionism. As labor moved toward Afrikaner nationalism, the South African Communist party was left with a small rump of white labor, estranged and under pressure from the masses of white and black labor alike. Despite occasional bows to white racialism, Communists had to stand for racial harmony and against either white or black nationalism. In Rhodesia and the Congo it was virtually impossible for the Communists to penetrate black labor, largely un-unionized and cut off from white society. Save for South Africa there were neither Communist parties nor, except in the case of Ethiopia, Communist diplomatic representatives who might act as covert focal points for local Communist groups. Eschewing African nationalism as divisive, the Communists regarded the continent as the special preserve of the European Communist parties.

These parties were not very much interested in the colonies. The British Communist party especially was too involved in union politics at home to care about "wogs." African students in England were attracted not to the ingrown, sectarian and essentially vulgar British Communist party but to the Marxist and demi-Marxist intellectuals of the Fabian Society and the universities, especially the London School of Economics. Here many Africans acquired an eclectic, intellectualized and essentially nonviolent perspective on the world, which they tried to fit in with their own predilections. Their disinterest in becoming involved in what they regarded as a white man's movement was heightened when George Padmore, a leading Pan-Africanist intellectual, broke with the party in 1934, charging it with using Africans and African nationalism for its own ends. As a result of these factors and of colonial government censorship and control over personal movement into and within the colonies, there was no penetration or even serious interest by the Communists in British Africa prior to the war era.

In French Africa things were somewhat different. French-speaking Africans were, if educated at all, Gallicized to the point of taking up the intellectualized approach to politics of French students and intellectuals. Africans in Paris flirted with Communism as well as with socialism, nascent Christian Democracy, and other creeds. After all Communism was intellectually respectable on the Left Bank in a way that it was not in London. During the Popular Front era in France the French colonial service was for the first time penetrated by Communists and socialists. Many individual colonial officials of various political persuasions set up informal, semiclandestine "study groups" for their African friends and colleagues. The gecist's, alumni of the Groupes Etudes Communistes, were important in the postwar formation of the Rassemblement Démocratique Africaine (RDA) in French West Africa and in many subsequent political activities as well. But no Communist party as such was built up in French Africa. African intellectuals sought instead to use Communism for their own ends. In Belgian Africa no political activity of any kind was permitted, and Belgian Communists were rigorously excluded. The party of course had been illegal in Spanish and Portuguese territories since the accessions to power of Franco and Salazar in the 1930's.

This was to change in the postwar period, although slowly and only after several false starts. The RDA, founded in 1946 as an African nationalist movement by Marxist-influenced

African leaders, formed an alliance with the French Communist party, followed its lead on many issues, and copied its structure and tactics. But, once the French government began to put pressure on the French Communist party and especially on its African allies following the ouster of the Communists from the government in Paris, the cost was too great, and in 1950 Houphouët-Boigny broke the alliance. But, although this particular experiment had been a failure from the Communist standpoint, the continued strength of the RDA gave Communist theoreticians and politicians a new respect for the possibilities of organizing Africans. In China Mao Tse-tung had long been pressing the idea of a national revolution led by the Communists but based on the peasantry, and carried on with the help of the national bourgeoisie—those individuals in non-Western nations who in objective economic status were capitalists or tied to capitalism but who were primarily nationalist and anticolonialist in their allegiances. Though (contrary to popular belief) Mao's united front tactics received tacit Moscow support throughout the thirties and forties, it was not until 1949 that Mao's theses were openly acceptable to most of world Communism. A new belief in the revolutionary and anti-imperialist potential of peasants and national bourgeoisie was growing.

Even so, Nkrumah of Ghana and Nehru of India were still being denounced as bourgeois nationalists in the immediate postwar period. Although the leading Soviet expert on Africa, Professor Potekhin, could say in 1949 that in "tropical and southern Africa the leading role in the national liberation movement now belongs to the national bourgeoisie and national intelligentsia," he was still denouncing Dr. Azikiwe of Nigeria as professor of a "colonial edition of the reactionary American philosophy of pragmatism" and the NCNC program as "the ideology and policy of petty bourgeois national reformism."

The death of Stalin in 1953 marked the real opening of debate on Communist colonial strategy as well as on many other issues in Communist society. The independence of such African states as Libya and the Sudan could no longer be considered "merely formal" or "fictitious" but had to be recognized as real. In 1955 the propaganda triumphs of Communist China at the Bandung conference showed the Soviet Union how the anticolonial nationalism of the new and developing nations might be turned to her advantage. In that year the Soviet Union implemented this new vision by allowing the Czechs to send arms to Nasser's Egypt in order to outflank the Baghdad Pact. This was a theoretical revolution in that it involved the admission that not all non-Communists were anti-Communists but that there could be degrees of friendship and animosity. The lesson later learned by the United States was already being learned in Moscow: neutralism is not necessarily immoral. By 1956, Premier Khrushchev was ready to tell the Twentieth Congress of the Communist party that "the awakening of the peoples of Africa has begun." The independence of the new states of Africa was to be accepted as genuine. In 1958 Nasser visited the USSR, and in 1959 Haile Selassie of Ethiopia and Touré of Guinea followed in his footsteps.

In 1960 this doctrinal development came to a climax, when the November Moscow conference of the world's Communist parties accepted the formula of "national democracy." According to this thesis there exist societies which can be called national democracies. They are states which are anticolonialist, anti-imperialist, independent, based on the masses politically, and in their economic institutions generally leaning toward socialism. In many respects they resemble the peoples democracies of postwar Eastern Europe, except for the major difference that the latter were necessarily led by the Communist party, while this was not the case with the national democracies. These states, indeed, often upset Moscow when, as in the case of the United Arab Republic, they actually outlawed their domestic Communist parties. But the important thing was that these states—led usually by their national bourgeoisies with regimes often based on the peasantry—were on the side of the angels in international affairs and therefore deserving of Communist support. Under this rationale, further developed and much explicated in the famous platform of the Twenty-second Party Congress of 1961, which marked Khrushchev's zenith as a Marxist theoretician, the world was not simply divided into two camps. There were in fact five groups of states: the socialist powers, their allies, the national democracies, the allies of the imperialists and the imperialists themselves. Not all of the first three were in the camp of socialism, but all three were in the camp of peace and anti-imperialism.

To strengthen the anti-imperialist camp the Soviet Union, while eschewing global war, which would be counter to the aspirations and doctrine of peaceful coexistence, would support national liberation movements. These were movements which were directed toward freeing captive peoples from the yoke of imperialism. They might be led by the national bourgeoisie or the Communists or both. They would not necessarily seek to replace imperialist subjugation directly with a socialist state, but at the least their success would weaken the imperialists and result in the establishment of national democracies.

At the very same time, therefore, that tensions were rising between China and the Soviet Union, the Russians were accepting the neo-Maoist formula in which proletarian revolution was not the only possible or worthwhile type of revolution, and in which wars of nationalism against imperialism were to be given the highest priority. But since this time the Soviets and the Chinese have violently disagreed on two subsidiary issues: the extent to which national liberation movements can be encouraged and supported without risk of their leading to nuclear war, with the Chinese in theory less concerned over this possibility than the Russians, and the question of which governments can really be classified as national democracies. Since the increasingly shrill tone of Chinese propaganda has labeled even the Soviet Union itself a revisionist state, few of Russia's protégés, including the African states it is willing to support, can qualify under the Chinese criteria, and therefore the Chinese can with theoretical and practical consistency plot their overthrow.

It is essential to understand this theoretical argument if one is to comprehend the nature of Communist influence in Africa today. Observers of both the left and the right have been engaged in arguments both tedious and bitter over whether or not Africa was "going Communist," both sides citing evidence, real and fictitious. This confuses the issue by mixing together three separate questions: the extent of overt Communist activity in Africa, the nature of the domestic, economic and political regimes of African states, and the nature of these states' foreign policies. The overwhelming majority of African observers have taken the position that there are few Communists in Africa (which is quite true) and that the vast majority of African nationalist leaders reject Communism (which is also true) and that any congruence between Communist ideas and African domestic and international policies is merely an independently caused, accidental parallel.

But there is a sense in which both sides are wrong. One's answer to any question about Communism in Africa depends on one's definition of Communism. If a Communist is a person who belongs to an organized Communist party or movement then Communism in Africa is virtually nonexistent. There are small underground parties in North Africa, though Nasser recently announced that the Egyptian party had "dissolved" itself. There is an illegal Communist party in South Africa (where almost any form of opposition can be loosely labeled "Communist" and summarily proscribed); it is the official sponsor of a journal called *The African Communist,* which sets the theoretical line for the whole continent. Three illegal African political parties of little strength are generally regarded as being under Communist control—the Parti de l'Indépendence Africaine in Senegal, the Sawaba party in Niger, and the non-loyalist wing of the Union des Populations Camerounais in the Cameroun Republic. The small but growing Nigerian Workers and Peasants party is considered to have important Communist elements within it. There are probably several thousand hard-core Communists scattered around the continent, active in opposition groups which are not basically Communist, or infiltrated or simply stranded within ruling parties.

But virtually every independent African nation is a one-party state and no opposition or even public deviation, Communist or otherwise, is tolerated. Many leaders of one-party states ranging from "conservative" Senegal and the Ivory Coast to "radical" Kenya and Tanzania openly condemn Communism as a danger, while on the other hand Nkrumah has allowed the existence of what amounts to an open Communist cell within the CPP as long as its members behave themselves, and in Algeria, although the Communist party is proscribed, the Communist party newspaper (with its editors unchanged) is now published as an official organ of the government party. But in any event the nationalist parties control most aspects of society and have firm mass support; the existence of more than a small clandestine Communist apparatus would be just as impossible as in Nazi Germany—the masses are already mobilized and under other leadership, or at any rate political expression is so tightly controlled as to make public deviation inexpedient or impossible.

But what difference does being or not being a Communist make anyway? A few years ago one could confidently say that being a Communist party member meant that one shared not only certain values but also a certain discipline, that ultimately one was under the direction of the Communist international in Moscow or its equivalent. But for most purposes this is no longer true. The growth of Titoism and of deviationism in general in Eastern Europe, together with the struggle for power in nonruling Communist parties throughout the world between the followers of Moscow and Peking has meant that, whatever their theoretical beliefs if any, Communist leaders are adjusting to the conditions and needs, internal and external, of the countries in which they rule or operate. Ho Chi Minh and Wladyslaw Gomulka, Janos Kadar and the new Rumanian elite, the leaders of French and of Italian Communism, all differ greatly from each other and from Premiers Kosygin or Mao. In the last year before his death the leading African Marxist theorist Frantz Fanon worked in and exulted over the Ben Bella regime in Algeria without feeling out of place. In the house of Communism too there are many mansions.

In fact, so many mansions exist that there is little to differentiate some leaders of national democracies, in Africa and elsewhere, from Communists save labels and largely meaningless quibbles over ideology. Ben Bella of Algeria called himself an Arab socialist and Castro of Cuba calls himself a Marxist-Leninist. Yet this difference could hardly have been deduced from an examination of life in the two countries (save perhaps for the greater lip service sometimes paid to religion in Algeria) and the two leaders were good friends personally and politically. In 1964 on a visit to the Soviet Union, Ben Bella was praised for his work in "building socialism" in Algeria, despite his outlawing of the Communist party. Except for talk of Arabism and Islam, what differentiates Tito and Nasser? Both Ghana and, somewhat less frequently, Mali refer to themselves as professing scientific, that is, Marxist, socialism rather than, or sometimes in addition to, African socialism, and Ghana, Guinea and Mali have all at various times sent "fraternal delegations" to Communist-party meetings in the Soviet Union. But while the creeds and practices of some of these countries might not be accepted as Marxism-Leninism by purists such as the late Professor Potekhin, their scientific socialism is simply part of a continuum stretching from the Soviet Union and China to some European nations. The one characteristic which all the national democracies and the Communist nations share is that they are not democratic by Western reckoning since all possibility of effective opposition is lacking. Though all share a theoretical bias against capitalism, their domestic arrangements are various, and Rumania has sought private American investment no less eagerly than Ghana.

When it comes to foreign policy, the national democracies

share many premises and attitudes with the Communist states. The national democracies of Africa claim to be nonaligned, but on most issues they reserve their most serious criticism for the West, in the United Nations and elsewhere. Western nuclear and conventional military power is regarded by them as the major threat to peace, and Western neo-colonialism as the greatest, though not the only, threat to African independence.

What has been happening is a convergence of nationalism and Communism both within the Communist camp and in the underdeveloped world. The Communist states of the world—virtually all of them underdeveloped to some extent themselves—have broken away from Communist orthodoxy and Moscow control while most nationalist developing nations in Africa and elsewhere have accepted many Marxist ideas about imperialism as a world problem and about the proper course of domestic progress, that is, through planned development managed by a bureaucratized intelligentsia. From the point of view of Moscow it should make relatively little difference whether or not a Communist party triumphs in a particular African state. Should Communism triumph in an African state that state's subsequent behavior might, given the current disarray of Communist theory and practice, be little different domestically or internationally from what it is now. Communist states in the same geopolitical position as the national democracies of Africa would guard their national freedom of action just as doggedly as they currently do. Such prestige and psychological lift as world Communism might gain from adding additional states to the formal roster of its supporters can be regarded as marginal, while too obvious conquests might be feared by the Communists themselves as provocative to anti-Communist forces in the West.

The Chinese do not and indeed cannot take quite the same position as do the Russians, however, largely because they view the world scene differently and have no interest in any form of "peaceful coexistence" with the West at present. Though, as in Southeast Asia, they are willing to support national liberation movements even when not completely controlled by Communists, they have a greater theoretical bias today in favor of Communist control. In large part this stems from their struggle with the Russians for control of the world Communist movement. If, for instance, they could replace the neutralist Kenyatta government in Kenya, with which Russia seems quite satisfied, with an outright Communist one led by their protégé, Vice-President Odinga, it would mean another, and a prestigious, vote for them in international Communist conclaves. Because they do not share the Russian fear of disrupting the fragile détente between the West and the Soviet Union, they are willing to work toward the overthrow of "moderate" regimes in Africa, and if they thought it was to their direct advantage, they would have no qualms about helping to destroy "progressive" ones which might be too friendly to the Soviet Union. For the Chinese as for the Russians, a nation's role in world affairs takes precedence over domestic orthodoxy and the Chinese will make friends where they can, supporting a monarchical Burundi and the royalist Watusi refugees from Rwanda when it serves their ends. Indeed their actions in supporting primitivistic terrorism in the Congo suggest that perhaps even more primary in their interest in Africa than the creation of friendly Communist regimes is a desire to destroy the whole fabric of society in the hope of picking up the pieces at some, possibly remote, future date.

The Soviet Union has been both cautious and bold in its economic aid to Africa. It is cautious in that while many individual projects have been spectacular (in some cases spectacular failures) most Soviet aid, contrary to widespread American opinion, has been designed to meet the priority economic needs of the countries involved rather than for splashy propaganda purposes. It has ranged from the huge Aswan Dam in Egypt to cement works in Guinea and Mali and a canning industry in the Sudan. Even help in the creation of state farms, as in Somalia and Ghana, institutions which would have been built anyway, represents the kind of project which the United States might support save for lack of background in such ventures. Assistance to geological prospecting is another form of Soviet aid that is widespread, inconspicuous and useful.

Where the Soviets have been bold is in concentrating their aid in a few countries and in trying to use it for direct political manipulation. About half has gone to the United Arab Republic, and a large proportion to Ghana and Ethiopia. The USSR has often demanded or implied a political quid pro quo, to the disgust of many Africans, and has usually been rebuffed. Many of its promises have turned out to be empty: credits are often announced which are never used by the Africans because of the high prices or inferior quality or unsuitableness of the goods available. Indeed, many Africans have accused the Russians of being overly hard-nosed in their dealings, and Khrushchev in typically insouciant fashion once replied, "We are not a charitable institution. The Soviet Union gives aid on fair commercial principles."

Despite myths to the contrary, Soviet aid in Africa has not been notably more successful than Western aid. The Russians have encountered many of the same problems and frustrations due to bad planning and ingratitude at the receiving end that we have. They do not know Africa as well as Britain, France or even the United States. Their technicians do not much care for Africa or Africans and keep pretty much to themselves. The Ugly American (who was the hero not the villain of the fable) went out to the grass roots to get results. Russians are generally not eager nor encouraged to do so and there are few ugly Russians.

Much good work has been done for Soviet aims by its East European allies such as East Germany and Czechoslovakia, whose know-how and products more often meet the demanding standards of Westernized Africans than do those of Russia. The total Russian aid program in Africa has actually been small viewed on a continental basis, small not only compared to that of the United States, but small compared to the combined programs of Western Europe. Whether Soviet aid will continue to grow or will decrease under the same domestic pressures which are tending to diminish Western programs is open to speculation. Liberalization behind the so-called iron curtain has meant that the voice of the consumer is once again being heard in the land, however faintly, and aiding Africa has meant more of a sacrifice for Communist than for American consumers. Within the past year or two there have been indications that aid from European Communism might fall off sharply. The crisis seems to have been surmounted, but major expansion of Soviet and East European aid seems unlikely.

Soviet aid to African nations has been accompanied by an intensification of political contacts. Well-staffed Soviet embassies are found in every African capital, save in a few states such as Liberia which have so far dodged such relations. Eastern European Communist nations are also represented to an inordinate degree. All of these embassies seek, of course, to maintain or set up contact with the masses of the population as well as with the host governments, but whether they are notably more successful in overcoming their own bureaucratic inertia and the suspicions of Africans than is the United States is doubtful. Russian meddling in Guinean politics led to the precipitate removal of the Russian ambassador in 1961. Russian embassy personnel may be slightly better at getting along with Africans than Russian technicians but the performance of neither is as spectacular as some Americans assume. Moscow is a world capital where nonaligned African states should logically be represented and many African states bear the expense of embassies there. Yet the burden of African relations with Russia, even more than their relations with Western nations, seems to be on a personal, heads-of-state basis.

Russian intellectual and cultural interest in Africa has been steadily increasing in recent years, for obvious political reasons. Soviet universities have begun to do extensive work in African studies, particularly in linguistics and economics. The

African Institute, founded in 1959 by Professor Potekhin, is now a semi-autonomous branch of the Soviet Academy of Sciences. The Soviets have produced an *Encyclopedia Africana* designed to be the Marxist rival to the late Lord Hailey's monumental but now somewhat dated *African Survey* as a basic reference on Africa. But Soviet African studies are still in their infancy as compared with those of Western nations, largely because of limited opportunities until recently to do field work. The founder of African studies in the USSR was a linguist, Professor D. A. Ol'derogge. Professor Potekhin, their long-time dean, did not visit Africa until late in his career, when he spent some time in Egypt in 1953. For political reasons he could not get to sub-Saharan Africa until after Ghanaian independence in 1957. His major works are based on secondary sources.

Reliance on such materials is still dominant among Soviet Africanists, but this is of marginal consequence since the primary purpose of Soviet African studies is to formulate a correct party line toward African events and to disseminate it to Russians and anyone else, including Africans, who will listen. The major problems in determining this line are crucial for Soviet relations with Africa: Can a Marxist accept that absence of classes in Africa which African socialism postulates (the answer was originally a tentative "Yes," but now Marxists claim more evidence for feudal relationships in both the past and the present), and can there be such a thing as "African" socialism? Potekhin and his successors have preferred to substitute a term not unknown in Africa itself—"The African road to socialism"—thus implying merely a different historical path to an identical end.

Though Russians are now visiting Africa in larger numbers and acquiring competence as Africanists, the Soviet Union is still behind the West not only in academic expertise but even more so in its lack of any counterpart to the thousands of Western missionaries, administrators and traders with long years of intimate African background. This Western advantage is not necessarily disappearing; there is no Russian counterpart to the thousands of Peace Corps veterans who will soon have served throughout Africa, for instance. It would be foolish to underestimate the scope of Africanist resources within the Soviet Union and its allies, but equally foolish to overestimate them.

From the beginning Soviet African studies were closely tied to the attempt to acquaint Africans with the Soviet Union. Professor Potekhin was the head of the Soviet Association for Friendship with Africa established in 1959. The Soviet Union and its allies seek to attract African students to their countries and there were some three thousand of these students in the Soviet Union alone in 1965. How satisfactorily do they get along in the Communist countries as compared with the way they manage in the West?

One must tread cautiously among the conflicting claims of propagandists of various persuasions to answer this question accurately. The students are generally not indoctrinated directly in Lumumba University (the former Friendship University for the Peoples of the East, in which Africa has long been included in Soviet usage) which enrolls over one thousand of them. But apparently they are under pressure to absorb Marxism-Leninism along with their studies elsewhere. Lumumba University presents fewer race-relations problems than do other institutions since it is in effect segregated. But, like their counterparts at Negro colleges in the United States, Africans even at Lumumba University have problems of relations with their white hosts. Relations between African students and other students and with Communist citizens generally have not been very good. This led to riots in Bulgaria in 1963 and in Moscow in 1964. But the contrast between these large-scale and dramatic clashes and the situation of African students in the United States can be attributed in part to the fact that Africans coming to the United States expect to find discrimination and can seek refuge in or take cues from the American Negro community, while discrimination in the Communist countries comes as more of a shock. Actually because of the exaggerated stories they have heard about the United States, some African students here find less discrimination than they expected (though, of course, this does not mean that they resent it any the less) and since Negroes are common they are at least not the object of the curious stares and even pawings they have received from people in Communist countries.

Generally Africans find less of a language problem in studying in the West, since they already have facility in English or French. That the placement and screening of African students going to Communist Europe is worse than that of those going to the United States most educators would find hard to believe, but apparently it is. This is due apparently to the Communists' scooping up of large numbers of unqualified students for propaganda reasons and then placing them arbitrarily in training programs for which they may have little or no ability or interest. When such students return home after disappointment or inferior training in Communist countries they may be bitter at the Communists, or at the home government which fails to recognize their meager skills, or both. Since many Africans still denigrate American academic standards as compared with those of Great Britain or France, it is hard to estimate how they will accept Communist degrees and qualifications, to say nothing of the political consequences of failure to recognize them.

It is thus difficult to generalize as to whether the European Communists or the West is doing better in the battle for influence through educational exchange. The Communists are perhaps catching up to the West's numerical lead by sacrifices in quality, but in any event the lead of either side is not great. Experience is showing that Africans are correct in asserting that they go abroad not to be indoctrinated but to learn and that overseas schooling does not control a person's later political development as much as some think. Thomas Kanza, the Congolese rebel foreign minister, is a product of Brussels University and a year at Harvard. Nkrumah is an alumnus of Lincoln University and the University of Pennsylvania, while many Africans have returned from behind the iron curtain disillusioned with Communism and more "pro-Western" than before. The present drive to concentrate African higher education in Africa may, despite dangers, be a healthy one not only for Africa, through saving money and gearing education more directly to African backgrounds and needs, but also for the perfervid competitors of the Cold War as well. On the other hand, it may mean that the struggle merely takes another form, since the expansion of African education will continue to require teachers from the competing nations.

More important than the question of educational advantage is the Soviet edge in some forms of propaganda. Not only does Soviet radio transmission to Africa overshadow the Voice of America in some respects (Soviet broadcasts are in African as well as world languages to a greater degree than are American broadcasts), but the Soviets also possess a similarity in rhetorical style to that of African nationalism which makes their propaganda seem more in key, and Africans are in little position to test the factual truth or falsity of most of the Communist assertions. Communists work hard at cultivating budding journalists. Persons from East African press agencies are being trained in Communist countries while news-gathering and distribution facilities are being set up with Communist technical assistance. Americans have done some work of a similar nature in West Africa but have generally lagged behind the Communists. The United States Information Agency is not able to provide general news services to African papers as readily as the Communists in part because of the opposition of commercial American news agencies to what they consider unfair competition, so that the American point of view gets across only with difficulty. American race violence gets special attention in the African press and many highly literate as well as demiliterate Africans accept such fictions as that both President Kennedy and Malcolm X were killed by the same racist imperialist forces which killed Patrice Lumumba.

The entry onto the African scene of the Chinese Communists has required a re-evaluation of much that everyone has said and believed about Communism in Africa. As has been noted already, though cautious in practice, the Chinese have a stake in revolution for its own sake if for no other reason than to gain adherents in their struggle with Moscow. Being Asian gives them a different racial image in African eyes than that of the West or of European Communists. This indeed is what the Soviets (and the Yugoslavs and the West as well) really fear most. The Chinese have been quiet but assiduous in cultivating relations with Africa. Chou En-lai during his ten-nation trip in Africa in 1963–64 adjusted his line to the African desire for stability and economic development. His economic projects were practical and his terms generous. Much of his claim that China's aid programs were in themselves nonpolitical were genuine, despite subsequent direct Chinese meddling in the affairs of many African states. His technicians work hard and live inexpensively and unobtrusively, and a number of victories have already been won in the war for diplomatic recognition vis-à-vis Taiwan. But the possibilities of Chinese aid really do not worry China's foes very much. The Soviet Union and its allies, to say nothing of the Western powers, have more to offer in economic and technical assistance. For those African leaders who want stability in order to consolidate revolutions already made, Red China is a disturbing threat. But the racial issue remains hidden dynamite.

There is no evidence that the Chinese are any more popular in Africa because of their skin color than Europeans, Arabs or Indians. In North Africa they are more alien than Europeans, and in black Africa it is a toss-up. A stranger is a stranger. Nor do they usually seek to exploit their race through the use of openly antiwhite propaganda. But they make the point just as clearly by indirection. They harp on the theme of Afro–Asian–Latin American solidarity and refer to the Soviet Union as a European power. They bear down on the notion that the real division of the world is between proletarian and wealthy nations, between what Henry Wallace and others have called the low-protein- and high-protein-diet peoples, between South and North rather than East and West. This is the doctrine in essence of African Marxists such as the late Frantz Fanon.

The implications are obvious, and obviously racial. The Soviets have long been wary of the racial aspects of Pan-Africanism. Bourgeois nationalism, though tactically acceptable, is dangerous enough in itself, but anything which splits the working class along racial lines necessarily terrifies the Soviets. What the Soviets fear is not only that Africans will discover that Russians too are white and class them with Europeans and Americans politically as well as racially; they fear the Chinese global strategy of creating a nonwhite international, under the acceptably Marxian guise of building an alliance of the proletarian nations and the pure Leninists against the revisionists.

Such an alliance is foreshadowed by the Chinese welcoming of Indonesian withdrawal from the United Nations added to their own indifference to membership, something which some observers see as laying the groundwork for a new, racially oriented world body. Such an alliance would destroy Russian leadership of Communism throughout the globe save perhaps for their immediate European neighbors. The Soviet leaders expect that they will lose battles for leadership in some countries sheerly because of the geographic propinquity of China and its power, but Chinese moves into Africa are a signal that the Communist ideological war is being joined on a global scale.

The effect of all this on Africa is problematical. The Chinese may be going through the same sequence of relations with Africa as the West and the Russians have. Aid projects that start out well can yet fail. There are already complaints about Chinese failure to line up fully to their commitments. Students may or may not find useful training and lack of discrimination in China (and present evidence indicates they are finding neither). All honeymoons come to an end.

But the Chinese are bolder than their predecessors. Though

their tactics are cautious their strategy is not. They have nothing to lose (save frightening other Africans) through overthrowing some of the pets of the West or the Soviet Union if as a result they can install governments more friendly to themselves. They aided Algeria when Khrushchev, playing anti-NATO politics and unwilling to anger De Gaulle, dared not. They have no interest in Europe, no détente with the West to preserve, and less fear of triggering a global military confrontation. America is already on their doorstep in the Far East. Conflict in Africa might relieve rather than add to the pressures on them.

African reactions to Chinese initiatives have been mixed. At first the existence of another party to the game of competitive aid and concessions seemed to be to Africa's advantage, someone else to play off against the others. But the game has suddenly grown fast, high-staked, confusing and very rough. After the murder of their prime minister, Burundi unceremoniously expelled the Chinese embassy that had done much, though not as much as reputed in the West, to feed the fires of rebellion in the Congo. The virtual Chinese takeover of the former French Congo during 1965 has awakened many to the danger of letting the Chinese onto the field at all; Brazzaville became a city of fear, with members of Chinese-inspired youth gangs brutally murdering even cabinet officials deemed hostile to their cause.

Recently the leaders of French-speaking Africa led by Houphouët-Boigny have, despite De Gaulle's silence and inaction concerning Peking's infiltration into his back yard, denounced Chinese interference in no uncertain terms. Other leaders such as Kenyatta are taking the hint. The public proclamation by the Kenya government in May, 1965, of the African socialism manifesto written by Tom Mboya coincided with several declarations by President Kenyatta that Kenya was not open to subversion from either East or West, and an increasing if possibly temporary political eclipse of Vice-President Odinga. Chou En-lai was handsomely greeted by Tanzania in June, 1965, when he returned President Nyerere's previous state visit to China. But though his attacks on the United States and his call for revolutions in Africa which China would be happy to support were listened to with respectful attention, Nyerere took the occasion to reiterate explicitly his nation's nonalignment and determination to remain independent from all foreign control. Nonetheless a trade agreement designed to substitute Chinese imports for many of the things Tanzania now imports from Kenya (which had confiscated a Chinese arms shipment being transported from Tanzania to Uganda) was negotiated during this visit. The Soviet Union by making a major effort to be invited to the Afro-Asian summit conference scheduled to be held in Algiers in 1965 demonstrated its intention to compete with China in Africa and to seek to reduce Chinese influence there.

But China is a major power. Though not rich it has fully recovered from the disaster of the "great leap forward," and what is a little to China economically can be a great deal to a small African nation. China can no more be completely kept out of Africa than can Russia or the West, as long as Africa is disunited. Not only is China's activity a reminder of the danger of nonalignment which seeks to turn the East-West struggle to African advantage by pitting the contestants against each other, but Chinese penetration is another, perhaps the penultimate reminder of the dangers facing Africa unless it can decide what being African means, as a first step toward seizing control of its own destiny.

XVII

AFRICA AND THE UNITED STATES

The American flag has never flown over any political dominion in Africa, yet no nation has been more involved in African history than the United States. Current American concern with Africa, whatever form it may eventually take, is natural and inevitable, and represents but another turning in a continuing historical cycle of American interest and disinterest in that continent.

The reason for American involvement is simple. Like so much which concerns Africa it is a matter of race. For centuries Africa's contacts with the outside world were determined by the existence, growth and decline of slavery in the New World, and this relationship has left a human bond among the continents. Former Foreign Minister Jaja Wachuku of Nigeria is fond of noting that Nigeria is the only country in the world with a larger Negro population than the United States.

American law and custom generally define as Negro anyone with one great-grandparent of African descent, that is, anyone who is one-sixteenth Negro. This fact is not merely a curious if distressing sidelight on that racism which is so fundamental a social force in America; it has had significant consequences for international politics, for it has given the Negro subcommunity in the United States a size and persistence it might not otherwise possess.

In the long and sordid history of slavery most African slaves came not to the American colonies but to South and Central America and the Caribbean. At the time of the American Revolution something like one-third of the population of the thirteen colonies was black, but this proportion soon declined; in the nineteenth century Negroes continued to outnumber whites in Brazil as well as in numerous nations of the Caribbean. However, during that same century the great wave of European immigration to the United States, Brazil, Argentina and elsewhere reduced the proportion of persons of African descent in the population virtually everywhere in the hemisphere. But the consequences of this change varied. In Latin America, where racism as an ideology (as opposed to the simple fact of discrimination) was not nearly so prevalent as in the United States, Negroes were largely integrated into the general population. In most areas those of mixed blood could, if economically fortunate, climb to complete social acceptance. But in the United States anyone of mixed ancestry remained irrevocably a Negro unless, as often happened, this heritage could be hidden and he or she could "pass" into the white community. The result has been that although Negro stock has been important throughout Latin America (five African languages are still spoken by small groups in the backlands of Brazil) the United States is the only major nation in the Americas with a large, identifiable, politically relevant Negro community of potential importance in relations between Africa and the rest of the world.

Slavery therefore did more than establish a demographic bond between the United States and Africa. It laid the basis for an American Negro interest in Africa which has waxed and waned throughout the years. The American Negro has been torn between assimilation in America and identification with Africa in a manner exhibiting striking if not complete parallels with the problems of American Jews vis-à-vis America and Israel, despite the fact that for Jews to become assimilated in America is, of course, infinitely easier. Early in the course of the American Negro's search for *his* identity, the issue of Zionism arose: should Negroes not only identify with and support Africa but return to Africa as Jews are urged by Zionists to return to Israel?

As early as 1788 a Negro group in Newport, Rhode Island, was proposing that Negro freedmen return to Africa. During the period prior to the Civil War there was widespread interest in Africa among those Negroes in a position to express themselves. The term Afro-American was widely used as a self-designation, and moves to settle Negroes in Liberia in the 1820's and thereafter secured considerable support among freedmen's groups as well as among white philanthropists and some whites who hoped to reduce the free Negro population by shipping them back to Africa. Liberia was a lodestar of Negro aspirations, and though Southern interests prevented its diplomatic recognition by the United States prior to the Reconstruction era it long enjoyed a special American governmental patronage in international affairs.

During the pre-Civil War period there began a three-cornered relationship among Negroes in the United States, the West Indies and Africa which has long fallen into desuetude but may yet revive as Negro political forces in the Caribbean gain self-confidence and Negroes in Barbados, the Bahamas and other British islands throw over more than three hundred years of white minority rule. Edward Blyden, an early proponent of West African nationalism, was born on St. Thomas in the Virgin Islands in 1832. He went to Liberia only after failing to get into college in the United States, and returned here on several occasions as a lecturer. After the Civil War West Indians began to migrate to the United States, where they provided important leadership within the Negro community, especially in business, a role which has declined only since the 1920's.

It was prior to the Civil War that Afro-Americans began the

missionary activities in Africa which, along with their closely related role in educating Africans in American Negro colleges, helped inspire the first stirrings of Westernization and nationalism in many areas of Africa. This role reached its height in later years, despite a general decline in American Negro interest in Africa, but the groundwork had been laid early.

The mid-nineteenth century marks a watershed in African-American relations. A large American trade with Africa—both West and East Africa—had flourished during the era of the clipper ships. It was a period during which legitimate trade predominated over the slave trade, illegal to the United States since 1808. Americans began to trade with Zanzibar in 1825 and predominated in commerce there for decades, while Liberia had a merchant marine which traded with the Western hemisphere. The Civil War sped the decline of this trade as did the spread of European colonialism and restrictionist policies, but the most important factor was the steam engine, which gradually replaced sail, hurting American foreign commerce generally and destroying Liberia as an international trader. After the Civil War, American interest turned to the Pacific and the past trading relations with Africa were virtually forgotten.

The post-Civil War period led to a turning inward of the American Negro community. The collapse of Reconstruction and the birth of Jim Crow focused Negro attention on the need to become accepted as equals in the American community. At the same time Africa was falling prey to the full force of colonialism. The great era of the slave trade had, strangely enough, been an era of equality between African and European traders and trading communities. Suppression of the trade and European political dominion over Africa now went hand in hand. Partially as a justification, conscious or subconscious, of colonization the colonial nations and their nationals spread exaggerated and even fictitious stories of African barbarism and savagery. The disorganization caused by the slave trade, especially in East Africa, was used as a measure of black unfitness for self-rule.

This propaganda had an effect not only in Britain, Europe and Africa, but also in America, and therefore among American Negroes. Under slavery, light skin color was a mark of high status: the illegitimate children of white masters became house servants, who were better treated than field slaves and sometimes (prior to the hysteria immediately preceding the Civil War) even received some education. Now the systematic denigration of things African reinforced and rationalized this color hierarchy among Negroes. To be light was good; to be dark—to be African—was bad. Most Negroes sought to be as like whites in appearance and manners as possible and eschewed anything reminiscent of their African heritage.

Now the tide is turning, though the problem of identification for American Negroes cannot be solved apart from Africa's own resolution of the conflict between the glorification of tradition and the acceptance of modernity. The new American Negro pride in things African has even led to some tendency to rewrite history and to overemphasize the extent to which a few lonely voices in the Negro community spoke up for Africa in decades past.

In this previous affirmation of Africa two names stand out—W. E. B. Du Bois and Carter G. Woodson. Du Bois's fame has overshadowed that of Woodson because of Du Bois's role in Pan-Africanism and in the founding of the National Association for the Advancement of Colored People. His famous lines in *The Souls of Black Folk,* written in 1903, have been rightly held to be prophetic, how prophetic only the future can tell: "The problem of the twentieth century is the problem of the color line—the relation of the darker to the lighter races of men in Asia and Africa, in America and the islands of the sea." Du Bois was influential in spreading pride in their race among Negroes; *The Crisis,* the official journal of the NAACP, gave much attention to African affairs from its inception. But Du Bois was a publicist and political agitator, not a historian. The scholarly groundwork for pride in their racial past, in both Africa and the Americans, was the work of the Negro academic

Carter G. Woodson. He founded the Association for the Study of Negro Life and History in 1915 and Negro History Week in 1926, and was the great popularizer of Africa among American Negroes. But Africa, like jazz, while it might be glorified by the writers of the "black renaissance" of the 1920's, was generally anathema to the middle-class leadership of the Negro community.

Despite the general American Negro disinterest in Africa throughout the period from the Civil War to World War I, American Negro churches and schools were in constant contact with Africa, receiving inspiration from Africa and stimulating African leadership. Proud of alumni such as Nkrumah and Azikiwe, Lincoln University can point to the presence of African students before the turn of the century. But a basic ambivalence continued to dominate American Negro attitudes toward Africa. In the 1920's, Marcus Garvey, a Jamaican by birth, founded the United Negro Improvement Association, with a platform emphasizing black separatism and return to Africa. Garvey, according to Nkrumah, was the most important single influence on his later life. However, at the time, Garvey's activities were resented by the assimilationist Negro leadership in the United States and found a following only among the masses. The financial collapse of the movement and Garvey's deportation in 1927 were hardly regretted by most Negro leaders.

The same impulses toward hoped-for acceptance by white America which led to the rejection of Garveyism were also responsible for the failure of Communism to make headway among the American Negro community, despite the economic and social disabilities under which it suffered. Against the wishes of its American leadership, the American Communist party in 1929 was forced by Stalin's interpretation of Lenin's doctrine on the "nationalities question" to adopt a platform of racial separation for the United States, coming out for a republic controlled by Negroes consisting of the "black belt" states of the South. This major blunder split the party and denied it access to major Negro support during the critical depression years of the early 1930's.

Even American Negroes who were concerned with Africa were not always sure just where they stood. Liberia was an especially touchy issue. It was revered by Negroes as the only free African nation; the Lone Star Republic was living proof that Negroes could rule themselves. But how well? Even Negroes conscious of the low standards of life and government in Liberia blamed them, not entirely without justice, on external pressures and supported Liberia against its enemies. Ethiopia was thought of as black, and much of the pseudo-historical glorification of the African past which preceded more sound historical verification of the real accomplishments of precolonial Africa focused on Ethiopia. It was important symbolically among Negroes in the United States and South Africa, as the use of "Abyssinian" and "Ethiopian" in the names of many Negro churches and organizations attests. However, the general attitude of the Ethiopian ruling class was that they were not Negroes but "Hamites" (a position which has only recently changed as a result of Ethiopia's political aims in postcolonial Africa) and American Negroes felt rebuffed and resentful as they became aware of Ethiopian sentiments. The Italian invasion in 1936, however, caused American Negroes to rally to the support of the Emperor and his embattled nation.

In general, though, American Negroes were only marginally more concerned with Africa than were white Americans prior to World War II, and whites were very little concerned. Africa was the special province of a few educators (the Phelps-Stokes Fund worked in Africa as well as among American Negroes), churchmen and intellectuals. Africa had almost dropped out of American sight.

The reasons for this are not hard to find. Most of America's population came from Europe. It was with Europe that she traded and engaged in a love-hate relationship based on common ancestry. Involvement in Europe's quarrels seemed unavoidable. America had commercial and political interests in the Far

East. Latin America rose and fell in American consciousness, although economic and political ties were constant and growing. But Africa? Africa was a land of savages, happily now under enlightened European control.

Even American missionaries (and American Protestant churches were quite active in many parts of Africa) helped spread the dominant attitude of superiority and indifference to African aspirations. On the scene many of them might seek to defend "native" rights against European rulers, but they too regarded the African as uncivilized and debauched and sought support from congregations at home by evoking a picture of the African as ignorant, unclothed, diseased and generally benighted.

American businessmen had little concern with Africa. American investments were primarily in mining in white South or Central Africa, and were little noted by the public. Firestone had come to Liberia in 1923 in order to grow its own rubber on a large scale. It later reorganized Liberia's difficult and politically embarrassing fiscal position, and for a time the Firestone plantation was Liberia's dominant economic activity. But mines and rubber plantations were virtually the only economic ties between the United States and Africa. The missionaries and businessmen and their relatives were never sufficiently numerous or cohesive to become the African equivalent of the "old China hands" so important in shaping and enlarging the American role in the Far East.

The American academic community likewise gave virtually no attention to Africa. Political scientists, highly legalistic and historical in their bent, generally restricted their attention to government in the United States and Europe. Sociologists were concerned almost exclusively with American social problems. Historians saw Africa only as a minor aspect of European imperialism and dealt with it only at second hand. Anthropologists, with the important exception of Melville Herskovits, were too busy about "New World" matters to concern themselves with Africa. American academic knowledge of Africa, such as it was, was mainly secondary, coming primarily from British sources, since academics shared the general American distaste for learning foreign languages usably well.

The American government had no diplomatic representatives in Africa save in Liberia (essentially a patronage post tied to American Negro politics), South Africa, and in Ethiopia prior to the Italian conquest and consular representatives were few. Before 1956 the African "desk" was part of a catchall Near East, South Asia and African division of the State Department, but for all practical purposes Africa was simply an extension of Europe.

World War II did little immediately to alter the picture. North Africa was a useful steppingstone to Italy and Europe. The United States increased its involvement in Liberia by building the airport at Robertsfield as part of a global air net that undercut the Axis-dominated Mediterranean. Most important, the American atomic bomb was made entirely of uranium from the Belgian Congo, uranium which local technicians had presciently mined and sent to New York for storage. But few Americans were or are even today conscious of these developments.

African independence broke upon the American consciousness with an even greater suddenness than on the consciousness of Britons or Europeans. The citizens of the colonial powers had relatives in the colonies, had seen African students, had read news dispatches about their colonial possessions, or, if nothing else, heard of them in school. If they did not know that the colonies were stirring, they at least knew that they existed.

Not only were Americans ignorant about Africa but change in Africa posed a basic dilemma for American policy, analogies of which still haunt it throughout the world. The ignorance could be cured; the dilemma could not be as easily resolved. For the United States is essentially a status quo power in a world of change. Her problem was and is how to make inevitable and perhaps desirable change in the rest of the world compatible with a domestic situation and world position with which she is basically satisfied.

It is difficult to discuss the shifts in American knowledge of Africa and the shifts in American policy independently, since to a large extent greater American knowledge of Africa went hand in hand with more political interest in it and, in a more subtle way, more American knowledge has meant greater sympathy with African nationalist aspirations, although a period of increasing disillusion may now be setting in.

The American academic community early responded to the challenge of postwar Africa. The war years had already set a pattern for area studies, and with government and foundation support similar programs were set up in the postwar period to deal with Africa. Northwestern and Boston universities pioneered in this field, and a host of others followed. While a crop of young academics trained as Africanists was in production, older academics extended their interests in Africa or shifted their attention there. In a few years the United States had a large and growing body of professionals concerned with Africa, whose status was formalized with the organization in 1959 of the African Studies Association, now numbering several hundred members.

Government, too, began to enlarge its interests. In 1958 a Bureau of African Affairs was set up in the State Department. Africa had come into its own. The status of Africa was given further prominence with the nomination of G. Mennen Williams, a prominent political figure in his own right, as Assistant Secretary of State for African Affairs by President John F. Kennedy. Meantime the State Department was feverishly training young and retraining older men as African specialists, and changing the image of an African assignment from a misfortune or a punishment to an opportunity for achievement.

As usual, the American press lagged behind. True to its tradition of allowing few reporters to stay in any foreign area long enough to know it well, it occasionally covered big stories in a sensational manner, and gave African dispatches increasing space and prominence, but it failed to develop a corps of men who could report Africa with the authority of its Washington or European experts or of African specialists on many European journals.

But while the academic experts might, either because of personal involvement with Africa and Africans or their more generally "liberal" bent, press the United States for a more "pro-African" foreign policy, and some State Department people might privately or publicly agree, American policy remained caught on the horns of the basic Cold War dilemma. The U.S. is by verbal tradition an anticolonial power, and it wished the political friendship of developing nations in Africa as elsewhere, but it was also the leader of NATO, and the major colonial powers were its allies in the Cold War.

It was this commitment to NATO, and thus to retaining the friendship and strength of America's allies in NATO, which was the major force conditioning American policy toward Africa in the years immediately following World War II and the formal establishment of NATO in 1948. To some extent this commitment involved acceptance of the assumptions of the "Eurafrican" point of view: that strategic bases in Africa would be useful in any future war against the Soviet Union, and that the economic unity of Africa and Europe was to America's advantage, since the economic resources of Africa would be in the hands of powers allied to the United States. The subsequent evolution of American policy is traceable less to any increase in American sympathies for the cause of independence in the abstract (though the sympathies were there and growing) than to factors which caused alterations in these basic assumptions.

One of these factors was of course the actual progress of Africa toward independence. The United States watched this development largely as a spectator, but drew from it the obvious conclusions. If the strategic bases and resources of Africa were to be increasingly in African hands, any power which wanted access to them had better be on as good terms as possible with the African nations. This conclusion was in conformity with a general belief that influenced American policy toward the whole underdeveloped world: the notion that the underdeveloped countries somehow held the balance of power in the East-West struggle and that economic and political ties with them must be forged even at the expense of the feelings of the colonial powers which had lost these areas. This point of view had a basic flaw, however. It assumed that, once freed, the new nations would be interested, in effect, in rejoining the Western side in the Cold War, albeit now as free and equal partners.

Morocco early demonstrated the fallacy of this assumption. Despite American aid projects which had as their *raison d'être* less economic development than bribery, Morocco's position in the Casablanca bloc eventually forced the United States to abandon the expensive air bases which it had built there under French aegis and which it had hoped to retain after Moroccan independence. Elsewhere the United States was more fortunate. Libya, a major recipient of American economic aid, permitted the American Strategic Air Command to retain its base at Wheelus Field, which until the revolutionary discovery of oil made the single most important contribution to the economy—although by 1964 internal political developments in Libya, strongly influenced by Nasser and the Arab League, were making the American position increasingly untenable. Ethiopia has also allowed the United States to make some use of its territory, and a major communications installation in former Eritrea plays an important role in American global strategy.

Most African nations of course need markets badly and will sell their products to the highest bidder, so the end of colonial control did not affect the economic relationship of Africa with the West insofar as strategic materials were concerned. But the basic fact remained that Africa under independent nationalist leadership could not be counted on as being within the Western camp in the same way in which it had been before, and the need for trade rubbed both ways, since independent Africa was willing to engage in close commercial relations with the Soviet bloc and make its resources available to the Communist powers on the same terms as to the West. So far trade with the Communist powers has not amounted to a great deal, but in so far as Africa's economic resources were a factor in the Cold War this represented a net loss to the West.

Similarly, there was always the potential danger that Africa might become a base for Communist forces once NATO control was lifted. This has proved to be even more of a chimera than the hope that Africa might act as a strategic base for the West, and no such bases ever came into existence.

Not only did the reality of African independence and nonalignment cause a change in American policy toward Africa, but this policy was also affected by a slow, almost glacial change in America's fundamental thinking about world politics. While the United States continued to urge the peoples of the world to choose up sides in a global struggle between good and evil (despite the overt repudiation of the Dulles doctrine that neutralism was immoral), the previous sense of urgency about individual nations and regions lessened as a result of the gradual realization of some basic strategic facts of life. Increasingly it was recognized that a major war between the United States and the Soviet Union would be one in which the underdeveloped nations, including those of Africa, would play little part. In an era when war with intercontinental ballistic missiles carrying nuclear weapons would first be signaled by suspicious radar sightings and would begin with massive destruction, the economic and manpower resources and the bases of Africa would be irrelevant. So too would be African public opinion. Communist successes in Africa might tempt the Soviets to military adventurism that could lead to war by overstimulating their confidence, just as it might tempt some Americans to wish to undertake a "preventive" war by stimulating their despair, but in any future war once the ICBM's were launched no one would care where Africa's allegiance lay.

The third factor influencing American policy was the existence and importance of the United Nations and of the African contingent within it. The American instinct was to support anticolonialism in principle but to be conservative about applying the principle, and to avoid specific stands in a continent where it had virtually no specific interests. Yet the very workings of the UN forced the United States to take stands (even abstentions have political significance and repercussions) on every issue that came up and thus to make decisions on matters which in traditional diplomacy it would not have been concerned with. All of these themes—American difficulty in choosing between its NATO allies and its putative African friends, growing American doubts about the strategic significance of Africa, and a mild anticolonialism which the U.S. sought to keep on a general level—are evident in the history of American policy statements concerning Africa and in American actions in the United Nations.

The Atlantic Charter had the same impact on Africans that Wilson's Fourteen Points had had on many Europeans and on the founders of the First Pan African Congress. It gave them hope that the Allies, including the United States, were fighting for a postwar world in which self-determination and democracy would be the rule. Specific American policy statements subsequent to this general propaganda document were largely in the form of tempering qualifications, and, prior to 1958 at least, they all revolved around a single point—that all ought to be free, but only when they were ready. Thus Secretary of State Cordell Hull in 1942 said: "All peoples . . . who are prepared and willing to accept the responsibility of liberty, are entitled to its enjoyment."

As applied to the colonial peoples of Africa this posed a basic problem. They might be willing to accept the responsibilities of freedom, but who was to say whether they were prepared—they or their colonial masters? If it rested with themselves, they were ready immediately. If it rested with their masters, they might never be considered ready. But suppose some objective observer concluded that in fact they were not prepared. How could they prepare themselves? Would the colonial powers prepare them? Not very likely as we have seen. No one was really prepared until nationalist pressures, if not locally then continentwide, made independence inevitable. Tying freedom to preparedness was to deprive it of any immediate relevance and to place it in a distant as well as hypothetical future.

By the 1950's American statements on Africa were becoming more frequent and important because Africa was becoming more important, and being given more and higher-level attention in American government. Nonetheless, the "yes but" line remained dominant. The United States was for independence, but emphasis was placed on the dangers of premature independence, and American overseas representatives were wont to make pro-colonialist statements as late as 1958. In 1957 Vice-President Richard Nixon made a tour of eight African capitals. One apparent motive and result was to increase American—especially governmental—interest in Africa and to shake up American representation there, but by continually talking of the "Battle for Men's Minds" and the dangers of Communism in Africa Nixon so placed this reforming urge within the context of the Cold War that Africans might be pardoned some cynicism about any new policy which might result.

The year 1958 was crucial in the history of American policy toward Africa. It marked the last major use of the theme of the dangers of "premature independence" by a major State Department figure and the initiation of a new tone and rhetoric at least in American policy. This resulted in part from the efforts of the Department's Bureau of African Affairs, although its first head, Mr. Joseph Satterthwaite, was hardly a fiery exponent of African nationalist causes. The year 1958 also reflected a growing change of attitude in the United States generally, a rising sympathy for African causes that was to have a brief efflorescence in the New Frontier of President Kennedy, who as a Senator had annoyed the French by his vocal support for Algerian independence.

Even Secretary of State John Foster Dulles was becoming more open to change. In November, 1958, he stated that the United States supported political independence for "all peoples who desire it and who are able to undertake its responsibilities. We have encouraged it and we rejoice in its evolution." The first part was the traditional American line, but the following sentence sounded a more positive note. In April, 1960, Mr. Satterthwaite put his rhetorical finger on the practical crux of the old argument about readiness, saying he believed it to be "an almost academic question. Peoples tend to acquire independence, ready or not, according to a time table of their own making." In September of that year outgoing President Eisenhower, addressing the United Nations, called upon the members "to respect the African peoples' right to choose their own way of life and to determine for themselves the course they are to follow." American policy regarding the desire of Africans for freedom had reached its full evolution, at least at the verbal level. Eisenhower's next words, however, were to introduce a new theme which was to have much more resonance in the future, for he also called on UN members to "refrain from intervening in these new nations' internal affairs . . . by subversion, force, propaganda or other means." Secretary of State Christian Herter, who replaced the deceased Dulles, gave the finishing touch to the initiatives of the Eisenhower administration by attacking President Nkrumah of Ghana for his violent anticolonial rhetoric in the United Nations. The incident, and talk in official Washington about Ghana's "pro-Communist" foreign policy, were soon glossed over, but they sounded a note which was to be heard again in the Johnson administration: American anger at being included within the ranks of condemned colonialists by nations which, according to our view at least, we had sought to aid and support.

The brief Kennedy administration represented what in retrospect may seem an ill-fated honeymoon in American relations with Africa. The young president had the reputation of being pro-African, and his Assistant Secretary of State for Africa, Governor Williams, had been active in civil-rights politics in the United States and now transferred much of his enthusiasm to the cause of African nationalism, much to the public annoyance of African colonial and settler regimes and the private annoyance and cynicism of many of his colleagues in Washington. Also noted for sympathy to the cause of African nationalism was the ebullient and energetic Peace Corps director, R. Sargent Shriver, a powerful figure because of his intimate White House connections. Above all, there was the new President himself. His youthfulness and *joie de vivre* struck a responsive chord in African leaders, whom he made a special point of inviting to the White House. Under his administration ambassadorships in Africa often went to younger men not out of the usual State Department mold. His tragic death saddened Africans of virtually all persuasions, the masses as well as their leaders. Their readiness to believe the legend that he had been killed by right-wing forces enabled them to retain their admiration for him as their relations with America cooled—indeed to accept his death as one of the causal factors in the change.

American diplomacy in the United Nations was strengthened by the appointment of Adlai Stevenson as our ambassador. His role as an opponent of Dulles and Eisenhower and his world travels gave him prestige and a reputation for honesty and sympathy among most rulers of developing nations, including those of Africa. He had to trade much on that reputation, which of course suffered as relations between the United States and the new nations declined, since American policy in recent years has not, from the point of view of African nationalists, advanced over that of the closing years of the Eisenhower administration and if anything has fallen behind the march of events, while the Congo rebellion has added new sources of disagreement.

In the late 1950's the United States, after much hesitation, began to take a position more favorable to the point of view of

African nationalists than to that of its NATO allies, but even so its major effort was devoted to finding a position both could support, and heading off Soviet-backed resolutions embodying the most extreme nationalist demands. The United States has opposed what it regards as injustices in Portuguese rule in its African territories, but has rejected what it considers extremist proposals to force Portugal to mend her ways. Mindful of its residual strategic interest in the Azores and unwilling to see changes anywhere made through force, it has taken a stand increasingly unsatisfactory to African leaders.

United States support for "self-determination" of Portuguese Africa, enunciated by Ambassador Stevenson in 1961, was reiterated by Secretary Williams in mid-1965. It accepts the principle of popular sovereignty without taking a theoretical stand in favor of independence, and many Africans suspect our position reflects American concern over the status of Puerto Rico and consider America to be unrealistic or disingenuous in its claims that the arms it sends to Portugal through NATO are not being used against the rebels. Similarly the United States has spoken in favor of popular sovereignty if not precisely of majority rule in what is now Rhodesia. Although the United States would not do anything to force Britain's hand there, it would undoubtedly wish her to remain firm in resisting white-settler demands for independence. But here again, as in the case of Portuguese Africa, this is not enough for African nationalists who have been putting strong pressure on Britain to somehow force a change in Rhodesia.

With regard to the overriding problem of South Africa, again the United States seems to have been slow in catching up with African opinion, and once having caught up, is now again lagging behind. After many years of accepting the argument that South African racial policies were a domestic South African matter, the United States in 1961 sharply reversed its policy and bitterly condemned apartheid in the United Nations. It has also consistently voted against the South African position on South-West Africa. On the other hand, the United States has just as consistently voted against imposing sanctions of any kind against South Africa (though it has refused to sell military equipment to her) and has voted against throwing South Africa out of various subsidiary UN bodies. The American position is that nothing will be accomplished by isolating South Africa, that it is still possible to influence her, and that isolation will only stiffen resistance and make communication more difficult. Such positions are increasingly deplored and resented by African nationalists.

But Africans no longer condemn the United States just for choosing NATO allies over Africans in clashes of interest between them nor for being soft on white minority rule. The United States is now the target of African wrath in her own right, largely as a result of the American role in the Congo. Early opposition in the UN between the American position on the UN Congo operation and that of the Casablanca powers gave way after Lumumba's death to harmony on the question of supporting Léopoldville against Tshombe's Katanga. But the African states most involved in the Congo continued to hate Tshombe and supported the rebellion against him in 1964, in heart if not always in deed. American support of the Tshombe government was deeply resented. The last straw was the American role in the airdrop of Belgian paratroops in Stanleyville in December of 1964, an action which most Africans saw as a simple case of whites killing blacks because blacks threatened whites. At the same time the United States has become increasingly disenchanted with neutralism in general. President Kennedy was bitterly disappointed by what he considered the wholesale parroting of the Communist line on world affairs by states attending the conference of nonaligned nations in Belgrade in 1961, and the Johnson administration has shown increasingly little patience with what it regards as misunderstanding and hostility from such quarters.

The United States rushed to recognize the new states (with the exception of Guinea), causing an inflation of American representation in Africa in place of previous neglect. But for a long time Africa was the neglected continent as far as foreign aid was concerned. The United States had to be cautious about intruding until nations became sovereign, of course, but even after independence tried to let Britain and France carry most of the burden, not wishing to push them out or to appear to do so. Early American aid programs in Africa were dictated by special considerations, primarily connected with the Cold War. As late as 1961, the bulk of aid went to Morocco, Libya, Ethiopia and, of course, Liberia. But soon aid missions and programs proliferated throughout the continent, with activity in French-speaking areas lagging somewhat behind because of French government hostility and lack of sufficient linguistically qualified personnel. It was early decided, with some misgivings, that the United States would make not political friendship but economic needs and potential the prime consideration in allocating aid, and in 1961 for instance it made good on an earlier tentative commitment to provide massive support for Ghana's Volta Dam project, despite Ghana's anti-American line in foreign policy. It also actively wooed Guinea and quietly gave military aid to Mali, also a Casablanca power, hoping to keep open the lines of communication. American aid continued to be given on a large scale to Ethiopia, despite its acceptance of Russian aid. In its earliest days in 1961 the Peace Corps concentrated on Africa. Its first project anywhere was in Tanganyika, and it made early and large-scale teacher commitments to Ghana and Nigeria. Though it is more active than ever in Africa, with Peace Corps teachers a major factor in the educational systems of nations such as Ethiopia, its focus of interest has followed the general drift of American policy and shifted to Latin America.

American foreign-aid philosophy has always been torn between giving massive aid to a few countries, hoping to get them to the point of self-sustaining economic growth, and spreading aid around to all who need it, more superficially appealing from a humanitarian point of view, but a policy which tends to solve the problems of no one. The American point of view in recent years, influenced by Chester Bowles among others, has shifted to the showplace, concentration-of-effort concept. India is its prime example in Asia, while in Africa both economic and political considerations have meant highest priorities to friendly Tunisia and giant Nigeria. Some form of aid is now being given to every independent nation in Africa. Some of these aid activities are large, but most are holding operations designed to demonstrate American good will and to maintain contacts should the money or occasion present itself when expansion might seem practicable.

Currently the whole position of foreign aid as an instrument of American foreign policy is under re-examination. The Johnson administration's budget request of 1965 for the Agency for International Development was the lowest in recent years, and this can be accounted for only in part by a desire on the part of the administration to use "pre-shrunk" figures as a matter of legislative tactics. Even the Kennedy-appointed Clay committee suggested reduction in American aid commitments, and concentration on Latin America, while letting Britain and France with their greater experience and trade connections carry the ball in Africa. Most of Africa's trade is after all with Europe, and the EEC, with which numerous African states are associated, is in part anti-American in motivation and impact. The United States has supplies of tropical raw materials within its own borders, in areas such as the Philippines in which it has a special interest, and in Latin America. All these factors seriously hamper American ability to help Africa through increased trade, and aid programs not geared to trading opportunities are largely futile.

But the signs of impending or possible American withdrawal from the major role she seemed on the verge of playing in Africa can only be read in the light of trends in world politics as a whole and in American politics. The United States has been turning inward as a result of the détente with the Soviet Union and the reassertion of European political independence. Lyndon Johnson has focused much of its attention on building a great society at home, while Castro and the Dominican Republic have made it acutely aware of problems in what it considers its own back yard. While all this has been going on there has been rising disenchantment with Africa—partly in reaction to the Congo crisis, partly as one element in the new wave of American distaste for neutralism. A new low point in African-American relations was reached in 1964 when bitter attacks against the United States in the UN as racist and imperialist, underlined by denunciations and anti-American demonstrations throughout the African and nonaligned worlds, brought forth an equally bitter counter-accusation of black racism from Ambassador Stevenson on the UN floor. It was evident to everyone in Washington that the sharp edge of the American response could be credited to the fact that it was the culmination of long-pent-up emotions of resentment toward Africans and the underdeveloped world generally which had been crackling in the atmosphere like lightning waiting to strike and had finally found a ground. Whether the cathartic effect of Stevenson's speech, for the American public and for American officialdom, has cleared the air or marks the beginning of a new and unhappy era in American relations with Africa remains to be seen.

The future depends partly on the character of American domestic politics. It is by no means coincidental that the American civil-rights movement has entered a new and hopefully a terminal phase in the same years that the African nations have gained their independence. The Supreme Court's desegregation decision of 1954, of course, did more than any other single event to spur the drive for a "new equality." But the rise of African independence, beginning with Ghanaian sovereignty in 1957, not only provided a major lift to the morale of American Negroes, giving them a new pride in their African ancestry; the existence of self-governing black states pointed up the anomaly of the Negroes' subordinate position in American society.

An era in which African and American politics exerted a reciprocal influence on each other had begun. The rise to power of the new African states, especially in the United Nations, meant outside pressures for equality. Many African leaders have had first-hand experience of racial discrimination in the United States as well as in Africa and elsewhere. They and others have lifted their voices in criticism of discriminatory racial policies in the United States.

What had been primarily a domestic problem now became virtually an international one. In a world in which nonwhites are not only in a majority but, after Bandung, a politically semi-organized one, the argument was increasingly made in the United States that racial discrimination was not only wrong in principle but damaging to the American cause in the Cold War. Cases of discrimination against African diplomats in the United States became international incidents and moves to remove such discrimination redounded to the benefit of American Negroes. American criticism of apartheid in South Africa became more difficult to square with discrimination at home.

At the same time that African power in world affairs became a political and psychological lever for improving the position of the American Negro community, the increasing political strength of the American Negro was used to benefit Africa. Africa joined the classic three "I's" of American politics—Ireland, Italy and Israel—as a place to visit and to identify oneself with if one was an aspiring American politician from a major industrial state. American political and economic policy toward Africa now had to meet the criticisms of leading elements in the American Negro community, and some African leaders, realizing this, have quietly interested themselves in the internal politics of that community. American Negroes have formed, under white liberal inspiration, such organizations as the American Leadership Council on African Affairs to press their views on the American government. By late 1964 James Farmer of CORE was visiting Africa and criticizing American policy in the Congo. Generally American Negroes have tended to identify with the extreme African nationalist point of view on Tshombe and similar issues, and Ghana has become a symbol to defend against all critics, just as Liberia was for a previous generation.

Increasing interaction between Africa and the American Negro community has not been without its controversies. One major question has been whether Africans really liked and respected American Negroes. Negroes tend to insist that they have a special rapport with Africans based on a common racial background, while many Africans are privately highly critical of American Negroes, whom they regard as lacking in ability and in pride. The alleged greater suitability of Negroes for American government positions in Africa is still a debated question.

The impact of the continuing Congo crisis and the consequent exacerbation of relations between the United States government and African nationalism upon the American Negro community is difficult to assess as yet. The tales of bloodshed coming out of the Congo over several years may have lowered the prestige of Negroes among whites just as independence raised it. But more significant than any such possibility is the political impact events in the Congo may have among American Negroes, many of whose leaders find themselves in increasing disagreement with Washington over the country's African policies.

Even more potentially explosive is the situation in South Africa. A racial revolt there could have a major influence on race relations in the United States and especially on American Negro political attitudes. As of now Negroes, and white groups concerned with civil rights, are exerting increasing pressure for American leadership against apartheid, but if the issue rises in public importance whites who are less than enthusiastic about the civil-rights crusade can be counted on to be among the opponents of

American initiatives against South Africa. As yet the issue has little salience in American politics, but the potential is there and growing.

In the last analysis, despite what happens in Africa, the American Negro is most concerned with what happens at home. Negro criticism of the Johnson administration's Africa policy is muted because of its confidence that he may, to the surprise of many, turn out to be the president who leads the United States across the river into the promised land of racial equality. When Roy Wilkins of the NAACP returned from Africa recently to counsel that perhaps Tshombe was there to stay, many political observers saw a connection between the old guard Negro leadership's trust in the administration and its distaste not only for the more militant tactics of groups such as CORE and SNCC but also for these groups' willingness to link African and American politics. As long as the Negro march toward equality in this country continues unchecked, any administration will have great freedom of action in Africa.

The real crisis could come if frustration and disappointment at racial progress in the United States were linked with a situation in which the United States was actively involved in a struggle with African nationalism. What would happen if race war broke out in South Africa and American troops intervened to protect American lives, while the American government speculated about the political affiliations of the rebels, is chilling to contemplate.

United States policy toward Africa must ultimately be decided as part of a reappraisal of America's global responsibilities. American involvement in Vietnam (lack of African sympathy for which is a major contributor to the present coolness of African-United States relations) represents one possible answer to the question of where it is in American interest to intervene to check political developments considered as abetting the spread of Communism. American intervention in the Congo in 1964, however limited and tentative, was another, as those who at the time openly expressed the fear it would become an African Vietnam realized. Only through calm evaluation of our interests can future American policy toward Africa be decided. This difficult decision will be one in which all Americans will have to participate without regard to color or ancestry, and one which will tax the patience and judgment of all equally.

XVIII

AFRICA'S SEARCH AND AMERICA'S RESPONSE

This is a book about Africa's role in the world, written by an American. Insofar as distance lends perspective it may be of use in helping Africans to see themselves as some others see them. Hopefully it will help Americans to see Africa from a viewpoint which avoids the perils of both African and American ethnocentrism, using that term in its broadest political as well as cultural sense. Much has been said about Africa's past and Africa's future, and, as in all writing about human society that even pretends to relevance, value judgments have been implied and positions taken by the sheer necessity of choosing among subjects and among words with which to discuss them. It should not be amiss, indeed perhaps it is even required, that there be some overt summary of what the author considers Africa's choices to be. It is perhaps even more necessary to say a few words on how the author considers that American foreign policy can best serve the interests of the United States and of the new Africa—interests which are compatible but by no means identical, an obvious point but one often lost sight of by men of good will on both continents.

It is the central thesis of this book that Africa's activity in world affairs is the expression not merely or even primarily of a congeries of national states seeking to maximize their interests through international politics, but of a self-conscious cultural and political entity, still in the process of formation, an entity which like a growing human being can only find and define its personality, its existence, in terms of its relations with other entities.

What are the choices and what will be the consequences for Africa and for the world of choosing certain alternatives rather than others? Two of the choices have to do with economics: Shall the new Africa emphasize agriculture or industry? Shall it be a doctrinaire socialist or a mixed economy? At first appraisal industrialization would seem to be the best road for development. Africa has vast reserves of hydroelectric power and is rich in minerals, whereas its land is generally rather poor for agricultural purposes. It already possesses developed industrial complexes in South Africa, Zambia and the Congo. Like all developing areas, it is conscious that the terms of trade favor the industrial rather than the agricultural producer. But while a large degree of industrialization must take place in Africa—to diversify its economies, make optimum use of existing resources, and, at the psychological level, to help build national self-esteem—an overemphasis on industry could be disastrous.

Markets for manufactured goods sufficiently large and profitable to make it cheaper to produce them locally than to import them will be a long time developing. Most of Africa's already developed industrial capacity is in the extractive industries, and mineral prices are subject to the same problems as agricultural prices in world markets, while in time even the richest deposits become exhausted, leaving social and economic desolation in their wake. Africa is short on capital and long—getting longer as population increases sharply—on manpower. As automation necessarily assumes more importance in industrial production it will become more and more apparent that what Africa needs in this century is labor-intensive economic activities to absorb her surplus manpower, for social as well as economic reasons. Increased attention to agricultural productivity could do much both to solve the problem of growing unemployment and to provide an immediate improvement in living standards.

Agriculture has other advantages than the purely economic. It could be the basis of a class of peasant proprietors who would give Africa a social stability and a base for political diversity which it will sorely need in the future, taking the place of an as yet nonexistent and slow-to-appear class of indigenous entrepreneurs. Even in doctrinaire socialist states, an agriculture based on cooperatives as well as state farms could enhance human dignity by offering a large number of Africans experience in controlling their own immediate destinies by giving them an alternative to being absorbed in centralized state-run industries.

But, even beyond this, agriculture provides more scope for expression of the African personality than does industry. The special problems of making Africa's difficult tropical soils more productive calls for both specialized agricultural techniques—an African subdiscipline of agronomy—and collaboration with the traditional wisdom of the African peasant, while industrial technology is essentially the same the world over. Additionally, the communal quality of African life and work discipline could fit more easily into even technically improved and modernized agriculture than it could into industry. African agriculture can be more distinctively African than African industry. Thus, insofar as the new Africa seeks to assert its own identity and traditions while raising its living standards, greater priority should be given to the farmer and the land.

At first glance there would seem to be little room left for a choice in Africa between socialism and non-socialism, since the rhetoric of African socialism is all pervasive. But, as we have seen, the very ubiquity of socialist slogans masks a variety of economic mixes in African nations. Despite general emphasis on socially owned enterprise, all these nations provide some room for foreign-owned or partly-owned industry and for some domestic mercantile activity, on however small a scale. Whatever the undesirable aspects of unalloyed large-scale capitalism, there is much to be said from a purely economic point of view for the creation of a class of African small entrepreneurs. The alternative is bureaucratization to the point of inefficiency and inflexibility, and the further expansion of a special caste of government employees who control all aspects of life. The real difference between technical efficiency and economic creativity needs to be better understood. The bureaucrat may strive for and even perhaps achieve the former, but the latter is also a necessary ingredient in economic development and it largely depends upon the entrepreneur.

Although socialism is held in Africa to be more in keeping with traditional African communalism than individualistic private enterprise, it is forgotten that the bureaucratic ethos is as foreign an importation as modern industry, and that among African virtues are ingenuity, flexibility and creativity. The examples of the Hausa traders and the market women of West Africa show what Africans can accomplish in mercantile activity if given an opportunity. Though African businessmen have been slow to shift their capital from purely trading activities to the kind of productive enterprise that would help promote economic development, it is somewhat premature to conclude that the transition is impossible. With sufficient technical and business training and official encouragement, and with creative assistance from the business communities of the developed nations, Africans could yet perhaps show their own governments a more adequate path to economic development than completely planned and centrally administered growth. As in the case of agriculture versus industry, what is at stake is not so much Africa's economic or political relations with the rest of the world (though they are affected by its commitment to socialism) but the extent to which African governments seek to enlist and develop the human potentialities of their own citizens.

The political choices like the economic choices offer Africans themselves the possibility of more or less personal autonomy and growth. Africa must choose between a more or less democratic and a more or less authoritarian (or even totalitarian) way of life, and its choice will turn primarily on its willingness to take chances, to have trust in the capabilities of its own citizens.

The arguments made for the repression of political dissent in the new states are plausible and cogent, and they echo those made throughout most of Asia and the Near East. But one must reiterate that despite cultural differences, Africans share a common humanity with the rest of the world. Being a political prisoner in an African dungeon is just as painful and degrading as being one in Eastern Europe. Unchecked power tempts to corruption in Africa as much as anywhere else. And majority rule there as elsewhere becomes a sham unless the majority can hear, publicly and adequately, all sides of the issues they are supposed to decide. "The Rule of Law," as the Chief Justice of Nigeria, Sir Adetokumba Ademola has put it, "is not a Western idea, nor is it linked with any economic or social system."

But the argument for democracy in Africa can be put on other than primarily ethical grounds. Not only is democracy (which necessarily includes the realistic possibility of serious political opposition—opposition to individual acts of the government if not to the whole regime) a common human necessity for the preservation of man's dignity in modern society, but it is also more conducive to economic and even political efficiency. Africans (or Europeans or Americans) misread the plain lessons of history as well as of common sense if they assume that free government can only be purchased at the price of efficiency. All that we know of government in Fascist Italy and Nazi Germany in the recent past and of life in the Communist nations today tells us that the suppression of dissent leads to an inability to cope realistically and flexibly with the demands a political system must meet.

Africans are right in insisting that there is no need to manufacture an opposition when substantial unanimity exists, and the example of Turkey shows that modernizing one-party movements can (although only with much difficulty) evolve into functioning democratic systems. But, if democracy is to have a chance to operate in Africa during the next generation, those regimes which believe in it must shape their institutions in such a way as to make it possible. The provision of the law setting up one-party government in Kenya which provides for multiple candidacies from within the party for legislative vacancies is a step in the right direction. Reports that some leaders are coming to feel that a free press and an independent judiciary (something which leads a precarious existence in many African states, especially the more "progressive" ones) are not incompatible with the national unity which the one-party system is designed to incarnate and perpetuate are encouraging.

So far many one-party states have continued to permit lively discussions of particular issues in parliament, and backbenchers have been able to criticize the execution and even the substance of government policies. This is conducive not only to freedom but in the last analysis to stability. A muzzled opposition soon becomes an irresponsible one. Regimes which do not provide for honest criticism set the stage for their own dissolution through explosive violence, and the specter of military dictatorship as an alternative to an unpopular or unstable civil government is increasingly present in Africa.

But the preservation of democracy in Africa is not merely a matter of what form of political rule shall prevail over the continent. The degree to which political freedom survives or fails to survive will have an important effect in shaping African culture and identity. One engaging feature of most African one-party states to date has been the relative openness of communication and the lack of enforced conformity in matters of opinion. So far the uniformity of views of most Africans on key issues has been like that of the nineteenth-century Americans whom De Tocqueville described—a nation of men and women sure of the virtue of their own ways and subject to a self-created tyranny of public opinion rather than one of government. Censorship either does not exist or tends to be spotty or inefficient, and the views of East and West, of other African states and even of local dissidents can usually still be aired. African one-party states have not become closed societies.

But Africans are increasingly suspicious of non-Africans and their opinions, especially in those states where a government press and radio echoes a demagogic anti-Western line. Africanization of the mass media and education, good in itself, poses a danger, for if it means self-indoctrination it can impoverish African culture and destroy the possibility of a mutually fruitful relation with the non-African world.

The question of the openness of the new African society cannot be separated from the question of race. North African societies will of course continue to be primarily white societies even if they identify culturally with anti-Western currents in world politics. The real decision will come in sub-Saharan and above all southern Africa. The virtual expulsion of whites and the definition of Africa as exclusively a "black man's continent" would have an importance far transcending the fate of the individuals directly involved. The real peril is that increasingly ideas—political, economic and cultural—will be given racial labels and that to the positive aspects of concepts such as Negritude and the African Personality will be added a negative rejection of all but the most overtly technological aspects of Western culture. A "Palm Curtain" around Africa is still a remote danger, but a real one nevertheless.

The danger that the Africa of tomorrow might become a racially chauvinistic society hostile to much of the outside world, above all the West, is heightened by the current struggle to create African political unity. The present controversies in the OAU over attitudes toward Nkrumah on the one hand and Tshombe on the other are only one surface manifestation of the deep-rooted split between those states which lean toward continued close ties with the West and reject doctrinaire socialism and anti-imperialism and those which feel that perhaps only through a revolutionary alliance of the underdeveloped nations against neo-colonialism can they create an identity of their own. African political unity, if that were the sole desideratum, could probably be most easily achieved under the rubric of anti-Western nationalism—still the continent's ideological lowest common denominator. To achieve unity on this basis would require the overthrow of the more moderate regimes, but this many Africans would welcome. To many Africans and many non-African students of Africa as well, nationalistic anti-Western extremism is the African "wave of the future." So far attempts to create such unity as a by-product of the Congo crisis have failed, but an international crisis stemming from an explosion in South Africa could lead to a radical reorganization of politics throughout the continent along the lines desired by the extremists.

It is of course the business of Africans alone whether they choose such a future for the continent—a continentwide semi-totalitarian state or federation of states ideologically based on racial chauvinism. But the coming into being of such a political entity would radically alter Africa's relationship to the rest of the world and would mean an isolation from much of human society far more profound than any temporary turning inward in the past.

Those desiring to create such a racialist state or federation would find a natural ally in Communist China. Unlike the Soviet Union, which has tended to work almost exclusively through existing nationalist governments, China could well become a partner in a drive to remake Africa in a manner more congenial to the extremists. China seeks leadership of the poor nations of the world in a revolutionary struggle against oppression by the well-off bourgeois West—in whose ranks China increasingly places the Soviet Union. In line with such an aim the Afro-Asian Peoples' Solidarity Conference held in Ghana in 1965 resolved to expand its membership to include Latin America and will meet in Havana in 1966. United in poverty, resentment of the West and a common drive toward establishment of ill-defined revolutionary societies, such an international grouping would have obvious racial overtones.

These choices—between industry and agriculture, between unalloyed socialism and mixed economies, between one-party dictatorship and democracy, between open societies and membership in a racist international—must be made by Africa, just as their consequences must be suffered by Africa. But what of America's role in Africa's future? What choices does it have? How can the United States, not by pressure or even by precept, but by the implications and consequences of its actions, help Africa to find a role in the world which is in Africa's best interests and those of America and the world as well?

The first question that must be asked about American policy in Africa is whether the United States needs an African policy at all. There is a sense in which the answer must be "No." The purposes of American foreign policy like those of any nation, especially any great power, are varied. It must foster America's primary interests, which consist of American political and military security and economic well-being. It must also seek to the extent possible to safeguard America's secondary interests, in world peace and world political and economic well-being.

To some extent, of course, safeguarding primary interests depends on safeguarding those that are secondary; how much so at any given time is a legitimate, indeed necessary, subject for debate. But the logical subordination must be maintained. In the last analysis, if fighting a bloody war is a necessary and a practical means to preserve a nation's political system it will fight such a war. Americans have fought two major and several minor wars in this century because they believed them to be necessary to the ultimate preservation of their freedom. Similarly, the well-being of other peoples, above all the interests of their governments (which may not be the same thing) must be subordinated to American interests if necessary. Any government's first duty—morally and practically—is to its own people. This is accepted by all nations. It is the rationale behind the general African commitment to neutralism and nonalignment, and Africans can and do assume that other nations, including the United States, act according to the same principle. This being so, one must begin any discussion of American policy in Africa by asking what—and how vital—are American interests there.

The United States today is undergoing a basic re-evaluation of its international position. What some have called "neo-isolationism," but which exponents like Walter Lippmann prefer to call anti-"globalism," is now in the air. George Kennan, John Paton Davies, Jr., Professor Hans Morgenthau, Senators Fulbright and Church, and others have called upon Americans to realize that they are not the God-given protectors and providers for all the world, that there are limits to American power and therefore to American obligations.

There are many reasons for the growth of this new attitude. The notion of the "Great Society" has called America's attention to the unfinished domestic business which has piled up since well before Pearl Harbor; President Johnson's political mind was formed in the early New Deal era and his special interests are domestic rather than foreign. The Soviet-American détente, polycentrism, and the Sino-Soviet split have caused the United States and the Communists to cease to appear to confront each other directly over every disputed social issue on earth. De Gaulle has cast doubts on the future of the Western alliance. Relations have deteriorated with rulers of underdeveloped countries, such as Nasser and Sukarno; regardless of particular future developments the honeymoon with the "unaligned" nations is over. The efficacy of foreign aid as a device for winning friends and influencing people is now seriously questioned. Problems in Latin America—highlighted by Castroism and American intervention in the Dominican Republic—have called attention to events nearer home at the same time that frustration with Vietnam, the Congo, and similar faraway problems increases. Americans are gradually coming to believe that perhaps they are spreading themselves too thin in an attempt to make a Pax Americana prevail over the globe against the wishes of Communists, neutrals and sometimes allies.

If there is merit in the notion that the United States need not, should not and cannot control events all over the planet, where does Africa stand on the list of American priorities? Obviously Europe ranks highest in the American scale. The United States has fought two major wars to prevent one nation, Germany, from forging the natural and human resources between the Urals and the Irish Sea into a power so strong it would necessarily imperil American security. The meaning of NATO is that the United States stands ready to fight another war to prevent such a combination under Russian aegis. A longstanding economic and sentimental involvement in the Far East has evolved into a confused and obscure conviction that though her existence as a power must be acknowledged, a hostile China cannot be allowed to draw all of Asia's manpower and resources into an overpowering combination under her control. Latin America is traditionally viewed as on America's side of the ocean, and the United States regards it as axiomatic that its growing strength cannot be allowed to fall prey to hostile powers or ideologies. In Africa alone the United States does not have a vital stake.

This is not to go so far as Walter Lippmann did in the 1964 version of his annual television encyclical to the American people and claim that the United States has no real interest in the Congo for instance. The United States would like to see all of Africa friendly to it and receptive to economic, cultural and even political ties. An Africa which "went Communist"—a highly unlikely and probably meaningless possibility—or joined a Chinese-led racial coalition against the West would be damaging to the United States psychologically and politically. But the world military balance of power cannot be significantly affected by anything occurring in Africa from now on—either in terms of arms, men or bases. In the event of an all-out war, a nuclear war, between the United States and the Soviet Union or Communist China no one would care what was happening in Accra or Zomba. Despite American investment in South Africa (now upwards of half a billion dollars) American economic interests in Africa, viewed in relation to her other nondomestic economic interests, are marginal, even trivial. The plain truth of the matter is that the main thing Africa has that the United States wants is its potential good will. And even that is perhaps less important than is sometimes felt. As thoughtful persons such as Dean Acheson are trying to tell Americans and as events are teaching them, a great power must seek not love and gratitude—rare items in international politics anyway—but rather trust and respect.

This is not to say that the United States should take as its model the haughtiness of nineteenth-century Britain or twentieth-century Gaullist France, nor emulate the contempt for others' opinions which enabled the Soviet government to break a moratorium on atomic testing during the Belgrade conference of the nonaligned nations in the confident—and correct—expectation of escaping serious censure by the neutralists meeting there. But the United States could well, as events in its recent relations with Tanzania and Indonesia show the Johnson administration intends to do, drop the pose of desperate suitor or scolding maiden aunt and conduct its relations with other states, especially developing nations, on a more businesslike basis.

Such a policy would in the long run have the effect of improving rather than hurting American relations with Africa. The total amount of American economic assistance might well be increased; a program of foreign aid given not on an inefficient and demagogic "crash" basis or as a form of bribery, but as a gesture of respect and help to those who are realistically working to help themselves, would enable Africans to respect both Americans and themselves by doing away with the demeaning relationship of international charity. Nor should it be considered an interference in a nation's internal affairs if the

United States refused to aid nations, such as the United Arab Republic, which spend an inordinate amount of their own scarce funds on military or external political purposes. American refusal to give further economic assistance to financially hard-pressed Ghana in 1965 seems to have been motivated by such a point of view. No one has a social obligation to subsidize a drunkard's drinking; on the contrary. American obligation to help Africa is part of its general obligation to the international common good.

To grant aid to Africa as a kind of reparations for the slave trade or as a concession to one element in our population would be to poison the wellsprings of American-African relations. It is of course up to American Negroes to decide to what extent they wish to embrace the concept of Afro-Americanism, and there is some merit in the contention of Negro leaders that throughout American history ethnic groups have acted as American pressure groups for their homelands. But past American experience with the results of pressures stemming from citizens specially interested in the problems of Ireland, Germany, Italy, Israel, Eastern Europe and even Cuba would suggest that such special identifications of Americans with other states may distort our foreign policy, and in the long run warp American relations with the nations involved.

What has just been said does not take into account a possible form of African-American interaction which would be intrinsically hostile and would involve a complete internationalization of American race problems. A shift of Africa toward a Chinese-led anti-Western coalition could coincide with rising despair or impatience among elements of the Negro population in the United States, with such elements looking to Maoism as an inspiration for a total rejection of American society and civilization. Portents for such a development are not entirely lacking. Recent months have seen the formation of a new Communist party in the United States, oriented to China rather than the Soviet Union and seeking to form ties both to the civil-rights movement and the groundswell of opposition in many quarters to American policy in the Far East. It is also noteworthy that one of the fastest growing and most dynamic leftist groups in the country is a nationwide organization of extremist campus clubs named in honor of the late Negro nationalist W. E. B. Du Bois.

If it is true that an intensification of American involvement in African affairs based on ethnic relationships can hurt rather than help American-African relations, this is doubly true of any special relationship based on ideological witch-hunting. The United States has a legitimate interest in competing throughout the world with hostile nations, such as China, through various means. But, given the confused political situations in many African states as well as African resentment of outside interference, it might be better for African-American relations if the United States normally does not try to combat Communist interventions and intrigues in Africa in kind, but lets them fall of their own weight, as evidence to date indicates they will. Regarding Africans as children to be protected by American wisdom is as obnoxious to Africans as is constantly lecturing them on their internal political and economic arrangements. An African counterpart to the absurd and degrading anti-Communist foray in the Dominican Republic could be just as dangerous to American interests as the creation of an African Vietnam.

The United States must be prepared to collaborate with other nations in defending the victims of outright aggression, but it cannot be the policeman of Africa. To seek to root out real or alleged Communist influences in African states would simply make it more likely that Africa would become the scene of a political struggle in which the Communists would hold the trump card of indigenous leadership and support, as well as needlessly involve American prestige in operations which, even if successful, would be at best petty and sordid. America's world position is not going to be decided by feuding tribal rivals masquerading as ideological crusaders unless the United States allows it to be.

In part as a corollary of this, and in the interest of African and international society generally, the United States must not encourage African states to engage in any arms race, even one whose alleged initial motivation is to provide local security against Communist insurrection or aggression; we must not make Africa a dumping ground for surplus American weapons.

What of the American position toward the increasingly totalitarian practices in many African states? The internal politics of African states are primarily their own affair, secondly that of their African neighbors, and only remotely any concern of the United States. If the United States can allow repression and terror in Haiti, Portugal, East Germany and North Korea, it can be permissive about it in Africa. But this should not prevent the United States from joining with appropriate international groups in the United Nations and elsewhere to condemn and investigate violations of human rights on a multinational basis, with the hope of correcting them. It is in this fashion, for instance, that the United States could best work toward ending conditions such as the Chinese Communst-inspired reign of terror which gripped Brazzaville in 1965.

Nor does the United States, or especially private American citizens, have to pretend that African oppression of fellow Africans is from a moral point of view substantially different from white oppression of Africans or white oppression of whites. There is of course a scale of arbitrariness on which wholesale mistreatment of persons because of the color of their skins—which they cannot change—ranks somewhat higher than mistreatment of them because of religious or political views which theoretically they could change, and on such a scale South Africa would obviously rank very high. But as a practical matter all tyranny is equally destructive of human dignity and those who suffer from deprivation of their rights on whatever basis equally merit our sympathy.

Nor do Americans need to pretend that bureacratization is any more efficient in Africa than elsewhere. The United States need not support and encourage states which stifle the freedom and intitiative of their own citizens. Africans like others must understand that diplomatic correctness and noninterference in other nations' internal affairs do not entail subsidization of regimes or activities of which we disapprove. Here as in every aspect of African-American relations the least element of neo-colonialism must be avoided. The overriding principle guiding American policy in Africa must be that African nations, save for certain special and temporary economic circumstances, can and must stand on their own feet economically, politically and culturally. They must, as the price of freedom, take responsibility for their actions and not expect to be treated as pampered client states but as equals. Only by treating Africans as equals, in fact as well as in diplomatic formality, can that last vestige of imperialism, the inferiority complex some African leaders manifest in their words and actions, be removed.

This means that America and to a lesser extent Europe as well must allow African states to go it alone for a while and make their own mistakes. Europe and the United States must decrease the intensity of their relations with Africa so that these can be restructured on a healthier basis. In effect Britain has long done this, and France is rapidly moving in this direction. The United States must resist the temptation to move into the "vacuum" (a nasty term for African sovereignty) in order to replace them and thereby become a neo-colonial power. The risks of noninvolvement—usually posed not so much as African collapse as Communist takeover—are not as great as sometimes thought. The costs, in exacerbation and suspicion, of becoming enmeshed are enormous.

But what of cases where African states have sought United States intervention in areas still ruled by white governments? What should American policy be toward Rhodesia, Portuguese Africa and the Republic of South Africa? Here the United States has a rare opportunity to act in accordance with the basic moral principles which underlie American democracy and are most consonant with a world in which the United States can feel at ease. The United States has no direct and immediate vital interests in southern Africa which would cause it to swerve from its belief in free institutions; because of its economic power and political prestige it has some hope that its actions will influence the course of events. Portuguese adherence to NATO is no longer of vital importance. In any event, future Portuguese-American relations will depend in large measure on developments in Portugal itself, developments which a morally justifiable American stand toward Portuguese Africa can do much to influence in our favor.

Nor has the United States any vital interests in perpetuating the Nationalist regime in South Africa as such. That nation is of negligible military value to the West in any future conflict and such value as it might have is largely vitiated by its inherent instability. Save for the special but not insoluble problems which would be raised for American fiscal policy by an interruption of South African gold production, American economic interests in Africa are not those of the nation but of a minute segment of it; their continued existence is of no significance to the American economy and is politically contrary to American interests generally. Failure to realize this would be a grave error. However, the inexplicable action of the Johnson administration in sending Charles Engelhard, most prominent of American investors in South Africa, as its representative to Zambia's independence celebrations indicates that it may be extremely difficult for the government to disassociate itself from American business interests in this region. Nor is the current South African regime, as it often claims, an anchor of the continent's stability. Quite the contrary. The policies of the Nationalist regime pose a constant threat not only to international stability on the continent but to the internal stability of many African states as well.

But by the same token that the United States is not bound to Portugal or South Africa it is not bound to any particular set of opponents or forms of opposition to the status quo in white Africa. The argument of African nationalists and their sympathizers that the United States must support opponents of these regimes lest the revolutionary forces and their African supporters turn to the Communists for support is just as much a form of blackmail and just as politically inconsequential as the notion that we must support white repression because Portugal and in some sense South Africa are our allies. The contention that we must support revolutionary nationalism is only a special application of the second of the two delusions which have plagued American policy throughout the world in sometimes complementary, sometimes contradictory fashion.

The first delusion is that wherever Communists or alleged Communists show their heads, the United States must make a negative and sometimes massive response, regardless of the moral and political circumstances and the nature of the regime the Communists are opposing. The second delusion is that, since Communist regimes have shown a willingness to support so-called national liberation movements and politically destabilizing elements in general throughout the world, the United States must outbid Communism by getting there first and itself supporting such movements against the status quo, again regardless of the moral circumstances or political consequences. Thus some would have the United States sacrifice Malaysia to Sukarno's nationalist imperialism or Israel to Arab nationalism on the grounds that revolutionary socialist nationalism is the wave of the future and we can somehow enlist it on "our side" against the Communists. In Africa this has taken the form of pressures upon the United States to seek African support by favoring those African regimes most congenial to a majority of African nationalists, or in some cases to a vocal extremist minority.

But both of these responses—the anti-Communist reflex and the pro-revolution reflex—are facets of the central consequence of globalist thinking, the turning of United States foreign policy over to the control of the Communist world by making American actions entirely dependent on what the Communists have done, are doing or might do. This is an intolerable position for a great power to allow itself to be put into, especially a power which purports to support international morality.

If the United States does in fact have some freedom of action in southern Africa despite domestic and foreign pressures from right and left, how should that freedom of action be used? It must first of all be recognized that American involvement must be proportionate to our already existing responsibilities. We are more heavily involved—as trading and investing partners—with South Africa than with Rhodesia or Portuguese Africa. Secondly, and more importantly, United States policy must be responsible, it must take into account the long-range consequences of American actions. There are areas of the world where American interests are so substantial and so direct and the pressures for action so strong that the United States must make ad hoc decisions, choosing between alternatives not of its own making, in the hope that the consequences will benefit both it and the peoples involved. This, however, is not yet the case in southern Africa, though time grows shorter day by day. The United States can and must ask itself what kind of final solution it hopes for in this area and relate its interim policies and decisions to that goal. Such a procedure is unfortunately neither congenial to the forces pressing the United States government from both sides nor to a State Department foreign policy mechanism which normally refuses to confront issues until they become crises, by which time American freedom of action is already drastically limited.

In the case of Portuguese Africa, the United States has already stated its position as being in favor of self-determination. Portugal, despite its legal claims, must admit that the weight of history is against considering noncontiguous territories separated by thousands of miles as being part of the same nation, and that the burden of proof is upon her to convince the world that the inhabitants of her African territories wish to continue in any particular form of association with her. The United

States should lend its support to international pressures to force Portugal to allow the peoples of this area to freely make known their wishes in this regard. At the same time the United States is under no obligation to support attempts to alter the political system of these territories by force. Only if Portugal were increasing oppressive measures against the African populations, retaining measures obviously contrary to human decency as generally and loosely defined by international law, or taking steps so as to preclude a free choice at some future date would American support of armed rebellion be justified.

Despite atrocities associated with the suppression of rebellion in these territories, Portugal is slowly moving, under international pressure, to ameliorate conditions. Such amelioration as exists is without doubt motivated by a desire to strengthen the Portuguese hold, but it need not be regarded as excluding a free popular decision. The evolution of the civil-rights struggle in the United States, for instance, shows that people who wish to be free will not be seduced but rather encouraged by improvement in their condition. The moral satisfaction many African nationalists—inside and outside the territories involved—would gain from throwing Portugal out by force though quite understandable need not override America's interest in a peaceful solution of the area's problems consistent with the welfare of the majority of those concerned, a welfare which postulates that the peoples of these territories will ultimately be able to choose their own destinies.

Rhodesia presents another case in which American policy to date can stand the test of events. The United States has upheld the principle of popular sovereignty as an ultimate goal and has denounced the foolhardiness of settler attempts to preclude this. On the other hand, deference to Britain in this area makes sense. The ultimate sanctions to be applied, especially from an economic point of view, are in Britain's hands. The United States must support, publicly and in advance, British measures to prevent a unilateral declaration of independence by any white government, but meaningful American initiatives in Rhodesia are as limited as is American responsibility.

Rhodesia is both a minor and a transient problem. It is the Republic of South Africa which is the key to American policy in southern Africa as it is to much of Africa's future, and it is here that the United States has its most important single opportunity to help fashion Africa's self-image for good or ill. This is one African area from which the United States cannot isolate itself. Our interest in this area is general, subtle and long range, but insofar as anything in Africa is important to the United States an equitable and peaceful resolution of the South African dilemma is vital.

It has often been said that American implication in apartheid, stemming from highly profitable and growing American private investment in South Africa, as well as from American failure to support sanctions against the policies of the Verwoerd government, does more to harm the American image in Africa than American aid and moral support for independent African states do to enhance it. Be that as it may, if South Africa should be politically and to some extent physically destroyed in a race war which was in part the result of American failure to take appropriate action in this area, and especially if, in such a situation, the Communist powers gave conspicuous aid to black nationalist forces—as they almost inevitably would—the result would be a major political defeat for the United States. More important in the long perspective of history, the probable result of such a tragedy would be a racialist African continent implacably hostile to the West. What the United States does or does not do in South Africa could profoundly affect not just Africa's identity but the future of mankind.

Future American policy therefore must be aimed at a just and viable solution of the South African problem. The first, though far from final, step toward such a solution is to do everything practicable to bring apartheid to an end, and to induce the South African government to allow events to move toward the creation of the kind of confederal, multiracial society discussed earlier, the only future for the area which is at once feasible, equitable and capable of being peacefully achieved. While the United States for reasons previously cited should not become involved in any program of sanctions or embargoes designed to overthrow the present government, it must work to create pressures which will convince the white community of the seriousness of its intentions without putting them in a position where their backs are to the wall and they see no alternatives save implacable resistance to change or complete loss of control over events.

The United States should therefore, in addition to continuing to ban arms shipments to South Africa, take the following steps: (1) actively discourage continued American investment in South Africa by public proclamation that it is contrary to the national interest, by announced unwillingness to take any steps to protect it or its employees in any fashion in any future crisis, by withdrawal of any overseas guarantees which may be applicable to such investment, and by any similar measures which are legally and constitutionally feasible; (2) take whatever steps are necessary to make it mandatory for domestic Fair Employment Practices Laws to be applied to the overseas operation of American firms, making American officers of such firms responsible for noncompliance; (3) on the grounds that the assets of the firms issuing them are inherently unprotectable, refuse to allow South African securities to be legally traded in the United States; (4) apply in a selective but increasingly broad fashion the laws against importation of goods produced by slave labor to products originating in South Africa. All of these measures might have to be publicized in South Africa through use of radio propaganda to overcome increasing censorship within that nation. But none of these actions would involve the United States in military action or other physical activity in or near South African territory.

Such measures, even without British or other Western support, could be sufficiently damaging to the South African economy to cause the government to make concessions without at the same time destroying economic and social order. Faced with loss of American capital, the government might be willing to make exceptions to racial policies in order to protect the position of American firms, exceptions which could set precedents and help undermine the whole system of segregation. Faced with a choice not between resistance and national extinction but between economic loss and inconvenience on the one hand and intrinsically minor—though cumulatively major—concessions on the other, South Africans might well choose to allow their economy and society to drift toward "creeping multiracialism" since no one concession would seem insupportable. Such a program would almost inevitably stimulate some concessions because in addition to the economic inconveniences and psychic pressures it would entail it would undermine the major bulwark of the present trend—the South Africans' conviction that time is on their side, that the West is slowly coming to admit that the South Africans are right, so that they can do whatever they wish without fear of serious economic reprisal or ultimate political isolation. The measures suggested have the further advantage, unlike an overall boycott or embargo, of being related to specific problems in such a way that they can be unilaterally suspended and reinstituted depending on South African reactions.

Such a policy might not work. If it did not the United States might lose face in the world but it would at least have the satisfaction of having acted morally; for, while the United States has no responsibility to end racial oppression in South Africa, it does have a responsibility not to collaborate in it, and the measures suggested are essentially acts of nonparticipation rather than direct attacks on the regime.

The initiation and success of a plan of selective boycott such as that suggested here is the only hope for the future of American relations with South Africa. If present South African society should dissolve in the bloodshed of a racial war, regardless of whose actions or failures to act are the cause, by the time the dust settles, black nationalists will not distinguish between Western nations which had sought to aid the cause of justice in South Africa and those which did not. Revolutions have a logic of their own, and the forces unleashed by civil war in South Africa would eventually create a situation in which the United States would be caught in the middle and in time would come to be regarded as as much a foe as any other white group, by whatever nationalist leaders emerged from the chaos.

But suppose such an American policy succeeded? This would be only a start, for any intervention of this kind necessarily implies a permanent commitment to the future of southern Africa. It would be the height of irresponsibility for the United States to prevent the South African government from trying to solve its own problems in its own way and then to walk away from the situation it created. If South Africa shows signs of moving toward confederal multiracialism, then the United States must be prepared to protect that evolution against the subversion of the impatient and the sinister, whether from within or without Africa, and must expect to take a leading role in any international action necessary to guarantee the stability of the constitutional arrangements of the new South Africa and to protect South Africa against external aggression.

In considering American policy toward Africa in general and southern Africa in particular we come full circle in the attempt to assess Africa's future. For Africa's future identity will be determined in large part by its reaction to what others, including Americans, do. We are not Africa's tutors, but neither we nor Africans can escape the fact that we, and our actions, are part of the environment in which the new Africa seeks to find its identity. Even if a peaceful and just solution for South Africa is found, Africa will still have the problem of relating its sense of its own uniqueness to the demands of life in a twentieth century in which technology has become the prime determinant of a universal culture. But a prosperous South Africa engaged in an intimate and fruitful dialogue with its neighbors on the continent could do much to serve as a bridge between the old

Africa and the new era of universal history. Not only would a modernized multiracial confederation dull the edge of racial chauvinism implicit in much African nationalism and reduce "the importance of being black," but the culture of its millions of urbanized and sophisticated Africans could serve as a prototype for Africans throughout the continent who are seeking to build societies at once African and modern.

A South Africa torn apart by strife might not become a Communist beachhead or lead to a major East-West political or military conflict, but it would turn Africa inward to feed its psyche on its wounds and frustrations and hostilities; it would cause Africa to become an isolated empire of bitterness or an adherent of a new international based on racism and economic backwardness. Instead of being a contributing member of a new world civilization, Africa would be instrumental in creating a world even more hopelessly divided into antagonistic blocs than it is today. Such an outcome would be a tragedy extending far beyond Africa's borders and involving more than just Africa's identity, for what is at stake is in large measure the future shape of world society.

INDEX

Index